International Banks and the Environment

RAYMOND F. MIKESELL
and LARRY WILLIAMS

International Banks and the Environment

From Growth to Sustainability: An Unfinished Agenda

SIERRA CLUB BOOKS   SAN FRANCISCO

LIBRARY OF CONGRESS CATALOGING IN PUBLICATION DATA
Mikesell, Raymond Frech.
    International banks and the environment : from growth to
sustainability, an unfinished agenda / Raymond F. Mikesell and Larry
Williams.
        p. cm.
    Includes bibliographical references and index.
    ISBN 0-87156-640-0
    1. Development banks—Developing countries.   2. Developing
countries—Economic policy—Environmental aspects.   3. Economic
development projects—Environmental aspects—Developing countries.
I. Williams Larry, 1937–   . II. Title.
HG1976.D44M55   1992
332.1′5′091724—dc20   91–30504
                                                              CIP

Production by Janet Vail
Jacket design by Bonnie Smetts Design
Book design by Abigail Johnston
Set in Sabon by Classic Typography
Printed in the United States on acid-free paper containing a minimum of 50% recovered waste paper, of which at least 10% of the fiber content is post-consumer waste

DEDICATION

*The authors dedicate this book to the
representatives of the nongovernmental
organizations throughout the world
who are working, sometimes at great
personal risk, to improve the quality of
life for the people of developing countries.*

TABLE OF CONTENTS

PREFACE

This book is the product of collaboration between a professor of economics at the University of Oregon and the director of the Sierra Club's International Program. The study draws heavily on Williams' rich experience as the senior international representative of the Sierra Club in meetings with officials of governments and nongovernmental organizations in Third World countries, with U.S. administration officials and congressional committees concerned with the environmental policies of multilateral development banks (MDBs), and with officials of MDBs themselves. Williams has traveled widely on behalf of the Sierra Club as a consultant or adviser to the Asian and African development banks, and has examined USAID programs in Botswana, the Sudan, Kenya, Rwanda, and Thailand.

Mikesell's experience includes a number of missions to Third World countries sponsored by the United Nations, USAID, and the Departments of State and Treasury, and he has served as a consultant to the World Bank. Mikesell has written a number of scholarly books on economic development, natural resources, international finance, and world trade. Currently he teaches environmental and resource economics and is Chair of the Sierra Club's Economics Committee.

In reviewing and evaluating operations and policies of the MDBs, the authors have applied the principles of sustainable economic development. This requires combining the best information on the economic and social problems of developing countries with what has been learned about environmental protection and the management of natural resources in the interest of sustaining the welfare of both the present and future generations. The MDBs have had an increasingly important influence on Third World development over the past four decades. As documented in this book, they have made and continue to make many mistakes. Also documented is their growing understanding of the environmental consequences and the social costs of flawed development policies. In our case studies of MDB-suppported development projects and programs we have identified those that have had adverse environmental impacts, and have made a number of recommendations for avoiding these impacts and for promoting sustainable development. Despite our criticism of past performance, our approach is intended to be constructive and optimistic regarding the future performance of the international development banks.

Although MDBs finance only a small portion of the total development activities of Third World countries, they can have a powerful influence on the quality of development. Therefore, we are concerned with not only the individual projects that MDBs and other external assistance agencies support, but also with how these organizations can promote environmentally sound policies and programs initiated by the governments of developing countries.

In writing this book, we have had several audiences in mind. First is the growing number of people who are concerned with the environmental policies of Third World countries, both because of their interest in the economic and social welfare of the inhabitants and because of the effects of these policies on the global ecology. People in the developed world are asking whether the development assistance these agencies provide is making a substantial contribution both to sustainable economic and social progress for three-fourths of the world's population, and to the viability of the earth's atmosphere, oceans, soils, and biodiversity, on which all life depends. Our second target is the NGOs in both the industrial and the developing countries that are monitoring the projects and programs supported by MDBs in order to forestall further environmental damage and natural resource mismanagement. We have sought to provide a framework and a set of guidelines for evaluating the effects of the major categories of development projects. A third group for which this book is written consists of economists and other social scientists with an interest in economic development and in the role of external assistance agencies in promoting it. Traditional development theory and practice are rapidly adapting to the principle of sustainability, which has important implications for how we should promote economic and social progress in poor countries, and for the way such progress should be measured. Therefore, we have sought to make a contribution to the academic literature on sustainable economic development, which we hope will advance rigorous thinking and teaching in this area.

We also wish to thank the many members of the U.S. Congress who have offered their considerable support to the international development reform effort. We would especially like to acknowledge the work of U.S. Representative David Obey and U.S. Senator Patrick Leahy, chairmen of the respective congressional appropriations subcommittees that fund and provide much of the oversight for USAID and the MDBs; Senator Robert Kasten, a member of the Appropriations Committee; and Representative Nancy Pelosi for her leadership in taking on the difficult but successful fights to pass the law requiring MDBs to write impact statements in exchange for U.S. support. We are indebted to Bruce Rich and his fine staff at the Environmental Defense Fund, who provided the documentation for many of the MDB case studies used in this book; and the many people in the World Bank, the Inter-American Development Bank, and the Asian Development Bank (who may prefer not to be named) for their information and assistance.

Finally, we want to acknowledge the cooperation of Danny Moses of Sierra Club Books, and the assistance of Cathy Fogel, Assistant International Representative, and Stephen Mills, Conservation Assistant, of the Sierra Club. We also want to thank Letty Fotta for her secretarial and editorial contributions; and our wives for their patience and good humor during the long research and writing process.

Raymond F. Mikesell and Larry Williams

LIST OF ACRONYMS

ADB: Asian Development Bank

AfDB: African Development Bank

ARD: agriculture and rural development

BACT: best available control technology

CIDIE: Committee of International Development Institutions on Environment

CODELCO: Coporacion Nacional del Cobre de Chile

CVRD: Companhia Valle do Rio Doce

EAP: environmental action plan

EBRD: European Bank for Reconstruction and Development

ECAFE: Economic Commission for Asia and the Far East (UN)

ED: Environmental Department (World Bank

EIA: environmental impact assessment

EIS: environmental impact statement

EMC: Environmental Management Committee (IADB)

EPA: Environmental Protection Agency (US)

EPD: Environmental Protection Division (IADB)

ESMAP: Energy Sector Management Assistance

EU: Environmental Unit (World Bank)

EWS: early warning system

FAO: Food and Agriculture Organization

FY: fiscal year

GDP: gross domestic product

GEF: Global Environmental Facility

GNP: gross national product

IADB: Inter-American Development ment Bank

ICVA: International Council of Voluntary Agencies

IDA: International Development Association (World Bank)

IEPS: initial executive project summary (World Bank)

IFC: International Finance Corporation (World Bank)

IFPRI: International Food Policy Research Institute

IIED: International Institute for Environment and Development

IMF: International Monetary Fund

IPM: Integrated Pest Management

ITMP: Indonesian Transmigration Program

IUCN: International Union on Conservation of Nature and Natural Resources

MADIA: Managing Agricultural Development in Africa

MDB: multilateral development bank

MNC: multinational corporation

NGO: nongovernmental organization

NRDC: Natural Resources Defense Council

O&M: operating and maintenance

OAS: Organization of American States

OECD: Organization for Economic Cooperation and Development

OECF: Overseas Economic Cooperation Fund (Japan)

OED: Operations Evaluation Department (World Bank)

OIDC: oil-importing developing countries

OPEC: Organization of Petroleum Exporting Countries

PFP: policy framework papers (IMF)

PL: public law (US)

PNG: Papua New Guinea

RED: Regional Environment Division (World Bank)

SAL: structural adjustment loan

SAR: staff appraisal report (World Bank)

SBCA: social benefit-cost analysis

SME: state mining enterprise

SOE: state-owned enterprise

SUDAM: Superintendencia para o Desenvolvimento da Amazonia (Brazil)

TFAP: tropical forest action plan

TM: Task Manager (World Bank)

UN: United Nations

UNDP: United Nations Development Programme

UNEP: United Nations Environment Programme

UNIDO: United Nations Industrial Development Organization

USAID: United States Agency for International Development

VALCO: Volta Aluminum Company

VRA: Volta River Authority

VRP: Volta River Project

WGMA: Working Group on Multilateral Assistance (US)

WMA: Wildlife Management Area

WRI: World Resources Institute

International
Banks and the
Environment

CHAPTER 1

Introduction

Only recently have the multilateral development banks (MDBs)—the World Bank and the regional development banks for Asia, Latin America, and Africa—discovered the importance of the environment and resource conservation for the welfare of the developing countries they assist. Deterioration of the environment and of the resource base has been taking place at an alarming rate for several decades. The destruction of tropical forests, the contamination of waterways and coastal areas, the appalling pollution and human degradation in Third World cities, and the increasing human-caused desertification of countries in the shadow of famine all are signs of this deterioration. The MDBs' involvement in these and other environmental problems is the subject of this book.

The World Bank's first faint awareness of the close relationship between the environment and economic development came during the tenure of Robert S. McNamara, its president from 1968 to 1981, who appointed the Bank's first environmental advisor in 1970. Twenty years later MDBs still have not satisfactorily embodied this policy-level recognition in their lending programs. Many changes are needed before MDBs can realize their full potential for improving the Third World environment. The banks have made progress, especially during the past couple of years, in examining the possible environmental impacts of the projects they plan to support, but awareness of the environmental implications of bank loans has not yet significantly improved their lending portfolios. Policies, guidelines, and procedures have been formulated for this purpose, but testing and revising those guidelines based on experience will take several years. The MDBs must learn to make loans for irrigation projects that will increase agricultural output without damaging the soil, causing severe hardship on families displaced by reservoirs, or polluting waterways used by farmers and villagers downstream. They must make loans for forest projects that will use resources productively without destroying the ecosystem or the cultures of indigenous people living in the primary forests, and for industry, power, transportation, and mining that will preserve the quality of the resource base, including the air and water.

To improve performance, MDBs must learn from both satisfactory and unsatisfactory operations of the past. For this reason we have reviewed in some detail the environmental consequences of development projects and programs supported by MDBs over the past three decades. We have done this according to the major economic sectors involved and, to some degree, according to the economic and social status of the countries receiving assistance. Experience with an agricultural project in a relatively advanced developing country such as Argentina or Venezuela, for example, will not be the same as that in a very poor Sub-Saharan country such as Mali.

Our major concern in this book is with the world's poorest countries, where environmental and natural resource depletion problems are greatest. We evaluate the performance of projects and programs and, by implication, of the MDBs based on the degree to which they promote sustainable development. This criterion, analyzed in Chapter 3, reflects a double objective, including not only a project's avoidance of environmental harm and depletion of natural resources, but its contribution to a country's economic and social progress.

A major objective of our analysis is to distill from experience with past MDB-supported projects and programs a set of guidelines for satisfactory performance in the future. These lessons and guidelines apply equally to the governments of developing countries that formulate economic and social policies and implement them through national administrative agencies. Since nongovernmental organizations (NGOs) are playing an increasingly important role in influencing the decisions of MDBs and governments, our findings and conclusions have relevance for them as well. Moreover, the information here should be of special interest to the governments of developed countries, which maintain substantial control over the policies and procedures of MDBs and have to an increasing degree become aware of the environmental consequences of the activities of MDBs. Finally, governmental concern reflects the growing public awareness of the national and global consequences of environmental deterioration. The writings of hundreds of scholars have contributed greatly to this awareness, and we hope our book will be a significant addition to this literature.

For the past several years MDBs have emphasized environmental standards and sustainable development as major objectives in their announced policies. They have participated in a number of international environmental conferences under the auspices of the United Nations (UN) and other intergovernmental organizations and have sponsored many workshops on environmental and natural resource issues, to which they have invited representatives from various private environmental organizations. The MDBs, in particular the World Bank, have assembled staffs of environmental specialists in the physical and social sciences, which have produced a body of high-quality literature. In fact, MDBs have written or sponsored a large portion of the published and unpublished documents we have consulted in preparing this book. In general, then, the environmental departments of the MDBs are quite knowledgeable regarding good environmental practices and the mistakes and omissions associated with MDB lending activities in the past. Large institutions are rarely capable of self-criticism, however, and it is not surprising that they have published few criticisms of their own loans.

Although MDBs as a group have a greater influence on Third World development than any other source of external assistance, they do not provide the bulk of foreign aid (defined as loans and grants to foreign government and nongovernment organizations for noncommercial purposes) to developing countries. In 1988 loans by the World Bank and the three regional development banks totaled about $27 billion, while bilateral development aid from governments (excluding export credits) was $48 billion, and private voluntary agencies contributed about $4 billion (OECD 1989, 150, 231). Although a substantial amount of government bilateral aid is for nondevelopment purposes such as famine relief and military assistance, most developed countries have development assistance agencies, such as the US Agency for International Development (USAID), that provide loans, grants, and technical assistance to Third World countries. These bilateral agencies operate in much the same way as MDBs in making loans for development projects and programs, and most take into account the environmental impacts of the projects they finance. In fact, USAID was the first large public development assistance agency to require environmental impact assessments (EIAs) as a condition for funding projects. The environmental problems associated with the lending activities of bilateral aid agencies apply equally to MDBs; thus some of their experiences appear in our case studies.

In Chapter 2 we describe the operations of MDBs and the evolution of their policies, with special reference to the environment. We critically examine the procedures MDBs follow to carry out their announced environmental policies, and we recommend more effective ways to assure the environmental soundness of the projects they support. We also consider ways in which MDBs and the International Monetary Fund (IMF) can use nonproject loans to promote governmental adoption of responsible environmental policies for all their economic and social programs, not just those supported by external assistance.

The structures of the World Bank Group (the World Bank and its two affiliates, the International Development Association [IDA] and the International Finance Corporation [IFC]) and of the three regional banks are similar, as are their policies and operations. This is largely because of the dominant role the United States played in founding the World Bank Group, the Inter-American Development Bank (IADB), and the Asian Development Bank (ADB). The organizers of the African Development Bank (AfDB) decided to adopt a similar pattern. Although not officially regarded as a development institution, the IMF has in the course of its evolution acquired some of the same functions as the World Bank. When the European Bank for Reconstruction and Development (EBRD) completes its organization process and begins making loans to Eastern European countries, it will encounter many of the same environmental problems that the other MDBs presently face. We examine the actual and potential environmental functions of each of these organizations.

The Sierra Club and other conservation organizations have published harsh criticisms of MDB loans in books with incriminating titles, such as *Bankrolling Disasters* (Sierra Club 1986) and *Funding Ecological and Social Destruction* (Bank Information Center 1989). Bank bashing is not the purpose of this book. Our purpose is to examine the record of MDB involvement in environmental problems as an evolutionary process. We believe that these institutions are making progress in safeguarding the environment in the projects they support, but that this process is moving too slowly. We also believe that the banks have an important obligation and potential to educate and to induce the governments of their member countries to adopt sound environmental and resource conservation principles. This means not only avoiding ecological and social subversion in designing and implementing individual projects, but integrating the principles of resource conservation and sustainability with country development policies and plans. Short-term output gains or other temporal objectives should not preclude long-term economic and social viability. The wasteful destruction of tropical forests for cattle ranching illustrates this principle well. Yet more basic development decisions may also be involved: whether to expand hydroelectric power by creating large dams and reservoirs or to promote energy conservation and less energy-intensive industries. The MDBs are in a strategic position to influence government development decisions to assign a high priority to the conservation of resources for future generations. Without attempting to provide a comprehensive blueprint for development, we suggest approaches to sustainable development that MDBs and their client governments should adopt.

The idea that a poor country inhabited by non-Western people can aspire to a level of economic and social development comparable to that of Western Europe and North America within a few generations did not become widely accepted as a realistic goal until after World War II. Our theories and strategies for the economic development of poor countries have emerged largely over the last four decades, but only during the past decade has the importance of resource conservation and sustainability in the development process come to be widely recognized. Most popular textbooks on economic development still fail to mention the environment or the concept of sustainable development. Development economists regard environmental considerations as a constraint on development planning, rather than as an integral part of the development process. Social scientists are only beginning to understand the necessity of integrating environmental and resource conservation principles into the development process; development practitioners conducting MDB lending activities have yet to grasp the concept. The idea of sustainable development has guided the decisions of government policymakers in the developing countries even less. In Chapter 3, therefore, we explain how environmental principles can be integrated with traditional development policies and practices. Preparation of environmental impact assessments (EIAs) is a major component of this process and should become an integral part of the formulation of all economic or social projects involving natural resources and social welfare. The MDBs are just beginning to require EIAs for projects they support and need considerable experience in adopting and carrying out procedures before they can realize the full potential of EIAs.

Understanding the environmental issues that confront MDBs in their lending operations requires a knowledge of the environmental and resource problems in each of the economic sectors in which MDBs operate. Hence, an analysis of the environmental problems associated with projects and programs in the major economic sectors—agriculture, forestry, livestock, power, mining, and infrastructure—occupies the bulk of this book, Chapters 4 through 7. Much of the discussion draws on case histories of projects supported by MDBs and bilateral aid agencies, often recording environmental failures with disastrous consequences. To a substantial degree, a project or program's adverse environmental consequences have also meant economic failure because of the interdependence of the two. In the past, MDBs have emphasized engineering and financial feasibility in evaluating projects for loans but have neglected to emphasize environmental feasibility. From our knowledge of the misguided development efforts of the past we can formulate guidelines for future sustainable development.

As the leading agents for economic and social change in Third World countries, MDBs should not be satisfied with simply assuring the environmental purity of the projects they support. They should use their economic leverage to induce governments to integrate environmental and resource conservation principles into all economic planning and policies. Chapter 8 shows how structural adjustment loans (SALs), which are made by MDBs and the IMF and are not tied to specific projects, can be used to induce improved environmental performance by governments.

Our concern with the contribution of MDBs to sustainable development has led us to analyze a number of controversial issues in development strategy. These include the desirability of large dams, which is a subject of another Sierra Club book (Goldsmith & Hildyard 1984); the exportation of tropical timber; the differences between communal pastures and fenced ranches and between organic farming and farming using chemical fertilizers; and the effectiveness of alternative forms of external development assistance. In our discussions of these and other issues we seek to examine their implications for sustainable development without necessarily taking a rigid position on the issues themselves. In many cases the answers depend on the physical and social conditions in the area, while in other cases they require more research and experimentation. In fact, one of our recommendations for MDBs is that they give greater emphasis to research and pilot projects targeted to the problems of particular regions.

The MDBs have considerable independence in their lending operations, their presidents have long tenures, and their large and competent staffs earn generous salaries, all of which helps to explain their remarkably low turnover of personnel. The fact that MDBs' annual loans exceed the national incomes of most of their members indicates their financial power. Not only do these institutions have a good deal of influence in the client countries, but their leaders play an important role in shaping world financial policy. Nevertheless, the policies and operations of these multibillion-dollar organizations are subject to strong external influences from the administrative and legislative branches of the governments of the large member countries, from other intergovernmental organizations, and from private organizations of bankers, industrialists, and environmentalists, among others. External influence has played a crucial role in shaping the environmental policies and procedures of MDBs during the past decade, and much of the credit goes to NGOs concerned with the environment. These NGOs have operated skillfully and effectively through legislative committees, the administrative departments of their governments, and the officials of the MDBs themselves. The little-known record of successful lobbying by US NGOs is reviewed in Chapter 9.

In the course of this book we present hundreds of recommendations, conclusions, and suggestions regarding the many topics covered in our sector-by-sector review of environmental problems, in our treatment of strategies for sustainable development, and in our analysis of MDB lending policies and procedures. Many of our conclusions follow those of specialists in particular areas of economic activity; many are tentative and subject to change with further knowledge and experimentation. In the final chapter we summarize the most important of these conclusions on MDB policies and operations as they relate to our central theme of sustainable development.

REFERENCES

Bank Information Center. 1989. *Funding Ecological and Social Destruction: The World Bank and the International Monetary Fund.* Washington, D.C.: Bank Information Center.

Goldsmith, Edward, and Nicholas Hildyard. 1984. *The Social and Environmental Effects of Large Dams.* San Francisco: Sierra Club Books.

Organization for Economic Cooperation and Development. 1989. *Development Co-operation in the 1990s.* Paris: OECD, December.

Sierra Club. 1986. *Bankrolling Disasters.* San Francisco: Sierra Club.

CHAPTER 2

The Evolution of Multilateral Development Banks and the Environment

The first public multilateral development bank, the World Bank, began operations in 1946. Its primary purpose was to provide financing for the post-World War II reconstruction of Europe, but its lending resources were far too small to accomplish this goal. The Marshall Plan took over the task in 1947, leaving the World Bank to play only a minor role. The Marshall Plan was also able to provide assistance on a grant and concessional loan basis (low interest and long repayment terms), while the World Bank had to charge rates of interest in line with those it paid to borrow from private international markets. The Bank's Articles of Agreement authorized loans for development, and the first loan to a developing country, Chile, was made in 1948. However, the Bank did not become a substantial supplier of loans to developing countries until the late 1950s.

As of 1990, the World Bank had 138 members, of which twenty-two were Western industrial countries, 2 (Hungary and Poland) were Eastern European countries and the remainder were Third World countries.

Loan funds are derived from capital subscriptions by member countries, principal repayments on loan, interest payments on loans, and borrowings from international capital markets. The last is the largest source of funds, with new borrowings totaling about $11 billion in FY 1988; interest on loans totaled $1.7 billion in FY 1988, and principal repayments totaled $8.2 billion. The Bank is able to borrow from international capital markets on the strength of the unpaid capital subscriptions of its wealthy members, which serve as a guarantee for its obligations. World Bank loans to member countries totaled $16.4 and $15.2 billion in FY 1989 and FY 1990, respectively.

Since the World Bank cannot make loans to private firms, except with the guarantee of a member government, and since in most cases neither private firms nor governments favor such guarantees, in July 1956 the International Finance Corporation (IFC) was established as an affiliate of the World Bank to make loans and guarantees to private firms operating in developing countries. The IFC subsequently obtained the power to make minority equity investments in private firms in developing countries. IFC resources are derived from paid-in capital of members, borrowings from the World Bank and from international capital markets, and accumulated earnings. In FY 1990, the IFC made loans and investments totaling $2.2 billion to 122 firms in developing countries. Although the IFC is an independent corporation with its own staff and board of directors, its president is the president of the World Bank, and the two institutions cooperate closely.

To make loans to poor countries with limited ability to repay foreign debt, the International Development Association (IDA) was established in 1961 as an affiliate of the World Bank. The Bank and the IDA share the same staff and, except for repayment terms, have the same policies. IDA loans bear no interest and are repayable over a forty-year period, with a ten-year grace period. The IDA's capital is derived from grants provided mainly by the developed countries, and this capital must be replenished from time to time. The World Bank, the IFC, and the IDA constitute the World Bank Group. In FY 1988, World Bank Group loans totaled nearly $22 billion (see Table 2-1).

Initially the World Bank did not regard itself as a development institution. Rather it was a supplier of intermediate- and long-term credits for specific projects on application from potential borrowers, similar to private investment banks, which have no special responsibility for the economic welfare of the borrowers. Its major concerns were the credit-worthiness of the borrower, the technical and financial feasibility of the project, and the impact of loan repayments on the balance of payments of the borrowing country.

During the 1950s and early 1960s the Bank regarded the major constraints on loans to developing countries to be their lack of capital absorptive

TABLE 2-1

MDB LOANS AND DISBURSEMENTS IN FY 1988 (billions of dollars)

	Loans	Disbursements
World Bank	$15.7	$12.0
IDA	4.6	3.6
IFC	1.5[a]	0.8
IADB (ordinary capital)	1.5[b]	1.9[b]
IADB (Fund for Special Operations)	0.2[b]	0.3[b]
ADB (ordinary capital)	1.5	1.0
ADB (Development Fund)	1.2	0.7
AfDB (ordinary capital)	1.7	0.8
AfDB (Development Fund)	0.9	0.4
TOTAL	$28.8	$21.5

[a] Includes equity investments.
[b] Calendar year 1988.
Source: National Advisory Council on International Monetary and Finance Policies, *Annual Report* (Washington, D.C.: U.S. Department of the Treasury, 1989); and Inter-American Development Bank, *Annual Report 1989* (Washington, D.C.: IADB, 1990).

capacity and their limited ability to repay foreign debt.[1] The establishment of the IDA eased the problem of repayment for the poorest countries, but promoting capital absorptive capacity required improving government organization and the competence of government officials and raising the country's level of education and skill.

During this period the Bank made loans to developing countries only for specific projects, largely for infrastructure. In FY 1964 the Bank's lending for agriculture totaled only $27 million, or 3 percent of the total loans for that year, while transportation and power accounted for 85 percent. The emphasis on loans for infrastructure—which tends to be in the public sector in developing countries—was consistent with the Bank's policy of promoting private loans and direct investments as the major forms of external capital for developing countries. Power and transportation do not attract foreign capital directly but facilitate foreign capital investment in manufacturing and in resource industries such as mining. Lending for infrastructure is in line with the Bank's charter, which defines the Bank's function in terms of promoting private foreign investment, with Bank loans supplementing private investment when private capital was not available on reasonable terms.

This limited view of the Bank's functions gradually changed. The Bank began sending missions to prospective borrowing countries to gather information and prepare reports on prospective projects and economic conditions. It became clear to the Bank that promoting continuous dialogue regarding possible future projects for Bank funding had advantages over considering intermittent solicitations for loans. Thus, granting a loan for a power project could be considered as part of developing a power sector to which further loans would be made in the future. Unlike the United Nations, and to a considerable extent the US Agency for International Development (USAID) in the 1960s, the Bank has never embraced a particular theory of growth or development. (See Chapter 3 for more on growth and development strategies.) Nor has the Bank financed comprehensive, multiple-year development plans such as India's five-year plans, in which that country sets gross national product (GNP) targets and plans investments to achieve them over five-year periods. Although Bank missions have often influenced countries in formulating national development plans, the Bank has tended to emphasize sectoral planning over formal development plans involving the entire economy.

Bank lending expanded gradually, both in volume and to areas other than infrastructure, during the presidency of George B. Woods, beginning in 1963. However, the Bank began to relate its lending and technical assistance operations to the promotion of all aspects of development—not just industrial and infrastructure projects—only after Robert S. McNamara became president in 1968. Under McNamara the Bank greatly expanded lending to agricultural and rural development and began lending for social service projects such as education and family planning. Electric power, transportation, and industrial projects still accounted for half the loans by the World Bank and the IDA in FY 1972, but the percentage of loans for agricultural projects rose to 16, compared to less than 4 percent in FY 1964, and 6 pecent of the loans were for education, compared to less than 2 percent in FY 1964. The trend toward loans for agricultural and rural development and for social services increased even more during the 1970s. During the 1980s, the number of nonproject loans—related neither to individual projects nor to particular sectors such as industry or agriculture—increased rapidly, reflecting the Bank's increased concern with governmental policies as a major determinant of development progress. The Bank did not attempt to use its leverage to achieve overall changes in environmental policy, however; its efforts to promote environmental standards were still largely project oriented.

The Bank's orientation toward projects explains its slow introduction of broad development perspectives, such as environmental protection and sustainable resource management, to its lending operations. As stated in Mason and Asher's seminal history of the World Bank (1973, 310),

> At the preinvestment stage, those environmental aspects of projects that might have a direct impact on the economic and financial success of the project itself have regularly been considered—for example, problems of waterlogging and salinity in irrigation projects, watershed and erosion control in hydroelectric and multipurpose river development schemes, and pasture development and animal disease problems in livestock projects. This, however, has not been true of environmental aspects external to the project, such as the increased incidence of water-borne disease resulting from projects that change the pattern of water distribution and use. Only recently and rarely have broad environmental, political, sociological, and other facets that are external to the project been seriously considered at the project preparation stage.

Since the late 1960s environmentalists have criticized the Bank for neglecting the environmental impacts of projects it has supported. Those who have criticized the Bank for its failure to follow a concept of development process have also faulted it for ignoring environmental and social impacts. As Mason and Asher also write (1973, 469), "And now after several years of public concern for the ecological consequences of economic expansion, the Bank is taking a somewhat belated interest in this problem."

The Bank's interest in environmental consequences rose in part as it shifted from measuring a nation's progress by its GNP rate of growth to valuing reduced poverty and an improved quality of human life. When governments and lending institutions pursue broad social objectives, rather than merely economic growth, the importance of a project's environmental impacts, such as industrial pollution or the disruption of the habitats of indigenous people in tropical forests, becomes obvious. However, there is a difference between viewing environmental impacts as "a factor to be considered" in facilitating and implementing development projects and programs, on the one hand, and adopting sustainable development as the primary policy objective, on the other. The Bank's full transition to the latter objective has yet to occur in practice, despite the lofty policy statements of its leaders.

The World Bank's Environmental Procedures

In 1970, the World Bank became the first multilateral development bank to appoint an environmental advisor; its Office of Environmental Affairs was created in 1973. At the policy level, President McNamara's successors, A. W. Clausen (1981–1986) and Barber B. Conable (1986–1991), continued his support for the Bank's involvement in environmental problems. The Bank now has an Environment Department (upgraded in 1987 from office to department status) under the Vice President for Sector Policy and Research.

The Environment Department (ED) is concerned primarily with general environmental policy and research. The Bank's operating staff performs most of the environmental functions associated with making project and sector loans, especially in the regional environment divisions (REDs). These divisions are not under the ED but are part of the country departments. The Bank has abandoned its earlier practice of having projects reviewed by the ED at the end of the appraisal process because it feels that environmental concerns should be integrated into mainstream operations and not considered by a separate entity within the Bank. The goal is to imbue the entire Bank staff with sensitivity for the environment and sustainability.

The major criteria for loan appraisal have traditionally been (1) a satisfactory economic return on the project and (2) financial and technical feasibility. Concern with adverse environmental impacts has been viewed as a constraint on lending rather than as an objective in the lending and development assistance process. Under traditional criteria, environmental improvement and sustainability cannot have the same priority in loan appraisal as monetary returns on investment.

It is our impression that the people in the ED are dedicated to improving the environment and managing resources for sustainable development. But the ED has no direct responsibility for the environmental components of projects, for negotiating with borrowers, or for postproject evaluation. It has no veto over loans for projects it believes are environmentally flawed, nor does it have any opportunity to prepare independent reports on the environmental consequences of proposed loans before they go to the board for approval. The ED can only educate the country and regional staffs of the Bank in applying environmental principles and sustainable resource management in their lending operations.

The ED does have a role in preparing and reviewing environmental issue papers for borrowing members. These papers identify key environmental problems and their causes. Most are written by the Bank's country departments, with varying degrees of support from the ED. Environmental issue papers form the basis for environmental action plans (EAPs), which Bank staff and consultants prepare in collaboration with member governments. The ED also prepares working papers in the areas of natural resource management, environmental quality and health, and environmental economics.

ENVIRONMENTAL PROCEDURES FOR PROJECT LOANS[2]

The World Bank's procedures for appraising the environmental impacts of prospective projects revolve around the preparation and review of an environmental impact assessment (EIA) of the project. (The IDA's environmental procedures are the same as those of the World Bank.) The borrower prepares the EIA (described in detail in Chapter 3), monitored and often assisted by Bank staff, including personnel from both the country department and the ED. The task manager (TM) for the project screens the project with advice from the regional environment division. Projects are divided into four categories: (1) those for which a normal EIA is required, (2) those requiring limited environmental assessment, (3) those for which an environmental assessment is unnecessary, and (4) those for which separate EIAs are not required because the environment is the major focus of project preparation. Dams and reservoirs, power projects, irrigation and drainage projects, industrial plants, mines, pipelines, port and harbor developments, reclamation and new land developments, resettlement, and transportation projects usually require EIAs and are designated in categories 1 or 2. Projects concerned with education, family planning, health, and institution building do not normally require EIAs and are designated in category 3. Reforestation or pollution abatement projects would be in category 4.*

An initial executive project summary (IEPS) identifies the key environmental issues, the category recommended, and a preliminary EIA preparation schedule if one is required. Following an IEPS meeting, at which the project's category and timing and the issues for environmental analysis are confirmed, the Bank staff discusses with the borrower the scope and terms of reference for the EIA. The Bank's environmental staff, sometimes including a member of the RED, usually makes a field visit. The EIA for a major project may take six to eighteen months to prepare and review.

*Author Note: In response to growing criticism from NGOs the EIA Category 4 was recently dropped by the World Bank.

It should form a part of the overall feasibility study, with its findings directly integrated into project design. However, analysts with appropriate expertise—and in some cases independent experts not affiliated with the project—usually prepare it separately. This procedure raises the question of how EIA findings are integrated with the project design.

A borrower for a project in categories 1 or 2 submits a final EIA report before the Bank can appraise the loan project. The Bank encourages the borrower to release relevant information in the EIA to interested parties, such as nongovernmental organizations (NGOs) concerned with the environment. The Bank's project appraisal mission reviews both the procedures and the substantive elements of the EIA with the borrower, assesses the adequacy of the institutions responsible for environmental planning and management in light of EIA findings, and determines whether the EIA's recommendations are properly addressed in project design. The main findings of the EIA are explained in the text of the staff appraisal report (SAR). In addition, an SAR annex summarizes the EIA more fully, covering environmental baseline conditions, alternatives considered, possible mitigating and compensatory actions, capability of local environmental staffs, environmental monitoring arrangements, and the borrower's consultations with affected groups. The RED must give formal environmental clearance based on these factors before the regional vice president can authorize negotiations with the prospective borrower.[3] Measures critical to the implementation of the EIA may require specific conditionality in the loan documents (see Appendix 2-A). EIA recommendations provide the basis for supervising the environmental aspects of project implementation. If unexpected environmental problems surface at the supervision stage, the project design may need to be revised. Following completion of the project, the Operations Evaluation Department of the Bank receives a report evaluating (1) environmental impacts, both anticipated in the EIA, and unanticipated, and (2) the effectiveness of mitigating measures taken.

EIAs are also prepared for some sector loans. Since these loans are often made through financial intermediaries, subproject details may not be known at the time of the sector appraisal. In such cases, the borrower's project-implementing institutions must carry out the same type of environmental assessment required for project loans, but without the monitoring and appraisal activities of the Bank's staff. As noted elsewhere, nonproject loans have become increasingly important in the Bank. This tends to reduce the scope of the Bank's project-oriented environmental control procedures. Nonproject loans are discussed in Chapter 8.

LOANS SPECIFICALLY DESIGNED TO
PROMOTE ENVIRONMENTAL OBJECTIVES

In recent years the Bank has made a number of loans specifically designed to promote environmental objectives or to correct the adverse environmental impacts of previous projects. An agricultural sector loan to Pakistan in FY 1989 specifies waterlogging and salinity as the country's principal environmental problems from irrigated agriculture. The loan is designed in part to rehabilitate irrigation and drainage systems, to privatize public tube-wells, to improve management of groundwater resources, and to improve assessment and collection of water charges to encourage the efficient allocation of irrigation water. A loan to Algeria is designed to introduce integrated pest management to reduce the use of agrochemicals. A loan for land settlement and environmental management in Malaysia includes provision for protection and management of wildlife reserves. Loans to Malawi and Pakistan are designed in part to achieve more economic use of forest resources by such things as conserving fuel wood and protecting and managing indigenous forests. Chapter 10 discusses a large number of useful projects that might be undertaken principally for their favorable environmental consequences and that would promote sustainable development.

THE IFC'S ENVIRONMENTAL PROCEDURES

The IFC's stated policy is that projects it supports must satisfy the same environmental standards required by the World Bank and the IDA and that an EIA must be an integral part of the project appraisal process. In FY 1989 the IFC appointed an environmental specialist "to insure that projects conform with local environmental requirements, as well as with the World Bank's guidelines and policies on such matters as air emissions, waste water, solid waste, hazardous chemicals, wildlands, resettlement, and worker health and safety."

Environmental Policies of Other
Multilateral Development Banks

The principal MDBs other than the World Bank Group are the Inter-American Development Bank (IADB), the Asian Development Bank (ADB), and the African Development Bank (AfDB). These regional MDBs have organizational structures and sources of capital similar to those of the World Bank. Like the World Bank, they make loans on near-market terms with funds borrowed from international capital markets; governments of the member countries effectively guarantee these obligations. Each MDB has a special fund financed by grants from the industrial-country members for making concessional loans similar to IDA's: the IADB's Fund for Special Operations, the ADB's Asian Development Fund, and the AfDB's African Development Fund. Members are the regional developing countries and the industrial countries. Although industrial countries supply the bulk of the effective capital, meaning the unpaid subscribed capital that constitutes credible guarantees for the funds borrowed in the international capital markets, they do not have majority voting power.

Regional MDBs lend largely on a project basis but make some loans to economic sectors, such as agriculture, and to financial intermediaries. The allocation of project loans by economic sector has been similar to that for the World Bank; however, the World Bank makes a higher proportion of its loans in nonproject form. In contrast to the World Bank, regional MDBs do not try to exert much direct influence on their member countries' fiscal, monetary, trade, or other macroeconomic policies.

Since nearly all members of regional MDBs are also members of the World Bank, the question arises as to why regional institutions with functions similar to those of the World Bank were established. Some members of regional MDBs argued that decentralization along regional lines would provide administrative advantages and that institutional policies should reflect the problems and interests unique to particular regions. However, regional politics and a desire to obtain more capital than was available from the World Bank were the real reasons for the establishment of the regional MDBs.

THE INTER-AMERICAN DEVELOPMENT BANK (IADB)

The roots of the IADB go back to the Pan-American Union established late in the last century, when an inter-American financial institution was first proposed. Throughout the twentieth century Latin American countries have demanded some kind of regional financial institution to which their governments could turn for assistance. Following World War II, the Organization of American States (OAS) was especially insistent. Until 1958, however, the US government steadfastly maintained that most Latin American countries were members of the World Bank and the International

Monetary Fund (IMF) and that the US Export-Import Bank had been making substantial loans to Latin America, so there was no need for a special institution to finance Latin American development.

Latin Americans countered by arguing that the World Bank was supplying development credits too slowly and was applying unreasonably rigid standards for those credits and that the United States had given generous concessional aid to Europe during the Marshall Plan era and large grants to Asia during the post-war period but gave only small loans from the US Export-Import Bank to Latin America. US concern for the political future of Latin America and increasing interest in its cooperation with the United States during the Cold War brought about a change in the US government's position. In August 1958 President Dwight D. Eisenhower announced his willingness to consider the establishment of an inter-American bank.

There was widespread disagreement in the Inter-American Economic and Social Council of the OAS and no Latin American consensus about the nature of the institution to be formed. The US Treasury Department submitted a draft agreement for an institution patterned along the lines of the World Bank. The OAS adopted this format in April 1959, and the IADB was established in December of that year. The IADB is second to the World Bank Group in total resources and annual loans made (see Table 2-1). Although the presidents of the IADB have always been Latin Americans, the United States government has significant influence over the Bank's policies. Since failure to heed United States objectives could impair the periodic replenishment of the Bank's resources, the United States has an effective veto on important decisions. The United States government holds 34.5 percent of the votes in the IADB. Nonregional members, including the United States and Canada, hold 46 percent, with the twenty-five regional developing members holding the remainder.

As in the case of the World Bank, regional banks became aware of the environmental consequences of MDB-supported projects long after environmentalists began calling the attention of the international community to the serious problems in Third World countries. In the case of the IADB, a lack of high-level commitment delayed environmental action at the operations level. In 1979, the executive directors of the Bank approved an operations policy statement establishing guidelines for the Bank's environmental activities. But as late as 1985 the IADB lacked systematic procedures for environmental analysis and had yet to establish an environmental office (Runnals 1986, 209). In 1983 the IADB established an

Environmental Management Committee (EMC), composed of departmental managers, to review the environmental aspects of projects, but the Bank did not establish an Environmental Protection Division (EPD) with professional staff members until 1989. Apparently this was in response to conditions set forth in the Seventh Replenishment Agreement by the member governments, which provided an increase in the resources of the IADB's Fund for Special Operations.

The IADB's Environmental Protection Division began operations in January 1990 with thirteen professional staff members. The EPD works with operational and technical staff to evaluate the environmental impact of projects and to recommend remedial action (IADB 1990b, 9). It also advises the EMC, and its chief serves as the committee's secretary. The EMC continues to review projects before they are submitted to the loan committee and the board of directors and has the authority to recommend that a project be reformulated or even removed from consideration. The EPD participates in projects specifically designed to resolve environmental and natural resource problems. It is also responsible for ongoing relations with other governmental and nongovernmental agencies. Specialists on environmental subjects are on the staff of other IADB departments, and the Bank plans to spread responsibility for environmental activities throughout the entire institution.

The procedures for classifying and evaluating environmental impacts of prospective IADB-supported projects are similar to those followed by the World Bank and IDA, with some important differences. The borrowing country prepares an EIA, except for those projects designed specifically to improve environmental quality or having no direct or indirect environmental impact. The IADB project team identifies a project's potential environmental impacts and, in collaboration with the EPD, determines the project category based on those potential impacts. Also in collaboration with the EPD the project team prepares the terms of reference for an EIA if one is required and recommends studies and activities necessary to determine the magnitude and duration of the impacts. Additionally, the project team exercises a supervisory role in preparation of the EIA. IADB procedures require that opinions on environmental impacts be solicited from local groups that may be affected by the project.

Following preparation of the EIA, a feasibility study, and the final project design, the EMC prepares an environmental report, which is reviewed before the project is submitted for approval by the board of directors. The government of the borrowing country has the option of making public the entire EIA or only a summary of it. IADB representatives may also consult with NGOs, although the borrowing-country government does not always favor this.

If these procedures work, it seems likely that the new IADB environmental organization will have more operating responsibility than the World Bank's ED. However, some of them were only adopted in 1990, and we have no report on how well the system is operating. Much will depend upon the leadership and quality of the staff of the EPD.

THE ASIAN DEVELOPMENT BANK (ADB)

Because of geographical factors and political and cultural differences within Asia, that continent has never experienced the sense of community that exists in Latin America. Nevertheless, following World War II several Asian leaders became ardent supporters of regional cooperation and of the need to establish a financial institution that would make them less dependent on loans from the World Bank, which was dominated by the United States and Western Europe. Interest in the establishment of an Asian development bank grew mainly from discussions in the United Nations Economic Commission for Asia and the Far East (ECAFE) headquartered in Bangkok, Thailand. Japan expressed strong interest in the establishment of an Asian bank, not as a source of capital for itself but as a means of increasing its influence in Asia. Following the meeting of an expert working group convened by ECAFE in August and September 1963, a Ministerial Conference for Asian Economic Cooperation in December 1963 endorsed the idea of an Asian bank. A charter was completed in 1964, modeled after that of the World Bank. Again the US government was skeptical about the need for another regional institution, but political developments worked in its favor. In April 1965, President Lyndon B. Johnson called for a peace effort in Indochina, which he hoped to encourage by an economic development program underwritten by US aid. The Asian Development Bank was inaugurated in November 1966, with headquarters in Manila, Philippines, but with a Japanese president, Takeshi Watanabe, who had played a leading role in promoting the idea of an Asian bank during the 1950s.

The ADB was late to officially recognize the importance of the environment in its lending and in doing anything about it. Stein and Johnson 1979) described the ADB as lacking any formal commitment to environmental protection or to specific procedures for considering environmental impacts in loan preparation and negotiation. The ADB did not appoint an environmental specialist until 1981; a second environmental specialist was recruited in 1981, but it was several years before a system of review of Bank projects and the application of environmental guidelines were put into operation. In 1987 the Bank's executive directors endorsed the establishment of an Environmental Unit (EU) and the deployment of a third environmental specialist. Between May 1981 and April 1987 more than five hundred projects were the subjects of environmental reports, but such a small staff could not adequately review and make recommendations on the problems of such a large portfolio.

ADB publications make references to the preparation of EIAs for Bank-supported projects from the 1970s onward but contain no information on review procedures. Regional or country staffs have reviewed most Bank-supported prospective projects, with the Bank's environmental specialists commenting on the reports. The EU has prepared guidelines for each of a number of economic sectors receiving loans and a first-rate document on EIAs (ADB 1988b & 1989). A statement on the significant environmental impacts of each project is included in the Bank staff's final project appraisal, and an environmental specialist attends review committee meetings on projects with important adverse impacts. Before 1989, however, the ADB's EU had little more than an advisory role. Its specialists had no veto power on the approval of projects or on agreements on environmental practices incorporated into loan covenants. Members of the EU cooperated in missions and in the preparation of reports, but these were project team activities rather than independent oversight by the EU (ADB 1988b). David Runnals points out that the influence of the environmental staff was limited once a project reached the appraisal stage, partly due to the lack of a formal environmental clearance process. At the postevaluation stage the EU had even less influence (1986, 204–207). In April 1989, the EU was upgraded to division and later to office status (ADB 1990, 56). The new Office of the Environment (OE) undertakes the screening and appraisal of the environmental aspects of projects and is also responsible for environmental review during the implementation and postevaluation phases. This information, which was provided to us in a letter from an ADB official, suggests that the OE now plays a more direct and independent role in the project review and appraisal process. The OE prepares annual environmental and natural resource briefing profiles for each member country, identifying major environmental and natural resource concerns and providing examples of projects for possible Bank funding. NGOs are contacted and encouraged to cooperate with member governments on potential projects identified in the profiles (ADB 1987, 28).

In 1989, the ADB announced that it was integrating environmental considerations into its program (nonproject) lending. Recently the Bank has expanded its program lending as a means of promoting financial and economic reforms in member countries. The procedure, as outlined by the Bank, is to hold a policy dialogue with the member country to develop a framework appropriate for Bank support and to establish interim goals and a timetable for implementation. Part of the program loan is withheld, and released after interim goals have been substantially achieved (ADB 1990, 37). It is not clear from the Bank's statement whether environmental conditionality has actually been used in program loans.

The Bank also reports that NGOs increasingly help to implement the environmental content of loan projects (ADB 1990, 31). It has consulted with NGOs on project designs and used them as credit intermediaries and providers of technical assistance in a pilot project in the Philippines for financing small enterprises and cottage industries. NGOs also serve as field-level project managers in a fisheries loan to the Philippines that supports a community-based coastal zone management program. However, cooperation with NGOs depends heavily on the borrowing government's willingness to associate them with projects. Thus far, NGOs have participated at the project level only in a few countries, including Indonesia, Pakistan, and the Philippines, and their involvement has been largely confined to agricultural and rural development (ADB 1990, 33).

In a recent letter to the president of the ADB, George A. Folsom, deputy assistant secretary of the US Treasury Department, criticized the Bank for not exerting sufficient effort in integrating environmental protection and resource management with its lending program (Folsom 1990b). One criticism was that the staff of environmental specialists was too small, currently only five, and that it should be increased to at least fifteen. The letter also implied that the Bank had not implemented procedures (including provision for NGO participation in the borrowing countries) for ensuring that EIAs are completed for projects with adverse environmental impacts, that copies of the EIAs are available to board members at least 120 days in advance of loan consideration, and that copies of the EIA or a comprehensive summary are made available to the public. These procedures are in line with a US law (effective 19 December 1991) stating that US directors on MDB boards cannot support loans unless these procedures are followed (see Chapter 9). Folsom's letter also asks the Bank to make sure that the forestry projects it finances emphasize conservation of forest areas and protection of biological diversity and that land-use policies take into account their impact on forest resources. Finally, the Folsom letter urges the Bank to expand its programs in energy conservation, end-use efficiency, and renewable energy. Folsom made some of these points less directly in an address at the 1990 annual meeting of the ADB in New Delhi (Folsom, 1990a).

THE AFRICAN DEVELOPMENT BANK (AfDB)

Unlike the other regional MDBs, the AfDB was established in September 1964 without developed-country members and very largely by Africans themselves. According to the Bank's charter, membership was confined to independent African states, except that South Africa would not be eligible until apartheid there was terminated. This membership limitation was altered in the 1970s so that developed non-African countries could be admitted. Subscriptions by members were based on a formula that included population, GNP, foreign trade, and government revenue. The authorized capital was $250 million, half to be paid in the form of convertible currencies (international currencies such as dollars or sterling), the other half subject to call. The Bank was expected to be able to borrow in the international capital markets on the basis of capital subject to call, as can the World Bank and the other regional banks. However, the other MDBs were able to borrow at rates of interest little different from those on US Treasury obligations because they could count on the capital subscriptions of developed-country members to meet their obligations to foreign creditors. The international credit standing of African member countries was not high enough to provide a credible guarantee on amounts borrowed. In the early years, the AfDB had to rely on the paid-in portion of subscribed capital, which was supposed to total $109 million. Since many countries failed to make subscription payments in accordance with their agreement with the Bank, only $53.3 million had been paid in by 1968 (White 1972, 116).

The Bank opened its doors at Abidjan, Ivory Coast, in July 1966 and made its first loan in August 1967—a $2.3 million highway loan for upgrading two roads on the Kenya-Uganda and Kenya-Tanzania borders. The Bank's Articles of Agreement require that loans be made only for specific projects and that the Bank favor regional loans involving more than one member country.

So long as the Bank's lending capacity depended solely on the capital subscriptions of its African members, it had little resources for loans. The Bank sought to augment its capital resources by subscriptions from developed countries to an African Development Fund (ADF), similar to the special funds established by the other MDBs, that make concessional loans. Attracting contributions to the AfDB proved difficult, however, until the early 1970s when the Organization for Economic Cooperation and Development showed interest in assisting Africa and OECD member countries agreed to make contributions to the ADF. Subsequently, the Bank opened its membership to countries outside the region and the AfDB grew in both numbers and resources. As of December 1988, its membership included sixty African nations and twenty-three nonregionals, mostly industrial countries or countries with high credit standings such as Saudi Arabia and Korea. The African members made capital subscriptions of $7.0 billion and held 59 percent of the voting power; nonregional countries made subscriptions of $4.6 billion and held 41 percent of the voting power.

The AfDB is now able to borrow in the international capital markets on the guarantee of the unpaid subscriptions of nonregional members. Loans by the AfDB during FY 1988 totaled nearly $1.7 billion. In addition, as of 30 September 1988, nonregional members had made subscriptions to the ADF totaling nearly $4.5 billion; loans from the Fund during FY 1988 totaled $931 million. An increase in the Bank's ordinary capital resources is expected to boost the Bank's capital to $19.4 billion, of which 6.25 percent will be paid in and 93.8 percent will be callable capital.

As of August 1991, the AfDB, while endorsing environmental policies similar to those of the World Bank, had not taken steps to embody these policies in its operations. It has established an Environmental Unit but has no permanent technical staff. As of July 1991 the AfDB did not require borrowers to prepare EIAs for their projects, nor had it adopted procedures for working with NGOs in member countries or for influencing member governments to adopt procedures whereby NGOs can help review prospective loan projects.

In a letter dated 23 August 1990, George Folsom, deputy assistant secretary in the US Treasury Department, urged the Bank to hire a minimum of ten environmental specialists and to integrate environmental considerations into all of its lending activities. Folsom also advised the Bank to implement procedures to ensure that EIAs are completed for all projects that will significantly affect the environment. The letter is similar in other respects to that written to the president of the ADB, noted on p. 23 (Folsom 1990c).

According to the Bank's 1989 *Annual Report,* in that year the AfDB and ADF appoved $2.9 billion in loans and grants. Nonproject loans constituted 17.3 percent, while project loans accounted for more than 75 percent of total lending; agriculture constituted the largest individual sector (AfDB 1990).

THE INTERNATIONAL MONETARY FUND (IMF)

The charters of both the IMF and the World Bank were negotiated at the Bretton Woods Conference in 1944, and both came into existence in 1946. Like the Bank, the IMF was designed mainly to deal with post–World War II problems in Europe. According to its charter, its principal purposes were to promote exchange rate stability and to restore the convertibility of the world's major currencies. The IMF was expected to provide financial assistance largely to the European countries whose currencies and balance of payments were of greatest importance to world trade and finance. For a number of reasons these currencies did not become generally convertible until the 1960s. After 1971, when the IMF par value system (under which the value of each member's currency was tied to the dollar and the dollar tied to gold) was terminated because the United States abandoned the gold standard, there was little need for IMF exchange rate stabilization loans to industrial countries.

There was, however, a need to provide intermediate-term credits to developing countries that, unlike industrial countries, lacked sufficient reserves to maintain imports in the face of fluctuating exchange earnings. Thus the IMF emerged from the early postwar period as an institution dedicated almost entirely to providing balance-of-payments assistance to developing countries.[4] Because of the terms and the general-purpose nature of its loans, the IMF is not officially regarded as a development institution. But as the World Bank has increased its nonproject loans designed to influence development policies, and as the IMF has lengthened the maturity of its loans, the distinction between the functions of these institutions has blurred.

Both the IMF and the World Bank make structural adjustment loans (SALs) accompanied by conditions in the loan agreements designed to influence government policies to promote economic development. In some cases both institutions make SALs to the same country and collaborate to some extent in their lending and conditionality. The IMF tends to emphasize exchange rate adjustments and monetary and fiscal policies; the

World Bank is somewhat more concerned with government policies that influence the level and allocation of investment, the liberalization of markets, foreign trade policies, and public enterprise reform. However, both agencies are certainly interested in all policies that promote balance-of-payments adjustment and economic growth. As the IMF *Annual Report 1989* (38) put it:

> Although their Articles of Agreement define different purposes and mandates for the Fund and the World Bank, cooperation between the two institutions has always been emphasized, reflecting the important links between macroeconomic management and economic development. The severe problems facing members in the 1970s and 1980s have led to greater overlap in the activities of the two institutions, with the Fund paying greater attention to structural reform and the Bank making structural and sectoral adjustment loans. Against this background, principles have been developed and further elaborated during the past year, to promote closer collaboration between the two institutions in assisting their member countries.

In short, we find little real distinction in either the purposes or the operations of the SALs of the two institutions.

As of late 1991, the IMF had not brought environmental issues into its operations. The Fund staff has been asked by the US executive director to the IMF to formulate a plan for its involvement with environmental problems. For reasons discussed in Chapter 8, we believe the Fund can bring environmental policy considerations into its loan conditionality in a way that will be consistent with the Fund's objectives.

BILATERAL ASSISTANCE AGENCIES

Nearly all industrial countries maintain government agencies that make loans or grants, or both, to Third World countries for development assistance. Most if not all of these agencies have sought to promote environmental objectives in their operations. We shall limit our discussion of bilateral agencies to the US Agency for International Development (USAID), a pioneer in combining environmental promotion with foreign aid.

Although the US Foreign Assistance Act establishing USAID contains language linking development assistance and the environment, little was done along these lines until 1975. In that year the Natural Resources Defense Council (NRDC) sued USAID, alleging that the agency had failed to file environmental impact statements (EISs) for the projects it supported and had in other ways failed to comply with the National Environmental Policy Act. USAID began preparing EISs following a consent decree. In 1978, a Foreign Assistance Act amendment required USAID to prepare EIAs for its projects, together with evaluations of developing countries' environmental and natural resource problems. In 1980, USAID appointed an environmental coordinator for the agency as a whole, a coordinator for each regional geographic bureau, and an environmental officer in each field mission.

According to current USAID procedures, all projects are screened to determine whether they require an environmental review, including an EIA or an EIS. The EIA constitutes a detailed study of foreseeable environmental effects, both beneficial and adverse, and identifies mitigation measures that should be incorporated into the design of the project (see Chapter 3). An EIS serves the same purpose as an EIA, except that it focuses on a wider context and includes global effects. If the USAID administrator deems it necessary, formal public hearings may be held in the United States to discuss the environmental study. Also, the agency's environmental coordinator and its general counsel review and clear the EIS. Thus, unlike most MDBs, USAID can approve funding for a project only after its environmental officer concurs with its mission as to how environmental issues should be addressed in the project design (Chew 1988, 6).

USAID has the largest field staff of any development assistance agency, and many of its environmental assessment activities are at the mission level (Runnals 1986, 210–211). The Agency's development assistance in the form of grants and loans has been running $6 billion annually in recent years.

Lending for the Global Environment

According to their charters, MDBs are dedicated to promoting world economic and social progress. These institutions are responsible for more than the welfare of the individual countries that receive their loans. They are responsible for the global environment, transcending the environmental impacts on the countries where damage may occur. Thus, destruction of tropical moist forests in Brazil and extinction of animal and plant species in Central America create worldwide social problems far greater than the social costs to individual countries.

Economic activities that principally affect common international environmental resources rather than simply the domestic environment include (1) production of chemicals that destroy the ozone layer; (2) pollution of international waters; (3) reduction of biodiversity; and (4) emission of gases that cause global warming. MDBs recognize an obligation to limit funding to projects that will deteriorate the international environment and to favor those that improve it. However, projects that promote these objectives, while having substantial net global benefits, may not be sufficiently profitable to the countries undertaking them. Examples of such projects include substituting coal and oil with alternative energy sources, such as natural gas and hydro power, to reduce CO_2 emissions; establishing national parks to protect biodiversity; rerouting roads, pipelines, and transmission lines away from areas of high biodiversity; constructing port facilities to avoid oil spills and dumping of bilge water and sludge by ships; and eliminating materials that cause ozone depletion, such as chlorofluorocarbons (CFCs) in the production of refrigeration equipment. The industrial countries are negotiating international agreements to act collectively to protect the global environment, but developing countries cannot be expected to undertake projects financed by MDBs at conventional rates of interest when returns are not sufficient to justify the investment.

At the 1989 meeting of the Development Committee (a joint ministerial committee of the boards of governors of the World Bank and the International Monetary Fund), the World Bank was asked to investigate the feasibility of a special fund to finance such investments in developing countries. On the basis of discussions with potential donor governments and with officials in both the United Nations Environment Programme (UNEP) and the United Nations Development Programme (UNDP), the World Bank presented the Development Committee in May 1990 with a paper proposing the establishment of a Global Environmental Facility (GEF). At a meeting of twenty-five industrialized and developing countries held in Paris in March 1990, a 1 to 1.5 billion dollar GEF pilot program was established under the management of the World Bank with participation by the UNDP and the UNEP. The industrial countries pledged funds for the GEF to operate for a three-year period. It would provide concessional assistance (either grants or loans on very liberal terms) to developing countries for projects designed to (1) protect the ozone layer, (2) reduce greenhouse gas emissions, (3) protect international water resources, and (4) protect biodiversity. The program would be in addition to development financing programs already in existence and would be available only for projects that contribute to the global environment but that would not earn a return sufficient for financing through regular MDB loan programs.

Although welcoming the GEF initiative, environmental NGOs have been critical of delegating the World Bank to manage the Fund on the grounds that the Bank has not been successful in protecting the environment in its own lending program. In January 1991 representatives of several conservation organizations, including the Natural Resources Defense Council, the Environmental Defense Fund, and the Sierra Club, released a memorandum setting forth recommendations concerning the structure and work plan of the GEF (NRDC 1991). The major recommendations were as follows:

1. Independent, high-level offices in both the World Bank and the UNEP should oversee the GEF.

2. Outside technical experts, affected communities, and NGOs should participate at all stages of the projects to be financed.

3. The Bank should consult with outside technical experts to develop innovative GEF projects, particularly in the areas of energy efficiency, biodiversity, and conservation of tropical forests, wetlands, and marine ecosystems.

Patrick Coady, US executive director on the board of directors of the World Bank, expressed agreement with some of the recommendations made by the conservation organizations regarding the GEF. He endorsed the establishment of a Scientific and Technical Advisory Panel and stated that "We look forward to an active panel that provides a strong link between private environmental interests and the implementing agencies. We also expect the panel to play a meaningful role in the operation of the Facility, including project identification, design, and monitoring. . . . It would be useful if the documents that come to this Board include input from the Advisory Panel. We would also like the Panel to report to the Board on project review and monitoring. . . . We hope to see the broadest possible opportunities for the Panel to contribute to the work of the Facility" (Coady 1991, 2).

Coady further stated that "the primary measure of success of the Facility will be incorporation of global environmental considerations into regular and ongoing operations of the World Bank and other development institutions. At the same time, the GEF must not become just an 'add-on' to existing lending programs. We want to ensure that the grant funds are utilized carefully. We see it as the vehicle to institutionalize an environmental policy framework through which all development activities will be considered in the years ahead, after the mandate for this three-year pilot program has expired."

Coady called for public participation in the GEF and for the establishment of facilities to make information available to NGOs and to solicit and incorporate NGO concerns into the preparation of the projects. The US government agreed to join the GEF and provide $150 million in parallel funding, rather than to put the funds directly into the GEF. In this way, the US government can control the use of its contribution.

APPENDIX 2-A

Conditionality

Conditionality as applied to development assistance refers to conditions that obligate the recipient to adopt certain economic policies or measures that an MDB or bilateral assistance agency believes will promote the borrowing country's economic welfare and the objectives of the assistance. A form of conditionality exists in the negotiation of all project loans, which are required to be used as defined in the loan agreement. If the project is an irrigation dam, the loan proceeds may not be used for a highway or a government building. But conditionality often goes beyond the project design to determine the way in which the project is to be implemented and what its effect may be on the economy and the physical and social environment of the borrowing country. A donor may require that an industrial plant be subject to pollution abatement standards, or that a reservoir project pay compensation to and finance the relocation of the people displaced, or that a forestry project provides for the protection of the indigenous population. Conditionality may even extend to indirect impacts of a project, such as its effect on the distribution of income in the region or on the welfare of women and minorities. It may also require legislative or administrative action that has no direct relation to the project. Borrowing governments often resent such conditionality, but nongovernmental organizations representing those people potentially disadvantaged by the project may demand it.

Conditionality may also be applied to nonproject assistance. The International Monetary Fund (IMF) has attached conditions to its loans almost from the beginning of its operations. These conditions may include the depreciation of the borrower's currency, the reduction or elimination of its budget deficit, or the liberalization of its import and foreign exchange restrictions. The World Bank requires in its structural adjustment loans trade liberalization, the removal of certain subsidies, and a variety of economic reforms designed to remove barriers to growth and promote balance-of-payments adjustment. These conditions often contradict existing government policies or are contrary to the interests of politically power-ful groups in the borrowing country. IMF and World Bank conditional-ity are often blamed for reduced government social services or employment in the borrowing country. For this reason, NGOs have often objected to some conditionality imposed by the IMF or World Bank. On the other hand, NGOs may demand conditionality for protecting the environment or for preventing the adverse social consequences of certain projects and programs financed by MDBs.

Borrowing-country governments often condemn conditionality on the grounds that it interferes with their sovereignty. They also argue that it is likely to fail unless there is wide national support for the conditions demanded by donors. Donors, on the other hand, argue that aid will not achieve its purpose without the adoption of certain policies and could, in fact, be counterproductive by enabling a country to continue practices that are actually harmful to economic growth. A conflict might occur be-tween an MDB that seeks to make the projects and programs it supports environmentally sound and a borrowing government that favors short-term economic gains, even at the cost of destruction or degradation of its resource capital. Such a controversy might reflect a difference in social values, or the government might believe that short-term gains at the ex-pense of sustainability will enable it to remain in power. We believe that MDBs should follow a policy of promoting sustained development and environmental soundness without compromise.

NOTES

1. Capital absorptive capacity refers to a country's ability to design investment projects and integrate the projects into its economy in a way that increases the productivity of labor and natural resources. Many poor countries have limited absorptive capacity because their citizens lack education and training, they lack human-resource development ability, and their agricultural productivity is low.
2. The material in this section is based on a World Bank document entitled "Operational Directive 4.01, Annex A: Environmental Assessment," October 1991.
3. This authorization requirement suggests that regional environment divisions hold a veto power over loan negotiations, but we have found no cases where such a veto has been exercised.
4. Balance-of-payments assistance is designed to enable countries to finance their imports of goods and services over periods of two or three years when their export earnings are temporarily insufficient. Loans for this purpose are expected to be repaid from increased exports or reduced imports within three to five years. Such assistance differs from development assistance, which is designed to finance development projects or programs requiring several years to complete and put into operation. Loans for development assistance are usually repayable over a fifteen- to thirty-year period. Structural adjustment loans are designed to assist countries to take measures to change the composition or structure of their imports and exports that may require five to ten years. Therefore, repayments may be made over a longer period of time than for normal balance-of-payments assistance.

REFERENCES

African Development Bank. 1990. *Annual Report 1989*. Abidjan, Ivory Coast: AfDB.

Asian Development Bank. 1987. *Annual Report 1986*. Manila, Philippines.

———. 1988a. *Environmental Planning and Management and the Project Cycle*. Environment Paper No. 1. Manila, Philippines: ADB, October.

———. 1988b. *Guidelines for Integrated Regional Economic-cum-Environmental Development Planning: A Review of Regional Environmental Development Planning Studies in Asia*. Manila, Philippines: ADB.

_____. 1989. *Minimum Quality Criteria for Ecologically Sensitive Areas*. Environment Paper No. 4. Manila, Philippines: ADB, April.

_____. 1990. *Annual Report 1989*. Manila, Philippines: ADB.

Chew, S. T. 1988. *Environmental Assessments of Development Projects: A Preliminary Review of AID's Experience*. USAID Evaluation Occasional Paper No. 17. Washington, D.C.: USAID, June.

Coady, E. Patrick. 1991. Mimeo. Washington, D.C.: World Bank, 14 March.

Development Committee. 1989. *The World Bank Support for the Environment: A Progress Report*. Washington, D.C.: World Bank, September.

Folsom, George A. 1990a. Statement to the twenty-third annual meeting of the Asian Development Bank, New Delhi, India, 3 May.

_____. 1990b. Letter to Kimimasa Tarumizu, president of the ADB. Washington, D.C., 23 August.

_____. 1990c. Letter to the Babacar N'Diaye, president of the AfDB. Washington, D.C., 28 August.

Inter-American Development Bank. 1989. *The IDB*. 16, no. 3 (December).

_____. 1990a. *Annual Report 1989*. Washington, D.C.: IADB.

_____. 1990b. "Procedures for Classifying and Evaluating Environmental Impacts of Bank Operations." Mimeo. Washington, D.C., February.

International Finance Corporation. 1989. *Annual Report 1989*. Washington, D.C.: World Bank.

International Monetary Fund (1989). *Annual Report 1989*, Washington, D.C.: IMF.

Mason, Edward S., and Robert E. Asher. 1973. *The World Bank Since Bretton Woods*. Washington, D.C.: Brookings Institution.

Natural Resources Defense Council. 1991. "Recommendations on the Global Environmental Facility." Mimeo. Washington, D.C., 16 September.

Runnals, David. 1986. "Factors Influencing Environmental Policies in International Development Agencies." In *Environmental Planning and Management* (proceedings of the 1986 Regional Symposium on Environmental and Natural Resources Planning). Manila, Philippines: ADB, December.

Stein, R. E., and B. Johnson. 1979. *Banking on the Biosphere*. New York: Lexington Books.

White, John. 1972. *Regional Development Banks: The Asian, African and Inter-American Development Banks*. New York: Praeger.

World Bank. 1989. "Operational Directive 4.00, Annex A: Environmental Assessment." Mimeo. Washington, D.C. September.

_____. 1990. *Annual Report 1989*. Washington, D.C.

CHAPTER 3

Sustainable Growth and Development Strategies

The State of the Third World Environment

This study is concerned largely with identifying and analyzing the adverse environmental impacts of development projects supported by MDBs. But simply preventing such impacts will not guarantee sustainable development. Traditional societies with low population densities and abundant land were able to produce adequate food and maintain their natural resource bases by using restorative fallows and practicing crop rotation and simple irrigation. In recent decades, however, population pressure and diminishing amounts of arable land have driven farmers in developing countries to expand production in ways characterized as ecological suicide (Oram 1988, 14ff): by shortening fallow, practicing excessive deforestation, farming on erosion-prone slopes, and overgrazing. These destructive activities are more harmful to the ecology and the resource base than all of the environmentally flawed government projects designed to expand agricultural output. In many poor counties with high rates of population growth, doing nothing will guarantee the destruction of indigenous resources and result in declining per capita food production. What to do to expand agricultural production and at the same time halt or reverse resource degradation is the heart of the problem of sustainable development. The solution requires new technologies designed to suit environmental, economic, and social conditions. Promoting sustainable development requires MDBs to take positive action to change farming practices, not simply to avoid projects that create environmental hazards.

Environmental conditions in Third World countries are about as varied as the conditions of these countries' economies. Per capita income ranges from less than $200 per year in some African countries to $3,000 in South Korea and Venezuela. If we had an index that measured relative environmental well-being for each of the world's countries, the rankings would to a considerable degree parallel those for per capita gross national product (GNP), with some important exceptions. Much would depend on what was included in the environmental index: In addition to levels of air, water, and soil pollution, we should include the extent of resource degradation. Extreme poverty is closely related to environmental atrophy, but the prevalence of extreme poverty is not necessarily measured by per capita GNP. For example, Brazil has more extreme poverty than Costa Rica, though Costa Rica's per capita income is about three-fourths that of Brazil. The nature of environmental degradation may differ greatly among very poor countries and between urban and rural populations. Many industrial cities in poor countries (such as Bombay in India and Manila in the Philippines) suffer from extreme air and water pollution, uncollected solid waste, and biologically dead waterways loaded with sewage and industrial chemicals. While rural populations of poor countries may be spared from significant air pollution, many lack safe drinking water.

The environmental destitution of urban slums and rural villages, while contributing heavily to human suffering and mortality, is not as serious a problem for long-run economic development as is the destruction of the resource base. Given a change in environmental policies and a reallocation of government expenditures, air and water pollution could be largely eliminated in a decade or so. But the desertification that has taken place in Sub-Saharan African countries and the massive erosion of the soil in Haiti may require a century or more before production is restored.

Both types of environmental problems are caused largely by a high rate of population growth in very poor countries with limited land and other resources. In a sense, high population growth may be regarded as the single most important environmental problem. Generally, the rate of population growth also correlates with the extent of poverty. However, these correlations do have exceptions. Eastern European countries have had low or even negative rates of population growth in recent years, and their per capita incomes are higher than in most countries that we classify as

Third World. Yet industrial pollution in their cities is among the highest in the world.

Brazil is listed in the upper-middle-income category in the *World Development Report* (World Bank 1989, 164–65), with a rate of population growth about average for Latin America and considerably lower than in most African countries. Yet Brazil has serious environmental and resource management problems. Much the same can be said of Mexico, which has only a slightly lower per capita income and about the same rate of population growth as Brazil. A country's governmental policies, along with its general level of education, are important in explaining its environmental conditions. Thus Chile, with a significantly lower per capita income than Brazil or Mexico, has a far better environmental record. Chile also has a much lower rate of population growth and higher levels of education and adult literacy.

How can MDBs influence the future course of environmental health in Third World countries? Government environmental policies and administrative reforms supported by an environmentally enlightened public must induce industries, municipalities, transportation sectors, mines, and participants in coastal activities to improve pollution abatement. As in the United States, NGOs can play a vital role in bringing pressure on governments. MDBs can provide education and limited amounts of technical and loan assistance and insist that loan-supported projects be designed and operated in accordance with environmental guidelines. MDBs have made their most serious mistakes in resource projects—irrigation, hydroelectric power, forestry, and the resettlement of frontier lands such as the Amazon Basin—largely by failing to perceive the indirect consequences of the projects and programs they have supported. Although MDB-supported projects constitute only a fraction of the sources of pollution, MDBs have considerable potential leverage in the area of resource management—especially in agriculture, land and water use, and forestry.

The Meaning of Sustainable Development

Sustainable development has become a popular concept in literature on the environment and on economic development. It is applicable to any economy but is generally thought of in reference to Third World countries. While achieving sustainable development has replaced maximizing economic growth as the primary goal of development assistance agencies, it is more heralded than actually applied. It's a good concept, provided we all know what it means, but it does not have the same meaning for all who use it. *Our Common Future* (The Brundtland Commission report) defines sustainable development as "development that meets the needs of the present without compromising the ability of future generations to meet their own needs." But some regard the primary focus on meeting "human needs" as too anthropocentric and argue for "global sustainability" that includes all components of the biosphere, even those with no apparent benefit to humanity. Short definitions are inadequate and often emphasize elements on which there can be no general agreement. The purpose of this section is to present the essential elements of sustainable development on which all environmentalists can agree.

Sustainable development requires conservation of the resource base as a condition for continual expansion of goods and services — not only those produced by combining human labor, knowledge, and capital with natural resources but also those such as clean air and water and wilderness amenities of all kinds provided directly by the resource base. The resource base encompasses the atmosphere; the oceans, lakes, and streams; the land in all its uses; animal and plant species; and forests, minerals, and the complex biological interrelationships that make up the ecology. It includes all that humanity has inherited from the time our species began interacting with the environment. It excludes plant and equipment and consumption goods. Some would include humans themselves and their cultural and social systems, but there is no general agreement on this. Despite our interest in the behavioral patterns of Australian aborigines, there is much in primitive cultures that few of us would want to preserve.

We classify resources as renewable or nonrenewable (or exhaustible), although this distinction is not always clear in practice. Sustainable development requires that we renew and expand renewable resources continuously and that we do not hinder future development by depleting exhaustible resources. Paradoxically, modern technology makes it possible to continue consuming nonrenewable resources while increasing their supply. For example, the world's reserves of copper are many times what they were in the nineteenth century despite our consumption of enormous amounts of the metal. (Mineral reserves are those that can be produced economically at a particular time.) New discoveries and technological advances have made this possible by allowing us to mine lower grades of ore commercially. Over time we can reduce our consumption of copper, nickel, chromium, and other minerals that are relatively scarce without impairing industrial production simply by substituting products made from silicon, aluminum, and iron, the most abundant minerals in the earth's crust. We can also develop substitutes for energy sources, such as solar power for petroleum. Many materials specialists believe that technology will enable us to prevent the exhaustion of any one of many minerals from impairing growth, but the depletion of other resources will threaten sustainable development.

Sustainable development is important for industrialized and developing countries and, indeed, for the entire globe. Resource deterioration in the form of desertification, deforestation, and loss of soil and groundwater is critical in many developing countries. Unless all industrialized countries take conservation measures, the loss of agricultural land and the reduction of water and energy resources will inevitably impair output in the next century. In the long run, the principles of sustainable development must be adopted on a global basis if the human species is to endure.

RESOURCE ACCOUNTING

Proponents of resource accounting regard our natural resource base as capital, analogous to humanly produced capital. When we use a machine or a building, part of the output attributed to that capital asset is regarded as depreciation or depletion, income that is not available for consumption but should be saved and reinvested in new buildings or machines as old ones wear out. In an analogous way, we should regard that portion of the output arising from the use of resource capital that is equal to the reduction in its value resulting from loss of quantity or impairment of quality as depletion. Again, this depletion should not be consumed as income but rather saved and reinvested to compensate for the loss of resource capital. Humans deplete resources in many ways: by harvesting virgin forests; extracting mineral reserves; eroding agricultural soil; lowering groundwater levels; reducing the natural purity of the atmosphere and of the water in our rivers, lakes, and oceans; and destroying wildlife and natural plant species. Whatever the form of depletion, we should reinvest a portion of our income each year to restore the capital value of our resource base. Since we have destroyed so much of this resource base inherited from the past without attempting to replenish it, we need to cover a large deficit in our resource account by increasing investment and conservation.

Environmental economists have been arguing for a revision of the national income accounting system that would recognize depletion of the natural resource base as a reduction in the national product. Robert Repetto has applied resource accounting to the Indonesian economy. The Indonesian government's statistics on gross domestic product (GNP) show an average annual increase of 7.1 percent from 1971 to 1984, but when allowance is made for resource depletion, GDP rose by only 4 percent per year (Repetto et al. 1989). Indonesia has been drawing heavily on her natural wealth—oil, gas, minerals, and timber and forest products—to finance development and pay for consumption expenditures. But this depletion of nonrenewable resources will reduce that country's future output and consumption, except to the extent that the proceeds from the natural resource industries are invested in other capital assets that will help to maintain output. Resource accounting can also be applied to nomarketable or common-use resources such as air and water. Pollution, for example, reduces the value of the resource base as measured by the human and material costs of pollution. This resource loss should also be deducted from the national product.

The rationale for using resource accounting is that it will make nations realize that resource depletion does not increase their national product and that, without adjustment for depletion, estimates of annual output and growth are overstated. Since natural resources are finite, resource accounting would help governments and the public to realize that resource loss cannot go on indefinitely without a decline in output, consumption, and social welfare. The US Congress was so impressed with this reasoning that in June 1989 it passed Public Law 101–45, Section 401, which provides that the administration "shall instruct the US Executive Director to each multilateral development bank and to the International Monetary Fund to seek the adoption of revisions in national accounting systems [that] reflect the depletion or degradation of natural resources as a component of economic activity." Similar instructions were given to the US secretary of state for delivery to the Organization for Economic Cooperation and Development (OECD) and the United Nations, and to the administrator of USAID for use in evaluating the economic performance of recipient countries. Commerce Appropriations Bill HR 2991 gives a similar directive to the US Department of Commerce, calling on the secretary to participate in the international effort to recompute national income accounts on a gross sustainable productivity basis. Such accounts would supplement but not substitute for traditional gross national product accounting.

These actions are an official recognition of the concept of sustainable development—that real growth cannot be achieved at the expense of natural resources.

FUTURE GENERATIONS

The policy against dissipating capital to prevent a decline in the future income of the *present* generation makes sense for a family, a nation, or the world. But sustainable development requires that we conserve resource capital to maintain output for *future* generations. This is the primary ethical justification for sustainable development. Sustainable development presents a conflict with the almost universal preference of individuals for present over future goods. This preference is measured by the rate of discount (interest). At a rate of discount of 10 percent, $100 worth of goods and services today is worth less than $40 ten years from now: When people borrow money at 10 percent for ten years, they agree to repay 2.5 times the amount borrowed at the end of the ten years. How, then, can the present generation be induced to sacrifice consumption so that future generations will inherit the present generation's resource base? In a democratic society in which government policies reflect the social consensus, sustainable development requires that society choose a goal that differs from the values individual members of society express in their private economic behavior. The government can accomplish this in the private sector by providing economic incentives to promote conservation of resource capital, and in the public sector by directly avoiding any net depletion or quality degradation of resource capital. The government can tax the consumption of fuel and of minerals likely to become scarce, and it can provide incentives for investments designed to maintain or enhance soil, forest, and water resources. Governments can also change the land tenure system to provide incentives for soil conservation. In many developing countries, peasants who do not own the land they work have little incentive to invest in farming methods that maintain soil productivity. Furthermore, low government-set prices for farm output discourage investment in the land. Governments should also abolish subsidies that promote deforestation.

In defining sustainable development, we must differentiate between maintaining the value of the total stock of resource capital and maintaining the physical quantity of each type of resource capital. Let us assume that 90 percent of a developing country's land is covered by virgin forest.

Sustainable development does not require that every harvested tree be replaced. The problem in Amazonia is not that the total amount of forest is declining, but that resources are being wasted. The forest is being burned and converted to uses that produce less value than it would have produced if left in a natural state. In a practical application of sustainable development, portions of the forest would be converted into agricultural and industrial uses, up to the point at which further deforestation would impair future output. The resource rents[1] from tree harvests (excluding payments to labor and human capital) would be set aside for investment to maintain the net capital value of the harvest. While such investment may take many forms, including investment in human capital, sustainable developing requires that priority be given to maintaining the value of renewable resources. For example, if farming is depleting soil, investment should be made in terracing and other forms of soil conservation. Where converting forestland for agricultural use has caused ecological damage, wilderness areas and wildlife refuges should be established and maintained to compensate for the damage.

PROMOTION OF SUSTAINABLE DEVELOPMENT

Many questions about what we must do to ensure the maintenance of the resource base so that future generations can enjoy the same or higher per capita incomes remain unanswered. For example, no technology is currently available for sustainable agricultural production in many tropical countries experiencing a 3 percent rate of population growth. It is sometimes suggested that development itself contains the seeds of its own termination, since it will in time deplete the natural resource base on which it depends. The Club of Rome expressed this pessimistic view in the early 1970s in its report, *Limits to Growth* (Meadows et al. 1972), in which it suggested that not only must the world limit population growth, but industrial countries in particular must give up the goal of constantly increasing their material standard of living. Although most population specialists and development economists agreed that reduced population growth is essential for any economic improvement in most Third World countries (and ultimately for the survival of the human species), there is no agreement that the world must terminate growth in per capita production. Such a conclusion suggests that sustainable development may be impossible. To sound an optimistic note, we have scarcely begun to realize the potential of technological advance, such as recycling and substitution, for conserving natural resources and for reducing human-caused pollution. The real obstacle to sustainable development may be political rather than economic or technical.

Foreign aid can promote sustainable development in developing countries if it is directed toward natural resource maintenance such as reforestation, soil protection, energy efficiency, and pollution abatement. Despite greater environmental awareness on the part of development assistance agencies, too much aid goes for direct or indirect financing of military expenditures, improper industrialization, expensive nonproductive government buildings and urban infrastructure, and bloated government bureaucracies. In some countries, *any* foreign aid may prove to be counterproductive without radical changes in government policies and leadership.

Traditional and Modern Development Strategies

Development assistance agencies are usually guided by some development or economic growth strategy based on a particular economic theory, or perhaps on a combination of theories. In the 1950s and 1960s, development economists formulated a number of growth theories, most of which were capital oriented in the sense that they made capital investment (and capital imports, in particular) a major determinant of economic growth (Mikesell 1968, Chs. 2 & 3). These theories had a great influence on UN institutions and on the US Foreign Assistance Agency, especially during the Kennedy and Johnson administrations. As a result, the World Bank, which had not adopted a specific strategy or theory of growth or development, came under intense criticism by the United Nations and by its economic commissions (such as the Economic Commission for Latin America) for its slow volume of lending and its failure to promote specific growth objectives for its members. The growth theories of the 1950s and 1960s supported the position that to achieve a certain rate of increase in per capita output in a developing country, a specific annual inflow of foreign aid would be required. For example, a report by a group of experts appointed by the UN secretary general (UN 1951, 75–79) estimated that an annual inflow of $14 billion in foreign capital would be required to support a 2 percent rate of growth in per capita national income in the developing countries over the 1950–1960 period. Such estimates were derived from theoretical growth models and became the basis of UN efforts to establish a large trust fund to be contributed by developed countries for grants to developing countries. Growth models also provided the rationale for US administration requests for congressional appropriations under the US Foreign Assistance Act.

Many development economists rejected capital-oriented growth models and their policy implications for foreign aid. They argued that economic growth and development are highly complex and involve much more than a certain amount of capital inflow. Although productive investment in a country correlates to the country's rate of economic growth, capital imports do not necessarily correspond to a rise in the growth rate on a sustained basis. World Bank officials also rejected the policy conclusions of the capital-oriented growth models. They argued that for capital imports to contribute to growth, a country must have sufficient *capital absorptive capacity,* which refers to the ability of a country to invest capital in a sufficiently productive way to earn an economic rate of return higher than the international rate of interest. Capital absorptive capacity differs greatly from country to country depending upon the amount and quality of its natural and human resources. It also depends on such factors as the country's economic organization (including market structure), the education and skill level of its population, government policies that determine economic incentives, the degree of competition in the economy, the mobility of capital and labor, and economic stability, including the absence of high inflation and severe recession. The Bank later broadened these conditions for capital absorptive capacity to include a social environment that would provide health, decent housing, basic education, sanitation, and foster a low birth rate—all essential to political stability and a productive work force. Most development economists now strongly endorse the idea that economic growth and development depend on a broad range of factors and not simply on the volume of foreign aid.

Today the MDBs, as well as most bilateral foreign assistance agencies (such as USAID), take an eclectic approach to the role of external assistance in development. Their attitude is that technical assistance and capital for imports should be provided to assist a country on the basis of a comprehensive examination of how that country ought to grow and on identification of the important bottlenecks to growth that external assistance could remove. There is no rigid formula for growth. Development is conceived not simply in terms of increasing per capita GNP but in terms of improving the lot of the abject poor and of providing a range of social services. MDBs encourage the adoption of government policies that will provide economic incentives to work and invest productively, promote free markets, reduce inflation, and avoid balance-of-payments conditions that interfere with foreign trade. While the former use of foreign aid to maximize the rate of economic growth has often proved incompatible with environmental protection and the conservation of natural resources, this modern approach fits well with the objectives of improving environmental conditions and promoting sustainable development.

Environmental Impact Assessment

Many governments, including the US government, have established procedures for investigating the environmental impacts of new projects. Nearly all projects approved for financing by MDBs now require an environmental impact assessment (EIA) if they are judged to be significantly hazardous to the environment. EIAs for large and complex projects involve engineering, biological, ecological, and economic studies that may cost a million dollars or more and require the services of specialists in several fields. NGOs should be acquainted with the procedures for preparing an EIA so that they will know how governments and MDBs evaluate proposed projects and can thus better raise pertinent questions on the environmental safety of the projects.

There is no standard format for EIAs. In most cases, borrowing governments prepare them in accordance with legislative or administrative regulations, but MDBs also sometimes prepare them. The major MDBs have published guidelines for EIA preparation, as have the UN, the OECD, and other international agencies (see References). Our analysis of EIAs is a composite of several guidelines. This analysis is intended not to provide technical instruction for the preparation of EIAs but to acquaint non-specialists concerned with monitoring and appraising the environmental consequences of development activities with the content and purposes of EIAs.

The EIA is not simply a document but is a process of investigation, analysis, and recommendation. Although that process should have a substantial impact on the planning and final design of the project, this is not always the case. There are, in general, two approaches to preparing an EIA. In the first, a team outside the group having major responsibility for project planning prepares the assessment. The team usually enters the process after completion of the initial project plan and uses the existing plan as the basis for its investigation of environmental impacts. The difficulty with this approach is that the environmental team is often under pressure to avoid recommending major changes in the basic plan. The EIA may then become little more than the basis for an impact statement that throws a favorable light on the environmental consequences of the project. Alternatively, the recommendations of the environmental team may be rejected and therefore have no influence on the final policy decision. We have been unable to find any cases in which an MDB abandoned a project on the basis of unfavorable findings in the EIA. Early EIAs prepared in the United States during the 1970s were entirely of this type, as were EIAs prepared by governments of developing countries.

The second approach is to make the EIA an integral part of the planning process and project design, with the same influence as the technical and economic feasibility of the project. This means that the initial outline of the project will reflect the maintenance of certain environmental standards. As project planning progresses, the plan will be adjusted to achieve these standards. During the 1980s, US government agencies, including USAID, have moved toward this second approach. For the most part, EIAs have been prepared as projects have been formulated, with environmental findings and recommendations for mitigation incorporated into the later stages of the technical and economic feasibility planning. However, full integration of the EIA with project planning requires joint operations by the environmental, engineering, and financial teams at each stage of the project design. Unless the identification and measurement of environmental impacts influence the project formulation at every stage, inducing changes or modifications in the basic structure of the project, the EIA may be little more than an appraisal after the fact. The EIA should also document environmental costs of the project that are not included in its actual monetary outlays, which can provide a basis for a full benefit-cost accounting of the project.

Just as a project reflects the development objectives of a borrowing government (which in turn reflect basic political decisions), so will the EIA process and its influence on the final design. This is likely to be true no matter how objective the technicians identifying and evaluating the environmental impacts may be. Decisions regarding measures for mitigating environmental impacts will involve trade-offs between maximizing output at the least cost, on the one hand, and preserving the resource base, minimizing pollution and hazards to health, or mitigating disruptive effects on traditional cultures and social patterns, on the other. For this reason, we stress the importance of having professional environmental staffs both participate directly in the EIA process and prepare an independent evaluation of the environmental impacts of the project before it is approved for funding.

Although EIAs may differ for different types of projects, an EIA should include the following basic elements (Econ. & Soc. Commission 1985, 10–16):

1. The environmental team should carry out preliminary studies at the same time the feasibility study for the project is being prepared, with both studies coordinated by the project manager. The environmental team should obtain basic information from the feasibility study and alert those responsible for the feasibility study to environmental problems that must be taken into account.

2. The environmental team should identify environmental impacts before completion of the preliminary design of the project. Testimony from all groups that the project may affect should be solicited. This process, sometimes called *scoping,* identifies problems that are likely to be significant and require special study. If no significant impacts are found, a decision may be made that an EIA is not necessary or that a full EIA need not be performed.

3. A baseline study should project the environmental changes likely to occur both with and without the project. The environmental team and the engineering team responsible for project design should conduct such a study jointly.

4. The environmental team should prepare an evaluation of the environmental impacts on humans, natural resources, production, ecology, social organizations, and cultures and should, to the maximum extent possible, convert those costs into monetary costs.

5. The environmental team, with input from technical specialists and the engineering team, should determine mitigation measures and cost estimates of mitigation measures for the environmental impacts indicated in No. 4 above.

6. The team should compare the costs of alternative measures for mitigating environmental impacts to the social benefits of those measures, using benefit-cost analysis (or other types of value analysis) before preparation of the final project design. Alternatives should include entirely different projects with less harmful environmental impacts.

7. A draft EIA should be issued before the final decision is made on the project design. If the project design has substantial unmitigated en-

vironmental impacts, social benefits of the project should be compared to social costs of unmitigated environmental impacts.

8. A final EIA should be available to the officials responsible for final approval of the project or of the loan for the project. A detailed summary (if not the entire EIA) should be available to the public well before final approval of the project or a loan.

9. Environmental impacts should be monitored throughout the project construction period. If necessary, changes should be recommended to conform with the expectations of the EIA.

10. There should be postconstruction monitoring of the project.

When a development project or program requires external financing, the external assistance agency — whether an MDB or a bilateral agency — will make the final decision on whether to approve the financing. The external agency will review the EIA and other documentation used in the preparation and may send specialists to work with government officials preparing the EIA. Normally, the external agency would not undertake a full EIA on its own but would review the project based on its environmental guidelines. The external agency may also notify the government agency responsible for preparing the project of its environmental concerns at different stages in the EIA process. Further changes in project design in the interest of mitigating adverse environmental impacts may be required in the course of negotiations between the external agency and the borrowing government. Frequently, these negotiations will involve a compromise between the positions of the government and of the external agency regarding certain environmental problems. In the case of MDBs, the governments of member countries might instruct their representatives on the board to vote against a loan because of adverse environmental impacts. Alternatively, additional conditions may be required before approval is given.

COMPARING ECONOMIC BENEFITS
WITH ENVIRONMENTAL COSTS

In the integration of EIAs with technical and financial project planning, judgments are often made requiring a comparison of the cost of environmental damage with the cost of measures for mitigating or avoiding the damage. In the final decision on a project plan potentially having significant environmental impacts, a judgment may also be made on whether the benefits of the project exceed the environmental costs. No matter how carefully and objectively an EIA is performed, it will not provide a formula for dealing with these problems, but an EIA can provide the information needed for making a rational judgment. Phrases such as "taking adequate account of environmental impacts" or in the language of a report sponsored by the World Bank, "making any trade-offs between economic and environmental objectives as explicit as possible" (1987) do not provide a basis for objective judgments. Only by rigorous analysis of social benefits and costs is it possible to reach scientifically objective conclusions.

The most widely used tool for determining whether a project is economically justified or for deciding among alternative means of realizing a particular economic objective is benefit-cost analysis. In simple terms, benefit-cost analysis is the comparison of the present value of annual revenues (benefits) from a project with the present value of annual costs over the life of the project. Present values are calculated by discounting each annual revenue and cost so that nominal amounts decline as we move into the future.[2] The rationale for discounting is based on two objective conditions. First, consumers prefer present over future consumption; otherwise, they would not pay interest to enjoy a home or car *now* rather than sometime in the future. Second, receiving money in the future rather than today means giving up interest that could be earned on the funds during the interim. This is called the opportunity cost of capital—that is, what capital could earn if it were invested rather than spent. Preference for present over future goods differs among individuals, but we know what invested capital earns—so the opportunity cost of capital is a more objective criterion for choosing the rate of discount used in benefit-cost analysis.

In most benefit-cost comparisons made in EIAs, only actual monetary outlays are included in costs. But benefit-cost analysis can be used to deal more fully with environmental and other social costs by including non-monetary social costs in project cost estimates. This is sometimes called social benefit-cost analysis (SBCA). The procedure may be used to determine whether the social benefits of measures to avoid adverse environmental impacts associated with a project are greater than the additional cost of these measures. Or it may be used to compare the cost-effectiveness of alternative measures for mitigating adverse impacts. SBCA requires making monetary estimates of damage caused by air and water pollution, ecological damage caused by loss of wetlands, loss of soil quality caused by multipurpose dams, and uncompensated welfare loss to people forced to abandon their homes to make way for reservoirs. Since MDBs rarely work with such estimates in EIAs, many of the most important environmental costs may be left out of the equation. Nathaniel Leff (1985 & 1988) has pointed out that MDBs have underwritten a substantial amount of research on SBCA as a decision-making tool but have neglected to use that tool. References to studies for valuing environmental costs are given in a separate section under References for this chapter.

A serious problem arises in dealing with environmental impacts that will occur well in the future, since discounting renders such environmental costs negligible. The impacts of projects on soil erosion, desertification, wetland destruction, and overuse of groundwater often occur decades after project completion. In such cases, sustainable development is not compatible with discounting future costs. However, we may deal with this problem by applying the principle of resource accounting to determine social costs. This requires that we include as part of the social costs the reduced value of the resource destroyed by the creation and operation of the proposed project. Moreover, we should not discount this resource loss even though the loss occurs over time. One way to deal with the problem is to regard the entire resource loss as if it occurred in the project's first year, thereby avoiding discounting the social cost of resource depletion.

An alternative to comparing economic benefits with the environmental costs of individual projects is establishing a set of rules that apply to environmental damage. Recommendations for specific rules will be discussed in forthcoming chapters dealing with particular categories of development projects. The following general rules might be adopted as consistent with sustainable development:

1. With the exception of minerals extraction, all development projects should make provision for restoring, or replacing with natural resources of equivalent productivity, those natural resources whose value has been impaired or destroyed. For example, forests destroyed by reservoirs created by multipurpose dams should be replaced with forests in other areas. Croplands destroyed by reservoirs should be compensated with productive croplands in other locations.

2. Natural resources should be regarded as the inheritance of humanity for all generations. Although the present generation may enjoy the net income produced from resources, it should preserve the capital value of all natural resources. For example, the resource (in-the-ground) value of extracted minerals should be reinvested, so that the capital value of the resource is not lost.

RISK AND UNCERTAINTY

Many, if not most, projects with adverse environmental impacts are subject to substantial uncertainty and the risk of not meeting expectations. The failure to account for engineering and financial risks in calculating the economc benefits of a project tends to overvalue the project's net benefits. No matter how carefully planned the project, its net economic benefits are frequently less than expected because of the costs of technical and financial feasibility studies, engineering errors, breakdowns, cost overruns, and disappointing markets for the products. Likewise, estimates of environmental damage or of the capability of measures designed to mitigate or avoid such damage are subject to engineering errors or to unexpected natural conditions. Therefore, these risks should be taken into account in the preparation of EIAs.

The normal way to deal with risk is to apply probability coefficients to both benefits and costs. Thus, if on the basis of experience with similar projects there is a 25 percent probability that benefits will be only half those estimated in the feasibility study, projected benefits should be reduced by at least 13 percent. On the other hand, if there is a 25 percent probability that the actual costs will be 50 percent higher than estimated, the costs used in calculating *net* benefits should be increased by at least 13 percent. The application of probability coefficients to expected benefits from resource projects is important for two reasons. First, reduction of projected net benefits will eliminate some marginal commercial projects in favor of noncommercial uses of the resource. Second, where there are economic losses on commercial uses, social welfare is reduced. A misallocation of resources reduces the national product if the labor and capital combined with natural resources fails to produce a net addition to the economic output. Society also loses the environmental benefits that the natural resources would yield if they were not developed. MDBs should use probability analysis in dealing with risky projects more than they do. Probability analysis is quite complex and involves a large number of variables, but its application in EIAs could save large amounts of social capital. Conservationists reviewing EIAs conducted by project sponsors should be concerned with whether and how risk is taken into account.

EIAs IN THE CONTEXT OF SUSTAINABLE DEVELOPMENT

EIAs in Third World countries should investigate both negative and positive aspects of projects in terms of their impact on sustainable development, with special emphasis on environmental impacts on soil erosion and on the chemical composition of the soil resulting from crops and livestock, and on water management. For example, growing cereal crops on a piece of agricultural land year after year using large amounts of chemical fertilizers may yield a high-value output for a time but result in soil loss and erosion over a period of several decades. A different type of agriculture, using crop rotation and natural fertilizers, may yield a somewhat lower-value output but actually improve the productivity of the land over time.

Three criteria for successful development should be applied in evaluating any project or program: (1) The project should be consistent with sustainability; (2) it should promote economic efficiency and increase output per unit input of productive resources (labor, capital, and natural resources); and (3) the benefits should be distributed equitably. A project or program meets the equity criterion if it does not increase inequality of income in the region where it is introduced. In the short run, at least, there may be a trade-off between efficiency and equity. A project that increases sustainable output may do so at the expense of employment, or it may increase the value of land in some areas and reduce it in others. The negative employment effects of any new investment tend to be short-lived, since the growth of output will generate an increased demand for goods and services and for the labor to produce them. More serious is the effect on land values, for example, of an irrigation project that increases the rents of landholders of the irrigated land, or of a reservoir that reduces the assets and incomes of people forced to evacuate while enhancing the land values and incomes of those benefiting from the project. These equity-oriented effects should be avoided in development projects and programs. Fees for the use of water approximating its cost, or subsidies to those forced to migrate, can help offset such inequities. Projects may be faulted if they benefit some members of society at the expense of others.[3]

NGOs or groups affected by development projects often criticize the projects on the grounds that they perpetuate income inequality or that they benefit the rich at the expense of the poor. If every development project were required to somehow change the distribution of income, say, to raise the percentage of total income received by the lowest quarter of the population, there could well be a conflict with efficiency. Income distribution in a nation is based largely on the structure of landholdings and on other asset holdings based on inheritance, on tax structure and fiscal policies, and demographic change. Development projects can meet the equity criterion if they are at least neutral in distribution of anticipated benefits. Whatever the arguments for reducing inequality of income and wealth, deliberately selecting development projects to reduce inequality is likely to be counterproductive. It is easier to reduce inequality through taxation and fiscal expenditure when output is growing.

Projects Most Vulnerable to Environmental Impacts

In many development projects, either no environmental problems are involved or the problems that do exist are mitigated. Projects causing few environmental problems concern education, population control, medical (except hospital-waste) improvement, research, and institution building. Types of projects for which mitigation measures can be readily prescribed include agro-industrial, crop intensification, fish farming, small-scale irrigation, water supply and sanitation, housing, rehabilitation of existing roads, communications, small-scale industrial, underground mining, transmission lines, and small-scale hydropower. Projects with significant adverse environmental impacts that pose severe mitigation problems are related to large-scale irrigation and water management, river basin development and drainage, new land development for agricultural and urban use, livestock, large-scale application of pesticides in agriculture, population displacement and resettlement, new roads in forests and environmentally sensitive areas, new airports, new ports, new harbors, large-scale water supply, sanitary landfills, power generation, open-pit mining, and large industrial plants.

Projects posing serious environmental problems require considerable analysis, including projections. Many of the issues faced are unique to a given project. In such cases, environmental specialists should have substantial input in preparing EIAs, and environmental technicians associated with the lending agency should closely monitor their work.

CRITICISMS OF EIAs PREPARED FOR MDB PROJECTS

Conservation groups have welcomed the preparation of EIAs for MDB-supported projects but have criticized some EIAs because they have either omitted or failed to take full account of a number of potentially adverse impacts. A common criticism is that the area to be examined for impacts is too small. A highway or multipurpose dam may have physical and so-cial impacts well beyond the area directly affected by the project. For ex-ample, deforestation or soil degradation caused by the resettlement of people attracted to the project area or forced out of the area by reservoirs or land development. Another common omission in consideration is the economic value of land or water resources that traditional users lose to the project. Such losses need to be compensated and included in project costs. Third, a detailed inventory of the ecological damage, including the loss of habitat for flora and fauna, is often omitted. The criticism of the terms of reference for the proposed environmental assessment of the Singrauli area in India, described in Appendix 3-A, illustrates these and other omissions.

The World Bank has had procedures for reviewing the environmental aspects of projects for about five years, but these procedures have not prevented the Bank from financing environmentally flawed projects, such as road building and power development in the Brazilian Amazon, livestock projects in Botswana, and irrigation projects in Africa and Asia. Criti-cism of the Bank's evaluation procedures is contained in a series of ques-tions that US Executive Director of the Bank James B. Burnham posed in response to NGO objections during the course of congressional hear-ings in 1983. The NGOs criticized the Bank for its lack of mandatory environmental guidelines and procedures, understaffing of environmen-tal departments, failure to integrate environmental concerns at the earli-est possible stage in project identification and preparation, failure to establish mechanisms for continual assessment and monitoring of environ-mental factors throughout the implementation phase of the project, and lack of adequate postproject evaluation of environmental performance (Runnals 1986, 202–203). These criticisms applied equally to the ADB and the IADB. In spite of considerable progress in MDB project evalua-tion, these criticisms are in some measure still applicable today.

In reviewing the procedures for avoiding or mitigating environmental damage arising from projects financed by MDBs, two impressions stand out. One is that actual practice departs significantly from models for EIAs prepared by policy research staffs of the MDBs themselves. The second is that there are no objective and usable standards for determining how much environmental damage is acceptable before a project is rejected, and how much mitigation is worth undertaking in view of the cost. These two issues are related, since rigorous procedures for environmental assessment necessarily imply quantifiable standards and criteria. Simply identifying and taking account of environmental concerns in the process of project design merely sets the stage for a negotiated compromise between those advocating environmental purity and those committed to maximizing economic benefits. "Splitting the difference" is not a socially acceptable way of dealing with issues that concern the future viability of poor countries.

EIAs AND RENEWABLE RESOURCE MANAGEMENT

The term *renewable resource management* is sometimes used synonymously with *environmental management* (World Bank 1988, v–vi). But renewable resource management goes beyond the design of a project to consider the effects of socioeconomic institutions and government policies on sustainability. In many cases, projects have created environmental damage because renewable resource management has failed. Therefore, in evaluating a project, the functions of renewable resource management should be included in the preparation of an EIA.

If projects are to succeed in promoting efficiency, sustainability, and equity, they must operate within a social, economic, and political framework consistent with the basic assumptions of the project design. For example, an irrigation project is bound to fail to realize these objectives if the government does not administer the project efficiently; if government employees are corrupt or discriminate on the basis of politics, race, or tribal loyalty; if farmers have no incentive or training to pursue proper environmental practices; or if a large migration attracted by the project destroys the forest and soil adjacent to an irrigation reservoir. Resource management should be concerned with these environmental conditions and should adopt policies and take administrative actions to deal with them. Many projects financed by the World Bank and other external assistance agencies have failed to realize the objectives of efficiency, sustainability, and equity because of an unfavorable sociopolitical environment. In some cases, government policies may not be in accord with these objectives.

The external financing agency may, of course, be aware of conditions necessary for the success of the project and may make recommendations and establish loan conditions requiring the borrowing government to adopt the necessary policies and administrative arrangements. But the government may ignore the recommendations and fail to live up to conditions in the loan agreement.

It may be that, given the policies and administrative competence of the government, *no* projects in certain sectors can be successful. At best, a proposed project may simply be a waste of money; at worst, it may lead to resource destruction. Under these conditions, no alteration or modification will make a project design viable; the project should be abandoned.

APPENDIX 3 - A

Criticism of the Terms of Reference for an Environmental Assessment of the Singrauli Area

Singrauli lies on the border between the states of Madhya Pradesh and Uttar Pradesh in India. Before the early 1960s, the area was relatively pristine, with rich tropical forest habitat for tigers, wild boar, bear, deer, and a variety of other fauna. It was home to more than 300,000 rural people, many of them tribal, who lived reasonably well by Indian standards from a sustainable, subsistence-oriented agricultural economy.

In the early 1960s, these people were forcibly displaced without adequate compensation by the construction of the Rihand Dam on the Sone River, which created one of the largest reservoirs in India. In the 1970s, the Indian government decided to build a series of coal-fired, water-cooled thermoelectric generating plants near the reservoir and adjacent coal fields. Since 1977, the World Bank has committed $850 million for development activities in Singrauli in four loans: two IDA credits approved in 1977 and 1980 for thermopower projects; a credit of $150 million in 1984 for the development of the Dudhichua coal project; and a loan for $250 million approved in 1985 for the construction of high-tension, long-distance transmission lines from Singrauli to Delhi. Other donors were also involved in projects in the area.

In 1987, the World Bank decided to finance an environmental impact assessment for the Singrauli area, presumably as a prelude to support for additional projects by the World Bank and other donors. Upon reviewing the terms of reference for the assessment, the Environmental Defense Fund, together with a number of major US and foreign environmental organizations, including the Sierra Club, submitted a detailed criticism of the terms of reference of the World Bank's proposed environmental assessment. Although the proposed review was not an EIA for a specific new project, the environmental groups' criticisms of its terms of reference illustrate common criticisms by these groups of EIAs. Quotations from the findings of the investigation by the Environmental Defense Fund et al., submitted to the Bank, are presented below (1987):

1. *Study Area*

The prime study area should be enlarged to [allow] focus on the environmental and developmental problems of the whole region, which would include a 50 kilometer band around the Rihand reservoir, not 15 kilometers as is suggested. While it is true that a provision is made for looking at major industrial installations outside the 15 kilometer band, critical problems of public health, resettlement and rehabilitation, water, air and dust pollution, etc., are in many instances equally severe in areas outside the proposed 15 kilometer band.

2. *Land Use*

The extremely vague description in this section ignores the tremendous human and environmental tragedy that has occurred in Singrauli over the past twenty-seven years. Only twenty-seven years ago, at the time of the completion of the Rihand dam, most of the Singrauli region was richly forested with sal, bamboo, kahir and salal trees, among other species. The area supported some 400,000 to 500,000 people, mostly tribals and scheduled castes in a sustainable, largely subsistence-oriented agricultural livelihood. The area was also a rich wildlife habitat, supporting bear, wild boar, and tigers, among other species.

The environmental assessment, therefore, should undertake some review of land use patterns over the past twenty-seven years, since the construction of the Rihand Dam was the real starting point for radical changes in land use patterns in the region. This is particularly important because there are still numerous survivors of the original forced displacement of the Rihand Dam who are living in the region and who have been subsequently displaced two, three, even four times.

Issues that require special attention include land use problems, pollution caused by ash disposal, and disposal of cooling water in the Singrauli Super Thermal Plant and in other super thermal plants in the region. The environmentally unsound practices in removing overburden at the Dudhichua and other coal mines must be examined. Another problem affecting land use is the nuisance caused by low hanging transmission lines around the village of Garbhandha, for instance.

3. *Water Use*

An issue that needs to be addressed is the current use of water from the Rihand reservoir. When Rihand was built, its primary use was to be for irrigation, but currently not a single acre is irrigated by Rihand. The reservoir is used exclusively for hydropower and cooling for the superthermal power plants. Community groups in the area assert that some water could be used from the reservoir for irrigation purposes for the benefit of the local population.

Another issue involves the effects of chemical and thermal pollution in the reservoir on cultivation of the shore area when the lake recedes following a monsoon. This area, known as pule, is quite fertile. Some 4,000 to 5,000 farmers are cultivating the pule area, growing wheat, corn and pulses.

Ground and surface water supplies for human consumption have suffered massive contamination in the area.

4. 'Socio-economics'

The dramatic problems associated with the forced, multiple, and repeated resettlement of some 300,000 people in the region [are] of the greatest priority [and] must be researched and assessed in detail in the proposed assessment.

There is only one sentence in the present terms of reference which refers to the issue of relocation, though this is the single most critical and urgent problem in the region. In the World Bank appraisal documents for its loans for the Singrauli Super Thermal Plant and the Dudhichua Coal Mine, no reference is to be found on questions of relocation, resettlement, compensation and rehabilitation, even though these Bank financed projects alone have forcibly displaced some 23,000 people.

The shocking social, economic, and health situation of some 100,000 contract workers in the greater Singrauli area is another issue that urgently needs a detailed assessment with a view toward implementing remedial measures.

5. Soils

Special attention needs to be focused on general problems of degradation and pollution of the soils in the region: waterlogging (from the ash dumps and cooling canals and ponds of the super thermal plants), pollution from cement dust and dust from stone crushers, windborne ash pollution, and coal dust pollution.

In the coal mine, special attention should focus on the deficiencies in current means of disposing of overburden. Current dumping practices are ruining still more forests and soil.

6. Sediments

The terms of reference did not focus on four issues that need attention:

a) around the reservoir there is a need in many areas for compensatory afforestation to conserve soil and lessen siltation;

b) one factor that helps contribute to siltation is linked to laying of transmission lines near the reservoir and the associated practice of clearing all vegetation on 220 feet of each side of the lines;

c) another factor in siltation is the constant seepage into the reservoir from the Singrauli Super Thermal Plant ash dump, as well as from others;

d) finally, inadequate management of overburden dumping in the coal mines may be contributing to siltation in some cases since topsoil and coal dust wash down in streams to the reservoir.

7. Meteorology

The critical issue of the cumulative regional effects — particularly with respect to public health and acid rain — of SO_2 and carbon compound emissions from the super thermal plants and industrial facilities needs to be carefully addressed. The assessment should include a review of existing emission control measures and those needed to ensure public health. Currently, it appears that none of the plants in the region have scrubbers to limit SO_2 emissions. One study for the Tata Energy Research Institute suggests that with the projected increases in generating capacity in the region, ground level SO_2 concentrations in the region could approach forty times the Indian government standards for densely populated areas.

Any discussion of meteorology should also examine the cumulative contribution of atmospheric emissions from the power and industrial facilities at Singrauli to global warming. The Singrauli region as a whole could become one of the largest concentrated sources of emissions contributing to global warming on the planet.

8. Air Quality

The issues associated with SO_2 and other atmospheric emissions need to be examined in depth.

Ash disposal through the atmosphere is a critical issue, since at least one other power plant in Singrauli, Renusagar, does not have electrostatic precipitators. Atmospheric pollution from this plant is tremendous.

In the dry season (April, May, June, etc.) there is terrible dust pollution from coal mines, cement factories, stone crushers, and last but not least, dried ash in ash dumps whipped up by the wind. The situation is worsened by the constant movement of trucks, vehicles, etc.

No effort is made to keep the dust down through use of water trucks, spraying, etc.

9. Ecology

Although the current terms of reference propose studies of the terrestrial and aquatic ecology of the Singrauli area, the greatest need of all is for a study of the human ecology of the area; i.e., of the current interrelations between the hundreds of thousands of inhabitants of Singrauli and their degraded natural environment, an environment which in the past provided a sustainable agricultural livelihood for many of them. Much of the ecology of the Singrauli area is now a lifeless wasteland, severely degraded by multiple forms of pollution and deterioration of soil, air and water resources. Although an inventory of terrestrial and aquatic fauna and flora is unquestionably a needed undertaking, it is equally obvious to any visitor to the Singrauli site that environmental deterioration is so severe that most forms of life in the area were eliminated or drastically reduced years ago, and that the current state of ecological destruction menaces the very health, livelihood, and survival of Singrauli's hundreds of thousands of displaced people. A study of the human ecology of Singrauli should review the ways in which multiple forms of environmental stress are affecting local populations and propose specific ecological rehabilitation measures and plans.

Under the baseline studies no mention is made of the public health situation, which is one of the most critical environmental problems in the area. Tuberculosis, chloroquine resistant malaria, [and] stomach, skin, and respiratory ailments are rampant among hundreds of thousands of people. It is urgent, then, that a separate public health study be prepared, and that it involve the full participation of voluntary agencies, health workers and doctors who have been working with local people.

10. *Planned [development]; Mitigating Measures*
The terms of reference for these sections call for a review of future plans for development, as well as for the development of an environmental management strategy which will analyze alternative mitigation methods. But no reference is made to the need for identifying and evaluating alternatives to the development plans themselves. This is a critical matter, since one of the most useful functions of an environmental assessment is the identification of alternatives that can accomplish similar goals at less environmental and social cost. It is particularly critical that the assessment review alternative energy investments to new super thermal plants in the region which would make available on a per rupee or dollar basis more energy. Some of these alternative energy investments are described (relying heavily on Indian government and academic studies) in the Bank's publication "End Use Electricity Conservation: Options for Developing Countries," 1986, Energy Department Paper No. 32.

11. *Impact Assessment*
The terms of reference in this section state that knowledge gained from the review of current and planned development activities and of baseline conditions will enable the preparers to make detailed environmental impact projections. A critical element of this analysis should be the review of the *cumulative impact* of development in the region. This is especially critical in the areas of region-wide air and water pollution.

12. *Institutions*

The terms of reference need to address the critical institutional issues of *implementation, coordination and enforcement* of the environmental and social rehabilitation plan, as well as of longer term planning measures and recommendations that the assessment will identify. In particular, it is essential that the assessment establish mechanisms to ensure that the foreign donors financing energy and industrial development in Singrauli work with the Government of India and local community and voluntary groups to address the environmental and social problems in the region in an integrated fashion with common standards and goals. It is incumbent on the World Bank, as the lead donor in Singrauli and in India, as well as the financer of the assessment, to undertake the initiative with Indian government agencies in setting up such mechanisms for coordinated implementation of the assessment's recommendations.

NOTES

1. The contribution of the resource is called resource rent. See Mikesell 1987.
2. If we have a series of equal annual revenues of $1 million and use a rate of discount of 5 percent, the discounted value of the annual revenue at the end of the first year is $.95 million; at the end of the second year, $.90 million; at the end of the third year, $.86 million; and so on. Adding the discounted annual revenues together over a period of ten years gives a present value of $7.1 million. If annual costs are $.90 million, the present value of the (equal) annual costs over the ten-year period is $6.94 million. Therefore, the benefit-cost ratio of the project is 1.1, and the net benefits are $.77 million.
3. Projects that benefit some at the expense of others violate a well-known principle of welfare economics called Pareto optimality.

REFERENCES

Environmental Defense Fund. 1987. "Letter and Accompanying Documents to President Barber Conable of the World Bank by the Environmental Defense Fund, et al." Washington, D.C.: EDF, December.

Goodland, R., and M. Webb. 1987. *The Management of Cultural Property and World Bank Assisted Projects.* Technical Paper No. 62. Washington, D.C.: World Bank.

Hufschmidt, M. M., D. E. James, A. D. Meister, B. K. Bower, and J. A. Dixon. 1983. *Environment, Natural Systems and Development: An Economic Valuation Guide.* Baltimore: Johns Hopkins University Press.

Joint Ministerial Committee of the Boards of Governors of the World Bank and the International Monetary Fund on the Transfer of Real Resources to Developing Countries (Development Committee). 1987. *Economic Growth and Development.* Washington, D.C.: World Bank, August.

Leff, Nathaniel H. (1985). "The Use of Policy-Science Tools in Public Sector Decision Making: Social Benefit-Cost Analysis in the World Bank." *Kyklos* 38, no. 2: 60–75.

————. 1988. "Policy Research for Improved Organizational Performance: A Case from the World Bank." *Journal of Economic Behavior and Organization* 9 (June): 393–403.

Meadows, Donella H., Dennis L. Meadows, Jorgen Randers, and William W. Behrens III. 1972. *The Limits to Growth.* New York: Universe Books.

Mikesell, Raymond F. 1968. *The Economics of Foreign Aid.* Chicago: Aldine Publishing.

_____. 1987. *Nonfuel Minerals: Foreign Dependence and National Security.* Ann Arbor: Univ. of Michigan Press for the Twentieth Century Fund.

Oram, Peter A. 1988. "Building the Agroecological Framework." *Environment* 30, no. 9 (November): 14–17.

Repetto, Robert, William Magrath, Michael Wells, Christine Beer, and Fabrizio Rossino. 1989. *Wasting Assets: Natural Resources in the National Income Accounts.* Washington, D.C.: World Resources Institute, June.

Runnals, David. 1986. "Factors Influencing Environmental Policies in International Development Agencies." In *Environmental Planning and Management: Regional Symposium on Environmental and Natural Resources Planning.* Manila, Philippines: ADB.

United Nations. 1951. *Measures for the Economic Development of Underdeveloped Countries.* Report by a group of experts appointed by the secretary general. New York: UN.

World Bank. 1987. *Environment, Growth and Development.* Washington, D.C.: World Bank.

_____. 1988. *Renewable Resource Management in Agriculture.* Operations Evaluation Department Report No. 7,345. Washington, D.C.: World Bank, June.

_____. 1989. *World Development Report.* Washington, D.C.: World Bank.

World Commission on Environment and Development. 1987. *Our Common Future.* Oxford: Oxford Univ. Press.

REFERENCES ON ENVIRONMENTAL IMPACT ASSESSMENT

Dixon, John A., Richard A. Carpenter, Louise A. Fallon, Paul B. Sherman, and Supachit Manopimoke. 1986. *Economic Analysis of the Environmental Impacts of Development Projects.* Prepared at the Environmental and Policy Institute, East-West Center, Honolulu. Manila, Philippines: ADB.

Economic and Social Commission for Asia and the Pacific. 1985. *Environmental Impact Assessment: Guidelines for Planners and Decision Makers.* Bangkok, Thailand: UN.

Organization for Economic Cooperation and Development. 1986. *Environmental Assessment and Development Assistance.* Paris: OECD.

United Nations. 1988. *Environmental Impact Assessment: Basic Procedures for Developing Countries.* New York: UN.

REFERENCES FOR PUBLICATIONS ON CALCULATING
MONETARY VALUES FOR ENVIRONMENTAL BENEFITS AND COSTS

Cook, Paul, and Paul Mosely. 1989. "On the Valuation of 'External Effects' in Project Appraisal." *Project Appraisal* (September): 143–150.

Decker, Daniel J., and Gary R. Goff, eds. 1987. *Valuing Wildlife: Economic and Social Perspectives.* Boulder, Colo.: Westview Press.

Dixon, J. A., and Maynard M. Hufschmidt. 1986. *Economic Valuation Techniques for the Environment.* Baltimore: Johns Hopkins Univ. Press.

Freeman, A. Myrick. 1981. *The Benefits of Environmental Improvement.* Baltimore: Johns Hopkins Univ. Press for Resources for the Future.

Ledec, George, and Robert Goodland. 1988. *Wildlands: Their Protection and Management in Economic Development.* Ch. 7. Washington, D.C.: World Bank.

Peskin, Henry N. 1989. *Accounting for Natural Resource Depletion and Degradation in Developing Countries.* Environmental Department Working Paper No. 13. Washington, D.C.: World Bank, January.

Peterson, George, L., and Alan Randall. 1984. *Valuation of Wildland Resource Benefits.* Boulder, Colo.: Westview Press.

Schwartzman, Daniel J., Richard A. Liroff, and Kevin G. Croke, eds. 1982. *Cost-Benefit Analysis and Environmental Regulations: Politics, Ethics and Methods.* Washington, D.C.: Conservation Foundation.

Smith, V. Kerry, and William, H. Desvousges. 1986. *Measuring Water Quality Benefits.* Boston: Kluwer Nijhoff.

CHAPTER 4

Environmental Problems in Irrigated Agriculture and Multipurpose Dams

A high proportion of MDB loans go to sectors that encounter severe economic and resource management problems—irrigation, land development and resettlement, forest management, livestock, power, highways, and industry. In some cases MDB-supported projects have had adverse environmental impacts, some of which qualify as disasters. However dramatic these cases, it is wrong to conclude that MDBs are the principal cause of environmental degradation in the Third World. On the contrary, over the last decade or so the MDBs have probably made a *net contribution* to the environment by building safeguards into loan agreements and by raising the environmental consciousness of member governments. In fact, environmental atrophy would exist in the absence of MDBs and is widespread in Third World economies not touched by external assistance of any kind. Moreover, most adverse environmental consequences of MDB loans have been caused by borrowers' violations of loan agreements or by the failure of MDBs to exercise proper oversight. Finally, MDBs have learned much from their past mistakes, and one would hope that NGOs will be vigilant in helping them to remember their derelictions and avoid repeating them.

Our analysis of environmental problems is not simply to provide an inventory of mistakes, omissions, and poor judgments on the part of MDBs and governments. Avoiding errors is less than half the solution to the problems. Environmental improvement and sustainable resource management require positive and often innovative policies and actions to promote development. As we stated in Chapter 3, project and program designers should consider environmental and sustainable feasibility as seriously as technical and financial feasibility. This approach goes well beyond identifying adverse environmental impacts and mitigating them without making the project financially infeasible. The overwhelming objective of development is net social benefit from an intergenerational perspective. This approach will often require MDBs to support projects for which the payoff is largely nonmonetary, in the form of social benefits and long-term sustainability.

MDBs have difficulty financing projects that do not yield a measurable net return on the investment. They need to begin to think more in terms of net social returns calculated according to the principles of SBCA and resource accounting, which requires deducting resource depletion and degradation from national income. By the same reasoning, a project whose main contribution is to restore a renewable resource can make an important contribution to national income. Environmental restoration can also contribute to national investment since resource renewal is a form of investment.

In this chapter we discuss MDB-supported irrigated agriculture and multipurpose dams. In our review of environmental and resource management problems we concentrate on some of the more important issues and suggest what MDBs and governments ought to be doing, as well as what they should be avoiding. No general solutions to sustainability problems apply to all lands and sociocultural conditions; therefore we may not be able to suggest specific positive actions in some cases, except the underwriting of more research and experiments.

Irrigated Agriculture

MDB lending for agricultural and rural development is second in volume to lending for energy but is by far the most important for improving the welfare of the poor and for sustainable development. Loans to the agricultural sector finance a wide range of activities, including irrigation and drainage as well as extension service and research, and credits for individual farmers. MDBs include loans for livestock and forestry in the agricultural category, but we shall treat them separately. From the standpoint of the number and complexity of environmental problems, large-scale irrigation is the most important project category in agricultural development. Most large irrigation projects involve the use of dams and reservoirs. Many dams serve other purposes in addition to agriculture; in many cases energy output from a hydroelectric dam is assigned more importance than irrigation. We deal in this section with irrigation, and in the following section with large multipurpose dams.

Irrigation is as old as civilization, and some of the problems in modern irrigation systems have their counterparts in ancient ones, as evidenced by archeological structures in now-sterile soils near abandoned cities. Nearly half of the world's population depends for its food production on some degree of irrigation; irrigation is increasingly necessary just to maintain present nutrition levels. While less than half the land with potential for irrigation has actually been developed for this purpose, the amount of land under irrigation in developing countries is currently increasing at about 3 percent per year (Tillman 1981, 5–6). An in-depth study of ten countries — Botswana, Kenya, Mali, Morocco, Orissa (India), Peru, Sudan, Thailand, Zambia, Zimbabwe — estimates the irrigation potential at about 20 million hectares, of which some 10 million hectares are already irrigated or were being developed for irrigation at the time of the study (Olivares 1987, 97). Thailand, Sudan, Morocco, and Peru have developed about two-thirds of their potential; Zimbabwe, Orissa, and Mali about one-third; and Botswana, Zambia, and Kenya are just beginning at 4 to 12 percent of their potential. Excluding India, China, and Brazil, the total irrigation potential of developing countries is about twice the amount of the 70 million hectares currently irrigated.

The MDBs have supported many public-sector irrigation systems in developing countries over the past four decades. World Bank and IDA loans for irrigation totaled $15.4 billion (cumulative) through 30 June, 1989, 30 percent of all loans by these agencies for agriculture and rural development. More than half of these loans went to Asian countries, with only about 6 percent going to African countries (World Bank 1989, 176–177). The greatest potentials for additional irrigation are in Asia and Latin America. Taking into acount soil conditions and the availability of water, Jose Olivares (1987, 97–99) estimates that only about 15 million hectares are suitable for future irrigation development in Africa. Although irrigation systems of various types number in the hundreds of thousands, it is estimated that more than 35,000 medium to large dams existed in the mid-1980s (excluding those in China); of these, some 11,000 were constructed in the 1951–1982 period at an average of 344 dams per year. More recently, during the 1975–1982 period, the rate of construction dropped to 258 dams per year, and of these, MDBs have financed less than 10 percent. The World Bank has supported only some 5 to 10 dams per year, or less than 5 percent of the average annual construction of dams worldwide (Dixon et al. 1989, 4–5). However, a number of these Bank-supported dams have been large projects, involving costs of half a billion dollars or more per dam.

Dam construction for irrigation purposes will undoubtedly continue in developing countries, but the annual rate seems likely to decline for several reasons. First, costs are exceedingly high and external capital available to developing countries has been declining. Second, rates of return on investment in dams have declined as the cost per hectare of irrigated area has risen relative to prices for agricultural products. Investment in irrigation would yield less than 12 percent on a large portion of potentially irrigatible land (Olivares 1987, 109). Finally, MDBs and govenments increasingly take into account the negative environmental consequences of large dams, and in many cases the net *social* returns are either very low or negative. Since a large number of irrigation systems in the developing world have not been well maintained and are operating poorly, food production could be increased significantly by improving or rehabilitating existing systems (Berry, Ford, and Hosier 1980, 16).

Irrigation was first developed in level river valleys or floodplains, where water could easily be collected in ponds by containing natural river overflows. Later, dams and canals were built and fields leveled to extend the area under irrigation. There are two distinct phases in irrigation: the collection of water from a natural source and the application of water to plants and soil. Improper methods of applying water can create environmental damage regardless of the source of the irrigation water. Water is applied to plants using three main methods: (1) surface irrigation, in which water runs over the surface of the soil and is allowed to infiltrate; (2) sprinkle irrigation, in which water is sprayed into the air and allowed to fall on plants and soil like rain; and (3) drip irrigation, in which water is applied directly to the root zone. Surface irrigation serves about 95 percent of the irrigated land worldwide; sprinkle irrigation is used mainly in developed countries (Hillel 1987, 50).

There are many ways to supply water for irrigation, including collecting rainwater in small ponds, an ancient practice; running canals from rivers; and creating large dams and reservoirs to irrigate many thousands of acres. In addition to surface water, groundwater supplied by tube-wells is a source for a substantial amount of irrigation. The type of irrigation used today depends on available sources of water, the nature of the soil and of crops produced, the organizational structure of farming, and the availability of capital. Each system of irrigation gives rise to special types of environmental and resource management problems. In many cases the desire to produce large amounts of electric power with multipurpose dams has determined the nature and size of an irrigation project.

The history of civilization provides many examples of irrigation failures. Six thousand years ago on the Tigris-Euphrates floodplain in Mesopotamia, Sumerian irrigation practices led to a salt buildup in the soil that contributed to the decline of the Sumerian culture. In many places in the world, archeologists have discovered the remains of elaborate irrigation systems that have had to be abandoned because of salinization, and of the civilizations they had supported that have disappeared with the irrigation facilities. Short-term gains in production from irrigation led to intensive settlement and resource exploitation, which in turn led to water resource depletion, pollution, and soil degradation.

Mistakes in surface irrigation often have to do with the amount and frequency of water application. Too little water might fail to benefit crops, but excessive flooding and soil saturation impedes aeration, leaches out nutrients, produces greater evaporation and salinization, and raises the water table, which suppresses normal root and microbial activities. Excessive water also aggravates disposal problems since pumping drainage back into a stream salinizes the water supply on which downstream users depend. Modern irrigation is quite sophisticated and seeks to adjust supply to the optimum rate required by the crop and soil conditions. With high-frequency irrigation provided by sprinklers or other modern systems, the exact amount and frequency of applications can be monitored (Hillel 1987, 51–77).

CRITICISMS OF IRRIGATION SYSTEMS

Agricultural economists agree almost unanimously that developing countries must expand their level of irrigation if they are to keep up with the growing demand for food and fibers, and with their need for foreign exchange to meet import requirements for growth. But environmentalists and some agricultural economists criticize existing irrigation systems and those currently being developed. First, some criticize the use of large dams and reservoirs and recommend that alternative irrigation systems be used. Second is the criticism of the design and operation of existing irrigation systems. Finally, some argue against multipurpose dam projects designed for functions such as power, flood control, commercial fisheries, and recreation in combination with irrigation, particularly when the design and operation of the project emphasizes the other purposes at the expense of irrigation. The criticisms cover adverse environmental impacts; lack of economic justification in terms of investment returns; and an inequitable distribution of benefits and costs among those affected. Although we will deal briefly with each of these categories, we will be concerned here mainly with the environmental impacts of large dams.

Many environmentalists have come out unequivocally against large dams. Nevertheless, many agricultural economists and water resource specialists favor large dams as the most efficient way to supply water for irrigating large areas, provided soil and other river basin conditions are favorable. Some World Bank technicians suggest that the Bank should limit its financing of large irrigation systems. This view may reflect more economic than environmental considerations, since most of these technicians believe that better design and improved performance can overcome environmental objections. Pierre Crosson, an economist with the resource research institution Resources for the Future, argues that a small-watershed focus—as opposed to focus on large developments—may not be the most appropriate way to protect sustainability (1987, 182). Edward Goldsmith and Nicholas Hildyard strongly disagree and recommend that foreign assistance agencies "cut off funds from all large-scale water development schemes they may be planning to finance or are involved in financing, regardless of how far those schemes have progressed" (1984, 331–332). They and others would limit irrigation to traditional small-scale methods that have worked successfully in combination with the practice of fallow (crop rotation). Others, supporting modern irrigation systems—whether large- or small-scale—argue that traditional agricultural systems may have worked well for a population that grew very slowly and had access to abundant land, but such methods would doom today's poor countries to a Malthusian existence.

Some criticisms of existing and planned public irrigation systems concern financial feasibility. Robert Repetto finds that gains in farm production and income from public irrigation systems in all countries for which data are available are far short of covering full operating, maintenance, and capital costs of new projects at current levels (1986, 7). This finding raises questions regarding the economic feasibility of many of the currently planned public irrigation systems, many of which MDBs are expected to finance. Existing systems have not been economical largely because of their poor performance, arising from poor management (including divided responsibilities), poorly trained operatives, corruption, and the water distribution system. According to Repetto, in nearly all systems the value of the water received by farmers far exceeds what they pay for it. This benefits the farmers but discourages efficient water use. Since water charges in most systems are not related to the amount of water used but rather to the area irrigated, using additional water on a given acreage costs the farmer nothing (Repetto 1986, Ch. 3). This leads not only to inefficiency and needless cost, but also to excessive water use, which creates waterlogging, soil erosion, and degradation of the quality of the water returned to the river. An estimated half of the world's irrigated land is badly salinized, with perhaps more than 1 million hectares of prime agricultural land becoming salinized each year.

Multipurpose Dams

A multipurpose dam is usually the largest and most expensive type of development project in Third World countries. Its potential for expanding agricultural output, supplying power for homes and industries, controlling flooding, and conserving water is enormous. So is its potential for environmental harm: destruction of forests, fish, and cultivatable land; human suffering and property damage from forced migration; waterborne disease; soil salinization and waterlogging; and downstream pollution. Figure 4.1 provides a graphic summary of the environmental impacts of a typical multipurpose dam. The association of large multipurpose dams with environmental harm has led some agricultural specialists to reject them in favor of small irrigation and mini-hydro projects.

Multipurpose dam projects often create problems because their requirements for efficient power production differ from their requirements for irrigation or other purposes such as fisheries. The contradiction may concern the size or location of the reservoir, or the control of the water flow in different seasons. Thus utilization of the river as an energy source frequently is not fully compatible with its optimum use for irrigation, flood control, or recreation.

FIGURE 4-1

MULTIPURPOSE DAM PROJECT:

LOSS OF ECONOMIC DEVELOPMENT OPPORTUNITIES

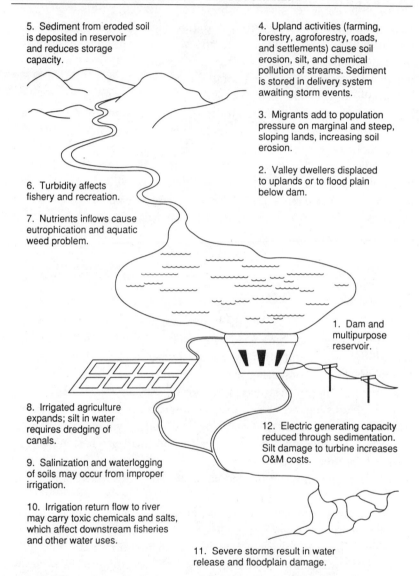

5. Sediment from eroded soil is deposited in reservoir and reduces storage capacity.

4. Upland activities (farming, forestry, agroforestry, roads, and settlements) cause soil erosion, silt, and chemical pollution of streams. Sediment is stored in delivery system awaiting storm events.

3. Migrants add to population pressure on marginal and steep, sloping lands, increasing soil erosion.

2. Valley dwellers displaced to uplands or to flood plain below dam.

6. Turbidity affects fishery and recreation.

7. Nutrients inflows cause eutrophication and aquatic weed problem.

1. Dam and multipurpose reservoir.

8. Irrigated agriculture expands; silt in water requires dredging of canals.

9. Salinization and waterlogging of soils may occur from improper irrigation.

10. Irrigation return flow to river may carry toxic chemicals and salts, which affect downstream fisheries and other water uses.

12. Electric generating capacity reduced through sedimentation. Silt damage to turbine increases O&M costs.

11. Severe storms result in water release and floodplain damage.

Source: John A. Dixon et al., *Economic Analysis of the Environmental Impacts of Development Projects* (Manila, Philippines: ADB, 1986), 9.

Reservoirs created for hydroelectric and irrigation storage are filling up with silt at rates two to three times faster than expected by the designing engineers. In India the expected life span of the Tehri Dam, the sixth largest in the world, has already been reduced from one hundred to forty years; the giant Tarbela Dam will be useless within forty years at current rates of siltation; and Pakistan's Mangla Reservoir, built with a one hundred-year life expectancy, may fill up with silt fifty years ahead of time (Repetto 1987, 172). These unexpected developments greatly limit the benefits of projects costing hundreds of millions of dollars. Biological degradation in tropical reservoirs may impair downstream water use (Garzon 1984). Project managers frequently do not take these and other factors into account when they estimate costs of multipurpose dams or compare those costs to the costs of alternative power sources and methods of irrigation.

Potential Environmental Hazards

Although we are skeptical about the desirability of large irrigation dams, many agricultural economists and water resource specialists favor large dams for specific soil and other river basin conditions as the most efficient way to apply water to large areas. In some situations, dams may be the most cost-effective means of irrigating large areas; it *may* even be possible to design and operate them without serious environmental damage, but unequivocal examples of this are difficult to find. At any rate, large dams will continue to be constructed with or without direct or indirect support from MDBs. Therefore, the following paragraphs are devoted to evaluating proposed irrigation projects and the environmental hazards that NGOs should consider in working to alter their designs or to oppose the projects altogether.

The first task in evaluating a proposed irrigation project is to determine whether the location is optimal from both environmental and efficiency standpoints. This requires reviewing economic justification for the site and any special environmental drawbacks. For example, does the site have unique or exceptional aesthetic qualities, or is it near an overcrowded area? Was the location determined by political factors, without regard for either environment or efficiency? It is also important to determine whether alternative projects could achieve much the same objective in terms of expanding agricultural production with less potential environmental damage, or whether such projects are viable in terms of the expected net social benefits.

The following discussion of relevant environmental factors in evaluating an irrigation project is divided into six categories: (1) soil modification; (2) water quality; (3) health hazards; (4) ecological values; (5) socioeconomic factors; and (6) archeological impacts. (See Appendix 4-F for a comprehensive checklist.)

SOIL MODIFICATION

Many soils and irrigation waters contain large amounts of salts, a major threat to sustainability in irrigated agriculture. Because salts limit crop production, excess quantities of soluble salts must be removed from the root zone area to sustain productivity. To prevent soil salinity from reaching harmful levels, a portion of the concentrated solution must be removed from the area where it can affect the roots. Sufficient water input from irrigation or rainfall can leach salt, providing soil infiltration and drainage rates are adequate. Except where rainfall is sufficient to leach the salts below the root zone, enough irrigation water must pass through the zone to prevent harmful salt accumulations—but not so much as to cause the problems discussed in the next paragraph. In addition, subsurface drainage is essential and, depending on the level of the natural water table and the character of the soil, drains may need to be installed. Depending on its quality, the drainage water may be used for irrigation. However, highly saline water pumped into rivers may create problems for those using the water downstream. Drainage water may injure fish and wildlife and could potentially affect human health. For example, drainage water from the west side of the San Joaquin Valley in California has damaged waterfowl habitat and agricultural lands. Most of the drainage water was discharged into the Kesterson National Wildlife Refuge, where it evaporated and left high levels of selenium and other trace metals in the drainage water, causing deformities in waterfowl (Ochs 1987, 239–248).

Quite apart from the problems of salinization, irrigation may cause waterlogging when groundwater saturates the plant root zone and prevents an exchange of oxygen between the roots and the soil. Excess irrigation and improper soil drainage may also elevate groundwater levels, consequently reducing productivity. In India waterlogging has made approximately 10 million hectares uncultivatable; in Pakistan an estimated 12 million hectares are waterlogged (Repetto 1987, 172–172).

WATER QUALITY

Poor water quality can cause adverse effects both in and outside the irrigated area. Depending upon the source, most water supplies contain salts; the concentration may vary seasonally. In some cases, high salinity may develop because of upstream irrigation or other water uses. Toxic chemicals, such as boron and arsenic, may also concentrate in the water, as may bacteria from sewage—which causes a variety of diseases such as cholera and hepatitis. Downstream water quality is affected by water impoundments in both large reservoirs and small ponds, by diversion of the irrigation water from the water course, and by the return flow from the irrigated fields. Water impounded in reservoirs has a different quality than that of the upstream water, and pollutants added to water below a diversion point are more concentrated than above the diversion. Diversion also severely impacts fish, thereby damaging downstream fisheries. During the dry season, the river flow may be so low that it creates stretches of stagnant pools containing poorly diluted wastes, which provide breeding areas for vermin and bacteria. Rivers used for consumption, if unable to flush wastes, are also health hazards.

Irrigation return flows bring water downstream with mineral concentrations several times greater than in the incoming water. The return flows may also contain pesticides and high concentrations of nitrates and phosphates that contribute to eutrophication, which causes waterweed proliferation. Nitrates derived from the use of fertilizers in the irrigated area may also contaminate downstream, causing illness in humans drinking the water. Some of the problems of salinization and water contamination are not unique to irrigation systems using large dams and reservoirs, but may also occur with the use of groundwater. The remedies are often complex and costly.

HEALTH HAZARDS

Water is a favorable medium for breeding and transmitting bacteria, viruses, and other organisms that cause diseases, the most important of which are malaria, schistosomiasis (or bilharzia), dysentery, hepatitis, yellow fever, and sleeping sickness. Impounding and conveying water for irrigation impairs the normal stream flow and gives rise to the growth of infectious agents, such as insects, snails, and other organisms that serve as hosts for bacteria and worms that invade humans. Canals and drainage ditches associated with irrigation projects also foster these health hazards. Diseases, such as dysentery and infectious hepatitis, tend to occur when irrigation canals and water impoundments are used for both human consumption and excreta disposal. These diseases are particularly prevalent where human populations concentrate around irrigation structures and reservoirs. Plans for irrigation systems should include sanitation facilities; disease prevention also requires the education of, and cooperation by, the population.

The effects of irrigation systems on health are not all adverse. The greater availability of water in times of drought can provide health benefits if the water's quality is sufficient for domestic use, and irrigation systems may prevent floods by channeling excess water into reservoirs. Floods contribute to disease by creating large numbers of small ponds. On the other hand, reduced flooding may affect downstream areas negatively. Forests depend on occasional floods both for creation of diversity and for regeneration of individual species of trees. Reduced flushing of downstream soils may lead to increased salinity levels. Floodwater farming and livestock management can also be adversely affected. Finally, decreases in fish populations may occur from low water levels in river channels (Scudder 1988, 54–58).

ECOLOGICAL VALUES

Irrigation systems destroy large forested areas and aquatic systems containing plants and animals, and this destruction carries over to the surrounding areas. Water courses diverted for irrigation reduce downstream flows and adversely affects flora and fauna; elevated water temperatures cause algae and waterweeds to proliferate, and nitrogen and phosphorous eliminate fish and animal species, which require oxygenated free-flowing water. On the other hand, reservoirs often attract waterfowl and can be used for fish hatcheries. The fish in reservoirs have in some cases made a significant contribution to food output.

SOCIOECONOMIC FACTORS

Socioeconomic impacts of irrigation are often more serious than the effects on the physical environment. Large irrigation systems with reservoirs covering hundreds of square miles require thousands of people to resettle. Compensation for lost property is often inadequate or nonexistent, and arrangements for relocation and productive employment for those forced to evacuate are often poorly planned, resulting in substantial human suffering and loss of output. The Narmada River Project described in Appendix 4-A illustrates this problem. Ideally, displaced workers and their families should be moved to an irrigated area, where they should be able to earn a higher income after paying reasonable fees for the water. However, this is rarely done. Rights to the land may already exist in the irrigated areas, sometimes held by absentee owners. Also, conversion from rain-fed agriculture to irrigation requires new methods of production and additional inputs, such as fertilizers, biocides, machinery, and seeds, which add greatly to operating costs. Maintenance of the irrigation system requires additional labor and management, as well as cooperation with other users for proper control and distribution of water. All of this requires technical assistance for training, and agricultural credits to purchase equipment.

Multipurpose dams that produce hydroelectric power, while not universally condemned by agricultural specialists, are commonly criticized on the grounds that the demand for a steady supply of power often conflicts with operation of the system for irrigating. In addition, some argue that power production benefits mainly those in urban areas, while the poorest segment of the rural population bears most of the human and environmental costs.

ARCHEOLOGICAL IMPACTS

The Aswân High Dam in Egypt buried a number of important archeological structures, only a few of which could be saved when they were moved to higher ground. In Anatolia (western Turkey), a massive project calling for the eventual construction of some twenty-two dams on the Tigris and Euphrates rivers will destroy hundreds of existing and potential archeological sites, possible sources for an enormous amount of information about civilizations going back thousands of years to the beginning of urban life (Ward 1990, 28–38). The first three dams to be built are expected to transform nearly 30,000 square miles of arid and semiarid land into productive agriculture and provide large amounts of power that will help reduce Turkey's annual $2 billion oil import bill.

World Bank Staff Criticisms of Bank Irrigation Loan Policies

Between 1970 and 1988 the World Bank provided financing for more than four hundred projects involving dams in one hundred countries—about 14 percent in Sub-Saharan Africa; 13 percent in Latin America and the Caribbean; 37 percent in southern Asia; 17 percent in eastern Asia; and 19 percent in Europe, the Middle East, and North Africa. Many of these dams have been the subject of widespread criticism, both inside and outside the countries where they are located, and there have been a number of critical evaluations of their environmental shortcomings within the Bank itself. Some of these criticisms were presented at a seminar entitled "Dams and the Environment: Considerations in Bank Projects" held at the World Bank on 18 June 1987. On the basis of appraisal reports prepared by Bank staff, about half the dams supported during the period 1972–1985 received explicit environmental attention, and environmental reports were prepared for only 49 percent of the total dams supported. A review of these projects by the conference participants reached the following conclusions:

1. In the Bank's project evaluation process, the decision whether to support the dam was based largely on economic justification. Although environmental factors were recognized, the evaluation did not include an adequate analysis of the environmental factors that could significantly affect sustainability and the social costs and benefits of the project.

2. In many cases, any consideration of the environment was too late in the procedure to have any impact on the design of the project—plans for the location and general features of the dam had already been determined. When environmental considerations are brought into the planning late, the environment is considered an *obstruction* to the design process rather than as a part of the process.

3. Most environmental considerations were limited to the immediate project area, not to basin-wide impacts of the project. Similarly, the influence of water releases from the project on basin-wide agricultural activities tended to be ignored.

4. Offshore impacts usually were not considered. Most large dams and water projects have significant effects (through changes in water flow, sedimentation, salinity, and other water-quality factors) on estuaries and associated waterways. These effects can be both positive and negative,

and the impacts on fisheries and other coastal resources may have been overlooked.

5. As most attention was placed on project analysis, even when there are plans for a series of dams (such as in the Narmada project), cumulative and feedback effects may have been ignored. In some instances it is necessary to take a regional or sectoral perspective to capture these cumulative effects.

6. In many cases, "indirect" factors, such as the secondary effects of new roads, which provide access that may lead to unplanned settlement and destructive cultivation, illegal logging and other vegetation clearance, poaching, or erosion, have received little or no attention in the Bank's dam projects. Sometimes these factors may have larger long-term impacts than actual dam construction. Even in those cases in which secondary effects were identified as issues, little was done other than to state that the government would look after the problem.

7. Environmental assessments rarely considered potential positive environmental effects that could be achieved by changes or additions to the design of the project. Examples include changes in dam site location, adjustments in dam height, development of fish ladders, clearance of vegetation from impoundment areas, adjustments to the minimum or seasonal downstream flow, establishment of parks or reserve areas to protect watershed and biological diversity, and property salvage.

The report concludes by pointing out that, while "until recently a high percentage of dams still receive little recorded environmental consideration," the Bank is making substantial progress in incorporating environmental considerations into its dam projects (Dixon, Talbot, & Le Moigne 1989, 11).

In a recent paper, World Bank staff member Gerald O'Mara (1990) criticized Bank-financed irrigation projects on the basis of both financial and physical sustainability. Borrowers have rarely complied with negotiated Bank agreements that provide, among other things, that managers of irrigation projects recover operating and maintenance costs (O&M) by collecting fees. This has been especially true of Indian and Pakistan irrigation projects, which constitute the bulk of Bank lending for irrigation. Other sources have had to subsidize O&M, but government funds for these purposes are sometimes not available. O&M includes not only operation costs of the irrigation system itself, but expenditures required to deal with the environmental impacts of the system. One of the reasons governments have not levied fees sufficient to cover O&M costs is that farmers are already so heavily taxed, directly or indirectly, that they cannot afford, or they are unwilling to pay, fees to cover these costs. Moreover, fees generally have not been related to the amount of water an individual farmer receives, but have been based on acreage farmed or on some other factor that does not contribute to an efficient allocation of water or to the equitable distribution of costs. Failure to relate fees paid to the amount of water used tends to encourage excessive water use by some farmers.

The same report recommends that the Bank focus more on the physical sustainability of irrigation investments and include environmental impacts in its feasibility studies. The report suggests that direct and indirect taxation of irrigated agriculture, achieved through price controls and restrictions on imported inputs for agriculture, be abolished and that a fee system be established to cover irrigation costs. This is desirable for other reasons relating to economic productivity as well. The report recognizes the difficulty in obtaining governmental compliance to a rational and efficient system of physical sustainability for irrigation investments. A firm commitment to this compliance may be impossible to achieve without Bank sanctions. The report suggests that "continued noncompliance would require cessation of all irrigation lending if the Bank is to retain credibility with respect to its irrigation portfolio" (O'Mara 1990, 22).

African River Basins and Hydroelectric Dams[1]

Agricultural development in tropical Africa is heavily dependent on river basins and their associated wetlands. Most of the basins experience seasonal flooding followed by drought, coupled with large variations in river flows from year to year. Annual flooding is the traditional method of irrigation and benefits millions of hectares of land under cultivation. Livestock pastures and fisheries are also heavily dependent on flooding. According to Thayer Scudder (1989), the construction of large dams interferes with natural flooding, and may thereby reduce productivity in areas downstream from the dam.

Most large African dams supported by MDBs are multipurpose dams designed with a heavy emphasis on producing electric power. Governments of the African countries have favored power production to promote industrialization, and until recently, at least, donor agencies have agreed with the objectives of the governments. In addition, the sale of power domestically or across borders has provided the foreign exchange needed to construct the dams. Also, according to Scudder, this emphasis on hydroelectric power production has inhibited the kind of river basin management that would promote the agricultural, fishery, forestry, and ecological conservation necessary for sustainable development. Large-scale irrigation projects, while contributing to productivity for a limited area, often are not cost-effective by themselves, nor do they compensate for the loss of agricultural production in other areas. Capital costs of irrigation sometimes exceed $20,000 per hectare, and even doubling the value of the crops produced in the area cannot support the interest, amortization, and high operating costs of the system. Moreover, pollution in the return flow from the irrigated area and the elimination of downstream flooding have an adverse effect on downstream farming, livestock production, and fish catches.

The power authorities of Africa, who have designed and administered most of the country's large dams, do not operate in accordance with the primary needs of local agriculture and, in particular, of the poor farmers. Both the design and the operation of the dams in response to seasonal changes in water flow tend to be biased in favor of power output. Agricultural productivity calls for a different design and different operational guidelines.

MDBs also show a bias in favor of the energy component of multipurpose dams. The World Bank's energy divisions have primary responsibility for the large African dam projects, including the Kainji Dam in Nigeria, the Kariba Dam in Zambia, and the Akosombo Dam in Ghana. According to Scudder, "The Energy Division has ignored the Bank's own environmental and resettlement guidelines during the construction of Kenya's recently completed Kiambere Dam" (1989, 27). (See following map for location of major African dams, most of which were supported by external assistance agencies.)

Dams, even large ones, can serve to promote efficient river basin management and expand agricultural production through controlled flooding. Natural flooding may damage crops by providing too much water, while too little flooding reduces harvests. Optimal management of water resources, therefore, requires that the design and operation of dams foster sustainable agriculture, not power production. Scudder states, "It is even

FIGURE 4-2

MAP OF AFRICAN DAMS

Source: Thayer Scudder, "River Basin Projects in Africa," *Environment* 31:5.
Illustration by Janet Dell Russell.

possible to combine hydropower generation with ecologically sound river management" (1980, 383). Although a few large African dams (such as the Manantali Dam on the Senegal River) are used for controlled flooding, "controlled downriver flooding synchronized with reservoir drawdown, is a relatively untried approach in African river basin development that deserves much more consideration because of the importance of flooding for the maintenance of some of Africa's most productive ecosystems, and because more people and livestock depend on natural floodplains in Africa than anywhere else in the tropics. The emphasis must shift either to small tributary dams or to mainstream dams that combine controlled downriver flood with regular reservoir drawdown" (Scudder 1989, 29). Unfortunately, most of the mainstream dams eliminate flooding altogether.

Improving the Traditional Irrigation System in Pakistan

The traditional irrigation system in Pakistan, a result of British engineering during the Colonial period, is a gravity-fed piped-water system with water drawn from natural pools in rivers. Altogether, more than 100 million acre-feet of water flow into irrigation canals in the Indus Basin and into a system of distributary canals that branch out to village watercourses, which in turn feed individual farmers' ditches. The design of the canal network did not provide for village watercourses to link it to the fields. Farmers, who had little understanding of channel design or the effects of watercourse deterioration on water loss, dug these. An estimated 40 percent of the water supply is lost through seepage, spillage, and evaporation before it reaches the farmer, with another 10 percent lost through inefficient irrigation.

Under a 1976 loan agreement, USAID and the Pakistan government initiated a five-year pilot project to demonstrate the feasibility of increasing food production by reducing irrigation water losses from village watercourses; improving the use of water through precision leveling of fields; and training farmers to improve farming practices. The initial loan was for $7.5 million, to be followed by a $15.0 million loan as needed, with the same amounts to be contributed by the Pakistan government. However, following congressional passage of the Symington amendment, the $15 million USAID loan was never made because US economic assistance to Pakistan temporarily ceased. Nevertheless, a 1981 USAID evaluation of the project found that thirteen hundred watercourses had been improved, reducing water loss and making more water available to farmers. The result was a significant expansion of crop area, increased cropping intensity, and higher crop yields per acre. Although the project had a number of problems, it reinforced the contention of several agricultural specialists that improving existing irrigation systems is often more economical than spending billions of dollars on new dams and reservoirs. The following statement in the USAID Evaluation Report is worth noting: "An immediate and very significant impact of implementation of the project, prior even to the attainment of any results from improved water management, was the incentive to the government of Pakistan to shift its development priorities from large infrastructure projects, such as dams, to water management—a previously neglected function" (USAID 1982b, 122).

Conclusion

It is difficult to find a large multipurpose dam that has not created severe environmental damage, or whose capital and operating costs have not been so high in relation to increased output as to make the dam uneconomic. Agronomists and other agricultural scientists—including those associated with the World Bank and USAID—are showing increasing skepticism about the value of large dams. Some questions remain, however: (1) Are there alternatives to large dams that will expand productivity sufficiently to compensate for high population growth; and (2) Is it possible to take measures to avoid the adverse environmental impacts of large dams while still enabling them to make a positive net contribution to social welfare?

APPENDIX 4-A

Case Study: The Narmada River Project[2]

The Narmada River Project in India was in the planning stage for several decades, but construction did not begin until 1987. The first phase of the project involves two dams on the Narmada—the Sardar Sarovar dam, expected to irrigate 1.8 million hectares of cultivatable land and generate 300 megawatts of electricity, and the Narmada Sagar dam, designed to irrigate 123,000 hectares of cultivatable land and produce 224 megawatts of power. In 1985 the World Bank approved loans and IDA credits totaling $350 million for the Sardar Sarovar dam, plus $100 million for the water delivery and drainage project. (Japan's Overseas Economic Cooperation Fund [OECF] agreed to provide $20 million in equipment credits.) The total population to be resettled as a consequence of land submerged by the dams is subject to dispute because some of the villages will be only partially submerged. The World Bank estimates fewer than seventy thousand for Sardar Sarovar and fewer than eighty thousand for Narmada Sagar, but other investigators give higher estimates.

The total cost of the two dams is estimated at $1.934 billion, not including water delivery and drainage, which are estimated at an additional half a billion dollars. The long-range Narmada River Basin Plan calls for construction of thirty major projects, including five hydropower dams, four multipurpose dams, and twenty-one irrigation projects. It would provide some 2,700 megawatts of hydroelectric capacity and require forty to fifty years to complete.

ANTICIPATED BENEFITS

Irrigation would substantially increase cropping intensities, mostly by enabling irrigated crops to replace rain-fed ones. The commercial value of the crops to be irrigated is expected to increase by 370 percent (in 1984 prices) over a twenty- to twenty-five-year period, while the value would increase by less than 30 percent without it (Searle 1987, 12). The value of food crops would rise by 306 percent, while the value of cash crops would rise by 272 percent (Searle 1987, 17). Among cash crops, the largest increases would be in cotton, groundnuts, tobacco, and mustard. More intensive cultivation in the project area would provide an estimated additional employment of 0.7 million man years, most to benefit landless laborers. Average farm income would rise by 380 percent because of the irrigation project (Searle 1987, 19).

The World Bank's financial evaluation of the project (which Searle was permitted to consult) confidently expected that the investment would yield the Bank's minimum return criterion of 12 percent. Chances of that rate's falling below 10 percent were placed at one in six (Searle 1987, 23). Power output would fluctuate, but capacity from the major powerhouse could be held at 300 megawatts indefinitely. Other benefits included the introduction of fisheries into the Sardar Sarovar reservoir, but some loss of fish downstream would offset this.

Approximately 11,600 hectares of recorded forestland would be inundated, but some of this is not actually forested. A wildlife escape corridor is to be maintained during the time when the reservoir is being filled. Apparently, little study was made of public health risks. The governments of the states responsible for the project—Gujarat, Madhya Pradesh, and Maharashtra—are required to take all necessary measures to minimize risks of malaria, filaria, schistosomiasis, and other water-related diseases. In short, the Bank report indicates that health risks are low.

The Bank's project appraisal mission also studied the potential for siltation and concluded that the reservoir has an expected life of between 180 and 340 years (Searle 1987, 26). According to Searle, project documents do not deal with the environmental problems associated with irrigation and drainage, but a work plan to be undertaken by the Narmada Planning Group will do so (1987, 26–27).

The three responsible states, the government of India, and the World Bank reached agreements regarding resettlement and rehabilitation of people displaced by the reservoir. These agreements embodied the Bank's own approach to the problem: Submergence can take place only after compensation, states must complete rehabilitation measures and arbitration rules are established in the event of disputes. Owners are to receive compensation for the value of private lands and buildings; displaced persons are to be offered new villages, together with irrigated agricultural lands and civil facilities; and grants are to be made to families being resettled. The people affected are to be assured they will regain the standard of living enjoyed prior to displacement; be relocated as village units, village sections, or families, according to preference; be fully integrated into the community in which they are resettled; and receive appropriate compensation, including community services and facilities (Searle 1987, 27–28). Displaced persons who have historically maintained their livelihood from the forest and its products will be moved to land that will include some forestland. Landless displaced persons are to be provided with permanent employment with an annual income above India's poverty line of $120 per year.

A number of problems were recognized in implementing these principles. These include inadequate food reserves to support the displaced persons until new lands are harvested or employment obtained; a shortage of land on which to settle those displaced; and a shortage of forestlands that can be released for resettlement purposes (Searle 1987, 30). Finally, it is not clear how the responsible states are to fund the costs of resettlement.

CRITICISMS OF THE NARMADA RIVER PROJECT

Few Third World projects have elicited more criticism than the Narmada River Project, either within India or internationally, between environmentalists and the World Bank. In India there is controversy within the government and between private scientists, engineers, environmentalists, and affected citizens, on the one hand, and the government, on the other.[3] The Indian government's Department of Environment and Forests refused to issue an unconditional environmental clearance for the dam because of the lack of crucial EIAs and the failure to prepare action programs for resettlement of all affected people. Several prominent Indian citizens have published detailed criticisms of the Narmada Project, and a number of treatises by environmental organizations critical of World Bank operations (including the Sierra Club, 1986, and Goldsmith & Hildyard, 1984) also criticize it.

The following adverse criticisms have been stressed by those who allege that the project fails to deal with the environmental impacts in a socially responsible manner:

1. The population that must evacuate the submerged land has not received adequate compensation and provisions for resettlement. Much

of the displaced population faces economic, social, and cultural depriva-
tion. More than one-third of the population consists of tribal communities that do not have legal claim to the plots they cultivate and, therefore,
will not receive any compensation. Nearly five hundred villages will be
affected, but no plans exist for the reconstitution of the submerged villages, so displaced people will be dispersed over a wide area instead of
being resettled together. Those who receive cash compensation instead
of new land will be unable to purchase an equivalent amount of land of
the same quality.

2. More than 54,000 hectares of forests will be inundated, and plans
for replacement by new plantings are lacking. Moreover, the loss of large
forest tracts presently used by livestock will create pressures on the remaining adjoining forest areas.

3. No provision has been made for the transfer of wildlife from submerged areas. Wildlife will be killed because there are no corridors through
which they may cross to other forested areas. Some animals will go into
agricultural areas and destroy crops. Some of the animal species are rare
and threatened with extinction—including tigers, panthers, bears, wolves,
lesser cats, pangolins, badgers, martins, flying squirrels, and porcupines.
Furthermore, there has been no systematic survey of the flora and fauna
in the area to be submerged.

4. Adequate provision has not been made for dealing with the waterlogging and salinity that will occur in the area to be irrigated. Based on
experience with other dams in the area, siltation rates have been grossly
underestimated.

5. Large irrigation projects in tropical areas give rise to health hazards
from such diseases as malaria, filariasis, cholera, tracoma, schistosomiasis, and others. Critics charge that the Narmada plans include no measures for disease prevention.

6. Over the long run, fish catches will be smaller with dam construction than without it because of the destruction of downstream fisheries.

7. For political reasons, consideration was not given to alteration of
the project, such as reducing the height of the dams and the use of lift
irrigation, both of which would avoid some of the adverse environmental
impacts.

8. Benefits will accrue to the wealthier landowners and urban power
users, while the poor villagers displaced by the reservoir will lose out. Of
245 villages to be flooded, 193 are in Madhya Pradesh, which ranks among
India's poorest and most backward states, while only 19 are in relatively

prosperous Gujarat. Most benefits from the dams will accrue to Gujarat (Fineman 1990).

9. Based on past experience with large dams in the region, critics view the expected rise in agricultural output from the Narmada project with extreme skepticism.

10. A full SBCA of the dams, which should include an allowance for the high risk, has not been prepared.

A recent NGO report entitled "Evaluating the Narmad Valley Projects" (Indian International Center 1988) criticizes the project on the grounds that the rate of return is not high enough to allow for risk and that a number of the costs have been left out of the calculations while the benefits have been overstated. The report also argues that the projected rate of return on the capital invested is not sufficient to cover the cost of domestic borrowing for a portion of the project. These allegations are important in considering alternatives that do not pose the same environmental consequences and risks. The Indian NGO report argues that repairing, excavating, and desilting existing village ponds and lakes, maintaining percolation tanks and wells, and introducing water-saving devices could provide substantial and more immediate benefits to the people of the area. The report also regards transporting water by pipeline across the Gulf of Cambay to be more cost-effective than the dam. Certainly, planning must be faulted if the Indian government and the World Bank have not fully explored lower-cost alternatives.

On 22 May, 1990 the Japanese Ministry of Foreign Affairs decided to halt additional funding for the Narmada River Project. But at the time of this writing, the World Bank continues to support the project; it is currently discussing a new $200 million credit from IDA, which would provide for watershed protection, environmental impact studies, and an updated resettlement and rehabilitation plan for the project. The continuing controversy over the resettlement arrangements has delayed Bank funding, however, and as of December 1990 the project was on hold. As of mid-1990, the dam was only 10 percent completed.

APPENDIX 4-B

Case Study: The Rahad Irrigation Project in Sudan[4]

The Rahad Project in Sudan, supported by the World Bank and other external agencies and costing in excess of $400 million, was designed to expand exports of cotton and peanuts and to improve the welfare of an indigenous population of eighty thousand engaged in subsistence rain-fed farming in an area of low average rainfall. The major source of water there is the Blue Nile, which carries water through a 90-kilometer canal to an irrigation system comprising 800 kilometers of major canals and a total irrigated area of about 300,000 acres located 160 kilometers southeast of Khartoum. As in other large-scale irrigation schemes in Sudan, tenants operate farms while a state corporation manages the project, providing all agricultural input, and markets and processes the cotton. In addition, the Rahad Corporation maintains close control over the selection of products. Each tenancy covers 22 *feddans* (1 feddan equals 1.04 acres) and is nonmortgagable and nontransferrable. The farming units produce mainly cotton and groundnuts on a rotation basis, and some fodder. In addition, there are five vegetable-fruit tenancies and twelve livestock tenancies.

Following the initial operation of the project in 1977, the incentive for growing cotton was very low, because world prices for cotton were low and the corporation paid low prices for it. Tenants prefer to grow groundnuts, which they are free to market outside the corporation. Producing sorghum, a major dietary staple and the predominant rainfall crop in the area before the project began, is even more desirable. Tenant behavior on the vegetable-fruit tenancies indicates that the farmers will work diligently and efficiently when they can market their own output. Cotton yields have been low, costs quite high, net yields to tenants low or negative, and net foreign exchange earnings for the country somewhat doubtful because of the high foreign exchange costs for required machinery and chemical inputs. Paul Harrison reports that tenants are worse off with the project than they were before (1987, Ch. 9). The agricultural chemicals used in the project represented an estimated 30 percent of total costs in the 1980–1981 production year. Most cotton fields were treated eleven times with insecticides applied from the air. Tractor-applied insecticides were used to control weeds, while the areas to be mechanically harvested were treated two times with defoliants applied by air. Tenants using knapsack sprayers treated horticulture plots with insecticides and fungicides on an individual basis. The costs of energy and equipment were high, and both involve mainly foreign exchange outlays.

Although a full appraisal of the irrigation program is not available, some Sudanese government officials have questioned the wisdom of investing in irrigated agriculture rather than in rain-fed agriculture and livestock from the standpoint of financial returns and national development priorities. When the project began in 1977, it cost $1,900 per feddan to develop irrigated land, compared to $100 per feddan to develop rain-fed land. Moreover, up to a 100 percent increase in yield could be obtained under traditional agriculture with improved seeds, weed control, and assistance in marketing (USAID 1982a, F5–6).

The estimated production gains from the project did not take account of the environmental losses. The project was subjected to ecological-environmental examination by the donors prior to completion of the project design. The following potential environmental impacts were identified at the time: (1) the creation of a habitat for waterborne diseases, including malaria and schistosomiasis; (2) adverse health effects of large amounts of agricultural chemicals (insecticides, herbicides, and so on); and (3) the disruption of migratory routes of native game to and from Dinder National Park. Secondary impacts, receiving little attention, included the displacement of traditional nomadic herdsmen and their livestock; the creation of a market for wood and charcoal, resulting in the degradation of forests adjacent to the development area; and the incremental increase in development pressure on Dinder National Park. A USAID evaluation report states that the project "represents the case where despite the identification and recognition of major environmental problems by donor and the host country, the project design and implementation plan were unsuccessful in addressing these problems through effective mitigation measures." Some unexpected environmental benefits, however, included creation of an extensive bird habitat in the irrigated area; creation of fish habitat in the irrigation canal systems; and reduction of grazing pressure from traditional nomadic herdsmen (USAID 1982a, F–4).

The principal health impacts associated with the project were waterborne diseases, illness from poor-quality drinking water, and adverse effects on human health and fish from the use of agricultural chemicals. Health effects, particularly from malaria, would have been far more serious without the intervention of the Blue Nile Health Project, jointly sponsored by the World Health Organization and the government of Sudan. Because villages were not supplied with sources of clean water, villagers were forced to obtain water from the canal. Provision was not made for planting trees to take the place of those removed in the irrigated area, and increased demand for firewood resulted in further destruction of forests.

Recent World Bank and USAID evaluation reports on the Sudan have tended to question the desirability of additional large irrigation projects in contrast to projects based on traditional rain-fed cropping and livestock and the rehabilitation of existing irrigation projects with emphasis on preventing resource degradation and promoting sustainability. A World Bank report stated that "in the late 1970s, the Bank turned to a more critical analysis of the consequences of the mechanized farming policy, the relative neglect of the traditional rain-fed sector, and shortfalls in irrigation performances." The Bank's recommendations in 1979 emphasized programs for improving productivity and sustainability in traditional rainfed cropping and livestock sectors. These programs included "(1) reform of existing communal tenure arrangements which were not conducive to the introduction of improved management practices; (2) the use of incentives (prices and taxes) to encourage better conservation practices; (3) diversification of small farm cropping; (4) higher takeoff by herders to reduce the grazing pressure on overstocked rangelands; and (5) research and pilot projects to develop appropriate technology for the traditional rain-fed environments which formerly had been neglected" (World Bank 1988, Annex 10, 4).

APPENDIX 4-C

Case Study: The Volta River Project in Ghana, 1962–1976

The Volta River Project (VRP) consists of a large hydroelectric dam and an aluminum smelter. Although the primary purpose of the dam was to supply power to the smelter to complement Ghana's bauxite industry, secondary objectives were expansion of agriculture, including an irrigation program (which was never implemented) in the resettlement area; expansion of fisheries in the reservoir (Volta Lake) created by the dam; and production of power for the local economy. The government of Ghana financed half the construction of the dam and power plant, and loans from the World Bank and loans and guarantees from US and UK government agencies financed the other half. The total cost was $196 million. Kaiser Aluminum and Chemical Corporation provided 90 percent of the $12 million equity financing for the smelter and Reynolds Metals provided 10 percent. In addition, the US Export-Import Bank made a $96 million mortgage loan to the Volta Aluminum Company (VALCO), which operates the smelter. The Ghana government operates the power plant as the Volta River Authority (VRA) and sells the power. Commercial power became available in September 1965, and the smelter began operations in April 1967. In addition to the sale of power to VALCO, power is also sold to the neighboring countries of Togo and Benin, as well as to users in Ghana. The smelter was expanded in 1972 and 1976, bringing its total cost to $220 million and its total capacity to about 200,000 metric tons of primary aluminum.

The World Bank was lukewarm to the project when it was first involved in negotiations for the dam and power plant in the early stages. However, strong US and UK government backing, for both economic and political reasons, probably influenced the Bank. The World Bank advised the Ghana government during negotiations over the price of electricity for the smelter. From what little is known about the loan negotiations, the

Bank seems to have been concerned primarily with the technical and commercial aspects of the project, rather than with the broader impact on the
Ghanaian economy. The project was supposed to promote the development of Ghana's bauxite industry, but since Ghana has no facilities for
producing alumina (the feed for aluminum smelters), it imports alumina
and exports bauxite and primary aluminum. Therefore, the project does
not use Ghana's raw materials. Ghana meets its requirements for aluminum products by importing rolled aluminum sheeting and fabricating it.

The VRP has not made a significant contribution to Ghana's net foreign exchange income (after servicing the loan). In 1976, total employment
at the dam, power plant, and smelter was estimated at about seven thousand, some of that part-time. Since VALCO takes a high percentage of
the power generated by the VRA, the VRA supplied only 11 percent of
the energy used by Ghanaian consumers, while oil supplied 85 percent
(excluding firewood and charcoal). There is little evidence that the project
has contributed significantly to Ghana's industrialization, since inputs for
the project come mainly from abroad. A benefit-cost study of the entire
project, including the smelter, yielded a benefit-to-cost ratio of only 1.04.
Since it allowed nothing for risk and used a discount rate of only 5 percent, this ratio is very unsatisfactory (Hart 1980, 71).

The environmental cost of the VRP to Ghana is quite substantial compared to the economic benefits. The original irrigation scheme for bringing water to 440,000 acres in the Accra Plain south of the dam was never
implemented, in part because of its high cost and unsuitability to the conditions. The resettlement plan for eighty thousand people in the area now
covered by Volta Lake was never completed. Not only were houses in
the resettlement area not built in sufficient numbers to accommodate the
migrating population, but dissatisfaction with housing led a large number of settlers to move out. A Food and Agricultural Organization (FAO)
survey in 1968 indicated that of the 67,500 people installed in resettlement villages, only 25,900 remained (FAO/UNDP 1981). Compensation
for crops destroyed and land submerged was inadequate and delayed,
partly because sufficient land was not provided at most of the resettlement sites. The maximum allocation per farmer was just over one hectare, which is insufficient for subsistence. A summary of the major costs
and benefits of the project, excluding power generation and the smelter,
shows costs of resettlement from $46 to $57 million; annual costs from
the loss of productivity due to disease and other social costs, $8.2 million;

and annual benefits represented by the value of the fish taken from Volta Lake, $8.0 million.

The development of a fishing industry on Volta Lake was a success, largely because of individual initiative. However, as a result of the dam, creek fisheries were destroyed and clam fishing substantially reduced.

Volta Lake became the site of serious health hazards. Diseases of major incidence were schistosomiasis (a debilitating disease) and onchocerciasis (river blindness). Loss of productivity through schistosomiasis alone has been estimated at $6.7 million annually (Hart 1980, 102).

In terms of the VRP's basic purpose to generate power for the operation of an aluminum smelter, the project has been a success. This is true despite occasional problems with the smelter and insufficient water to operate the plant at a level sufficient to meet demand during drought periods. In some years the smelter has operated at well below capacity. The failure of the project has to do with the social costs of resettlement, the diseases generated and spread by Volta Lake, and the loss of forests from creation of the lake. These costs greatly exceeded any possible benefits from the project to the Ghanaian economy. But at the time the World Bank and government loans were committed to this project in the early 1960s, little thought was given to environmental impacts.

APPENDIX 4-D

Case Study: The Nam Pong Project in Northeast Thailand

The Nam Pong Project is a multipurpose dam-reservoir for power, irrigation, flood control, and fisheries (Lohani 1988, 110). It consists of a dam and a power plant, a downstream irrigation diversion weir, and irrigation canals on both banks of the Nam Pong River. The project was expected to provide 65 million kilowatts of electricity per year and water for about 53,000 hectares of land, which had been used only for rainfall cropping in the past. Preliminary investigation and feasibility studies were completed in 1959 and the dam and power station officially opened in March 1966. At the time of the case study summarized here (1979), the irrigation system was only about half completed.

The project was planned primarily for power and irrigation, but power appeared to be given priority. Progress in the development of the irrigation system, including construction of canals and ditches, was slow, and yields have been substantially lower than target goals. Moreover, farmers needed training, credit, and guidance to achieve a successful transition from simple, rain-fed farming to complex irrigation farming involving new technology and new crops. The farmers also need credit to obtain on-farm physical irrigation facilities. Farm incomes in irrigated areas have been higher than those in nearby nonirrigated areas, but this is partly because the farms in irrigated areas are larger.

The project made a substantial contribution to fisheries; in some years income from fishing was about three-fourths the value of the power produced. Although provision was made for resettlement of farmers displaced by the reservoir and other facilities, there have been many complaints about inadequate payments, insufficient allowance for the costs of rehabilitation, and long periods of time between evacuation and compensation. Resettlement sites are located in areas with poor soil capable of a fair yield only in the first years of cultivation. Thereafter, soil fertility has declined, resulting in relatively low yields. Water for drinking is scant, leaving settlers with no water source within a reasonable distance of their homes. Agricultural extension services, more schools, health centers, and improved transportation are also needed. Although the prevention of flooding has led to substantial savings by warding off crop damage, there were adverse effects from flood control and increased flood occurrence in the upstream areas.

The Nam Pong reservoir is a popular tourist resort that provides income to the local population and for which there is little evidence of increasing water-oriented communicable disease. But there have been severe losses in forest and wildlife habitat around it. The authors of the project evaluation prepared ten years after its initiation drew the following conclusion (Lohani 1988, 111):

> The Nam Pong experience after more than a decade of operation shows clearly that the traditional approach to multipurpose dams/reservoir planning has been only semi-multipurpose with adequate attention to civil engineering features including hydropower and flood control, only partial attention to resettlement, irrigation, and community water supply, little attention to fisheries and recreational potentials, and very little attention to comprehensive socio-economic or 'human settlements' planning for villages and communities in the vicinity of the project. In particular, too few of the project benefits are received by people living in the project vicinity, and those who are flooded out (and thus make the maximum contribution to the project) received the least benefit of all, and even became worse off because of it.

APPENDIX 4-E

Case Study: The Aswân High Dam

The Aswân High Dam on the Nile River, completed in the late 1960s, is perhaps the best-known large multipurpose dam in the world. Little has been published about its environmental impacts, however, other than regarding the burying of important archeological sites. Although the dam has helped to substantially increase Egypt's cotton crops, its many adverse impacts have led some to question its long-term value (Lohani 1988, 42–48).

Before the Aswân High Dam was built, the Nile River deposited about 100 million tons of sediment each year on nearly 1 million hectares of land in the Nile Valley. The sediment was rich in minerals and nutrients important for soil fertility. With its silt trapped behind the Aswân High Dam, the once-muddy brown waters of the Nile are now green. This trapping of silt has had several important effects. First, to compensate for the nutrients once provided by the river's annual flood, Egypt must buy fertilizers on an ever-increasing scale. In terms of nitrogen content alone, the fertilizer value of Nile silt has been estimated at about $100 million annually (Goldsmith & Hildyard 1984, 60–61). Second, agricultural lands in the Nile Delta have been lost. The lack of river-carried silt has caused the Egyptian coastline to retreat and a large amount of agricultural land to be lost. Third, much water has been lost through evaporation: Lake Nasser is estimated to lose some 15 billion cubic meters of water per year—enough to irrigate 2 million acres of farmland. Fourth, waterlogging and salinity have increased substantially due to the lack of drainage in irrigated lands, not a problem when Nile River flooding provided irrigation. Finally, the Aswân High Dam has also resulted in the loss of fish and has caused adverse health effects.

APPENDIX 4-F

Environmental Effects Commonly Associated with Irrigation Projects

Significant adverse environmental effects that have resulted from irrigation projects include the following (exclusive of effects of dam/storage reservoirs):

A. *Environmental Effects Due to Project Location*
   1. *Disruption of Hydrology:* Changes in the hydrology of waterways intercepted by irrigation canals, without careful planning can result (1) in creating or intensifying local flooding problems and (2) in affecting adequate ecology including fisheries. Through evaluation of the local situations, such potential adverse impacts can be identified and the planning/design adjusted to minimize the effects.
   2. *Resettlement of Families Displaced by Project*
   3. *Encroachment into Forests/Swamplands:* This can be caused by the project structures or by filling of swamplands to gain more farmland area. Impairment of mangrove areas may be especially serious.
   4. *Impediments to Movement of Wildlife/Cattle/People:* Suitable crossing ways need to be provided.
   5. *Encroachment on Historical/Cultural Buildings/Areas:* Need to avoid/minimize/offset such effects by careful design.
   6. *Conflicts in Water Supply Rights:* Careful planning may be needed to avoid serious conflicts with other beneficial water uses (for example, implementation of excessive irrigation projects in the upper

Source: Environmental Unit, *Environmental Guidelines for Selected Agricultural and Natural Resource Development Projects* (Manila, Philippines: ADB, 1987), Annex 1–A, 3–7.

Chao Phya Basin in Thailand has tended to "dry up" established water uses in the lower basin during the dry seasons in drought years). Also, proposed transbasin diversions, although technically feasible, may create political problems.

7. *Regional Flooding and Drainage Hazards:* Will the structures be secure against regional flooding hazards? Is the regional drainage pattern inadequate to meet project needs? Should the project be enlarged to obtain reasonable flood protection?

B. *Environmental Problems Relating to Design (including assumptions on O&M)*

1. *Watershed Erosion:* Could the project efficiency be seriously impaired by inadequate attention to erosion control in upper watershed, resulting in excessive siltation problems? Is the project plan based on realistic expectations of silt runoff rates? Should the project be expanded to include such erosion control? Could erosion in farmland areas be a serious problem and, if so, should the project include regreening? Will the overall erosion rates result in excessive canal siltation?

2. *Water Quality Problems:* Diversion of water from surface streams by decreasing downstream flow can result in increasing the downstream concentrations of dissolved mineral salts and in increasing seawater encroachment into the stream systems. Also, downstream salinity may be increased from return irrigation flows. Such salinity increases may adversely affect many downstream beneficial water uses including community water supply and fisheries.

3. *Suitability of Natural Water Quality for Irrigation:* This includes such parameters as total dissolved solids, chlorides, sodium/calcium ratio, boron and others.

4. *Overpumping of Groundwater:* This can lead to numerous problems including water rights conflicts, salinization and ground subsidence.

5. *Adequacy of Drainage Planning:* Insufficient drainage can negate much of the project benefits, such as from salinity encroachment, and can decrease stream capacity from siltation.

6. *Land Tenure Problems:* How will the project benefits be distributed between farmers and landowners?

7. *Farmer Credit Limitations:* Do the farm families have sufficient

financial resources to make the needed investments in farm inputs and in land levelling/preparations?

8. *Feasibility of Cooperatives:* Does the project depend upon assumed functioning of cooperatives for farm inputs and for marketing beyond the reality of the "track record" for such cooperatives?

9. *Feasibility of Water User Associations:* Does the project depend on assumed functioning of such associations, both for water distribution and for O&M, beyond the reality of the "track record" for such associations?

10. *Disruption of Existing Farmer Cooperative Systems:* Does the project plan for farmer cooperation (for cooperatives and water users associations) make appropriate use of existing systems performing these functions?

11. *Use of Agriculture Chemicals:* Does the project plan provide for competent use of fertilizers and pesticides by the farmers so that proper amounts will be used and so that excessive chemical runoff does not occur causing depreciation of downstream water quality including problems of toxicity to aquatic fauna and/or eutrophication?

12. *Selection of Pesticides:* Will the project plan result in the use of environmentally acceptable (degradable) pesticides and avoid the use of hard pesticides which will accumulate in soils and stream sediments with potentials for serious effects on ecology?

13. *Land Use Conflicts:* Will the project result in conflicts with other necessary land uses such as cattle grazing?

14. *Inequities in Water Distribution:* Will the project ensure reasonable distribution of water throughout the service area, including provision of practicable turnout facilities?

15. *Canal Maintenance:* Does the design of canals provide for reasonable protection against weed growth which could seriously impair canal capacity? If canal banks are not lined and dependence for removing weeds is placed on assumed levels of O&M, is this assumption realistic? Also, does the design include canal gates needed for flushing?

16. *Passageways:* Does the design incorporate adequate passageways for wildlife/cattle/people?

17. *Scouring Hazards:* Does the design incorporate adequate protection against scouring hazards at culverts, control structures, and other special structures?

C. *Problems During Construction Stage*
    1. *Erosion Control:* Does the construction plan include adequate provision for control of erosion and for proper rehabilitation of exposed cut-and-fill areas?
    2. *Other Construction Stage Hazards:* Does the project construction plan incorporate provision for other potential adverse effects during construction?
    3. *Monitoring During Construction:* Does the project construction plan provide for necessary construction stage monitoring?

D. *Problems Relating to Operations*
    1. *Adequacy of O&M:* Is the O&M plan realistic in terms of experience in the project area? If there are questions on the O&M adequacy, how will canals be cleaned of silt? How will they be cleaned of excessive weeds, etc.?
    2. *Adverse Soil Modifications:* Is the project likely to result in adverse soil modifications resulting from (1) water logging, (2) soil salinization, (3) soil alkalinization, (4) nutrient leaching, (5) acid sulfate hazards, and (6) development of soil impermeability from excessive sodium?
    3. *Changes in Groundwater Hydrology:* Will the operation of the irrigation system change groundwater levels and adversely affect other beneficial water uses?
    4. *Water-Oriented Diseases.* Will the changes in surface water hydrology resulting from the canal system induce new communicable diseases or increase the incidence of existing ones, including insect vector diseases such as malaria and schistosomiasis? If the irrigation water is being drawn from a source contaminated with the schistosomiasis snails, are provisions made for screening out the snails before the water enters the irrigation systems?
    5. *Hazards of Toxic Chemicals:* Will the use/misuse of toxic agricultural chemicals, especially pesticides, result in impairment of local aquaculture or of downstream fisheries or in impairment of ecology through accumulation in soil and bottom sediments? Will misuse result in occupational health hazards to the farmers?
    6. *Hazards of Fertilizer Runoff:* Will the use/misuse of fertilizer result in excessive eutrophication in the irrigation system or in the downstream waterways?
    7. *Operations Monitoring;* Does the project operations plan and

budget include provision for minimum necessary periodic monitoring to ensure that all essential environmental protection measures are being done, and to recommend on needed corrections?

8. *Aquaculture Water Supply:* Will the project distribution system ensure year-round delivery of water to aquaculture operations whose success depends upon such year-round water availability?

E. *Realization of Enhancement Measures*

Recognizing that the water distributed by the irrigation system may be the only feasible source of water for other essential water uses in the irrigation service area:

1. Does the project include appropriate use of water for improving community water supply and sanitation facilities in the service area?

2. Does the project include an appropriate component for making optimal use of water for improving aquaculture in the service area, especially aquaculture which is feasible only with an assured year-round supply?

F. *Overall Critical Environmental Review Criteria*

1. Will the project cause unwarranted losses in precious/irreplaceable natural or other resources?

2. Will the project make unwarranted accelerated use of scarce resources in favor of short-term rather than long-term economic gains?

3. Will the project adversely affect the national energy/foreign exchange situation to an unwarranted degree?

4. Will the project result in unwarranted hazards to endangered species?

5. Will the project tend to intensify undesirable migration from rural to urban sector?

6. Will the project tend to increase the "income gap" between the poor and the affluent?

APPENDIX 4-G

Summary of Major Environmental Factors in Dam Projects

The following summary of major environmental factors in large dam projects appears in a recent World Bank document:

The Dam and Impoundment Area

Specific provisions must be made to eliminate or mitigate environmental damage in the impoundment area during and after construction. Some of these effects are the responsibility of the contractor and others are the responsibility of various government agencies.

Provisions should be incorporated into construction tenders so that the eventual contractor clearly recognizes its responsibility for construction related impacts. The Bank has formalized instructions for contractors that cover many points, including the following:

- location of borrow areas and borrow pits;
- air and water pollution from construction equipment, earth movement, and living quarters;
- screening of laborers for imported water-related diseases;
- solid waste disposal;
- siting of contractor facilities and other infrastructure to minimize destruction of the natural landscape; and,
- noise pollution.

Other environmental effects found in the dam and impoundment area may be the responsiblity of the contractor, the project authority, or various

Source: John A. Dixon, Lee M. Talbot, and Guy J. M. Le Moigne, *Dams and the Environment,* Technical Paper No. 110 (Washington, D.C.: World Bank, 1990), 15–19.

government agencies. These environmental impacts can be both negative and positive and include the following:

- *Population influx,* associated with the need for labor for construction, may cause problems including pollution and a variety of linked social effects including health, security, and impact on local cultures;
- *Direct effects on people:* reservoir creation may involve inundation of houses, villages, farms and infrastructure such as roads and transmission lines. When people are involved, involuntary resettlement is required. Involuntary resettlement imposes major social and economic costs;
- *Cultural/historical sites:* inundation of sites or areas of historic, religious, aesthetic or other particular cultural value, and sites of archeological and paleontological significance requires special attention;
- *Inundation of agricultural land,* especially highly productive bottom lands;
- *Inundation of forest land,* may mean the loss of valuable timber and species diversity. Salvage lumbering can recover some of this potential loss and provide other reservoir benefits; species loss may not be replaceable;
- *Inundation of wildlife habitat,* particularly habitat of threatened species with consequent impact on biological diversity;
- *Inundation of potentially valuable mineral resources;*
- *Inundated vegetation:* biomass left in the reservoir can affect water quality if the water is to be used for potable purposes, reservoir fishing (for example, through interference with nets), operation and longevity of dam and associated machinery (e.g., effect of floating debris, chemical reactions, and wear on turbines);
- *Water weeds:* proliferation of water weeds can increase disease vectors, affect water quality and fisheries, increase water loss (through transpiration), affect navigation, recreation and fishing, and clog irrigation structures and turbines;
- *Fisheries:* the dam will block fish migrations in the river, although fish ladders may sometimes be practical. Substantial new reservoir fisheries are often possible if carefully planned and managed. In the Saguling reservoir in Indonesia, for example, the reservoir fishery helped those resettled to restore or even surpass their previous income levels. Similar results have been observed elsewhere including Thailand (Nam Pong) and in Gujarat, India;

- *Water quality* within the reservoir is, in part, dependent on what happens upstream and retention time within the reservoir. Quality may be affected by salt accumulation, eutrophication from weeds and biomass decay, turbidity, pollution from agricultural, industrial and human wastes, and fish processing. By trapping sediment, the reservoir provides better quality water downstream with less suspended matter;
- *Health:* establishment of the reservoir and associated water management structures (e.g., canals and ditches) can create conditions fostering establishment and spread of water-related diseases such as schistosomiasis, onchocerciasis, encephalitis, and malaria. Prevention, where possible, is essential, since treatment to eliminate most disease vectors is difficult (or impossible) and expensive once they become established. In other cases, availability of regulated water supplies for municipal and industrial use (M and I) can have major beneficial effects;
- *Effect of drawdown regime,* which may create agricultural possibilities, as well as health, recreational, aesthetic, and access problems;
- *Seismicity* may be induced by large reservoirs;
- *Ground water level* in the surrounding area may be altered;
- *Local climate* may be modified by large reservoirs, especially in terms of humidity and local fog;
- *Temperature* of released water may be higher or lower than ambient river temperature (depending on pattern of release); this will have varying impacts on downstream water users;

Upstream Considerations

A variety of upstream considerations can affect the dam and its reservoir. While not directly "caused" by the dam, these effects may be induced or exacerbated by the dam. For example, dam construction and reservoir filling may provide access to a previously remote and inaccessible area. The induced population in-migration may lead to increased agricultural or mining activities with major implications for soil erosion, sedimentation, and water quality.

Increased population settlement and economic development in the upper catchment or watershed usually increase soil movement. The timing and ultimate impact of this increased movement on the reservoir varies greatly from case to case.

The major sources of sediment are the following:

- *Existing sediment:* sediment resulting from previous natural or induced erosion remains in the bed of watercourses and elsewhere in the watershed area, and will continue to flow into the reservoir, particularly in periods of heavy rainfall (especially in "young" geological areas, such as the Himalayas);
- *Unusual natural sedimentation:* natural events such as volcanic activity, earthquakes, mudslides, typhoons and "100 year precipitation events" may cause heavy sedimentation regardless of watershed management measures;
- *Road building and other construction,* not necessarily associated with the dam project, can cause soil erosion and associated sedimentation;
- *Erosion* from (usually unplanned) clearance of vegetation, logging, and cultivation by people who have moved into the watershed areas as a direct or indirect result of the construction of the dam project. This is largely a planning and regulation problem.

Changes in land use caused directly or indirectly by the dam and dam construction, primarily from increases in population due to planned or unplanned resettlement from inundated areas or elsewhere. These changes may also go on without the project; the question is the rate of change. In-migration from both downstream and outside the river basin area is often facilitated by the project (improved access due to new roads and water transport). The resource and environmental effects include the following:

- *Cultivation on unsuitable sites,* often unplanned, using unstable or otherwise unsuitable lands (e.g., steep slopes, poor soils) leading to soil erosion and sedimentation;
- *Logging,* usually unplanned and often illegal, which results in denudation, unsustainable exploitation of the resource, and erosion;
- *Poaching,* i.e., illegal, unsustainable exploitation of wildlife;
- *Denudation of vegetation* for cultivation, fuel collection, and logging;
- *Loss of wildland and wildlife habitat,* with impact on endangered species and reduction of biological diversity;
- *Negative impacts on aesthetic and scenic qualities* of the area and the potential for certain recreational uses. The reservoir, however, may create recreational benefits;
- *Pollution* from settlements and cultivation.

Changed watershed hydrology. The changes in land use patterns, if extensive enough, may affect the timing and magnitude of runoff, especially during major storm events. Changed vegetative patterns may also influence dry season stream flow.

Salt inflows from the watershed may accumulate in the reservoir and affect water quality. Similarly, catchment runoff may carry increased quantities of agricultural chemicals and fertilizer with resultant impacts on reservoir water quality.

Downstream Considerations

Numerous impacts are felt downstream. Many are positive and are the reasons why dams are built—increased irrigation, improved water control, hydropower generation and water supply benefits. Whether they are considered direct or indirect project effects, there are other environmental and resource impacts that can be both positive and negative. Among these are the following:

• *Impact on river fishery* due to changes in flow regime, effect of dam blocking fish migration, changes in water quality (e.g., loss of nutrients trapped by dam, pollution from irrigation return flow, and increased water turbidity);

• *Effect on traditional flood plain cultivation* through changes in flow and flooding regime, and loss of annual "top dressing" fertilization from limited flooding. Control of severe flooding can also yield benefits through reduced crop and property losses;

• *Impact on other water projects:* changes in stream flow and water releases from the dam affect dams and irrigation projects elsewhere in the lower basin. The impacts can be both positive and negative. Reduced silt content in water, for example, will lower downstream O&M costs and permit better water management; low silt levels also decrease potable water treatment costs. On the other hand, weed growth in existing canals may increase with perennial water supplies;

• *Impact on municipal and industrial water supply* downstream can have both positive and negative effects depending on water quantity and quality;

• *Stream bed changes* are one possibility, but not a common result of the changed water flow and sediment load. This includes the possibility of increased stream bed erosion below the dam due to "hungry" water (with reduced silt loads) being released from the dam;

- *Effect on estuarine and marine fisheries* and marine biota, including endangered species, through change in flow regime, change in water quality (e.g., pollution from toxic chemicals and salts from irrigation return flow to river) and loss of nutrients;
- *Salt intrusion* into estuarine and lower river basin areas may result from sustained or seasonal reduction in river flow;
- *Groundwater level changes:* higher levels due to the high water levels in the reservoir. Downstream, in old flood plain areas, the groundwater level may fall but in irrigated areas, it may rise;
- *Health problems* from water-related diseases or parasites (similar health problems may also occur in the reservoir itself), primarily from irrigation and associated canals;
- *Effects on wildlife and wildlands* through loss of or change in habitat may result in an impact on biological diversity.

NOTES

1. The material in this section draws heavily on Thayer Scudder (1988).
2. Much of the material in this section is based on studies by Graham Searle (1987); Claude Alvares and Ramesh Dillorey (1988); Bharat Dogra (1985); and Kalpavriksh (1985).
3. In May 1990 thousands of villagers met in New Delhi with Indian Prime Minister V. P. Singh to protest the building of the dams, mainly because they feared that thousands would be left homeless.
4. Much of this material is based on USAID (1982a).

REFERENCES

Alvares, Claude, and Ramesh Dillorey. 1988. *Damming the Narmada: India's Greatest Planned Environmental Disaster.* Penang, Malaysia: Third World Network.

Berry, L., R. Ford, and R. Hosier. 1980. *The Impact of Irrigation on Development.* Program Evaluation Discussion Paper No. 9. Washington, D.C.: USAID, October.

Crosson, Pierre. 1987. "Soil Conservation and Small Watershed Development." In *Sustainability Issues in Agricultural Development* (proceedings of the Seventh Agricultural Sector Symposium), edited by T. J. Davis and I. A. Schirmer. Washington, D.C.: World Bank.

Dixon, John A. et al. 1986. *Economic Analysis of the Environmental Impacts of Development Projects* (Environmental and Policy Institute, East-West Center, Hawaii). Manila, Philippines: ADB.

Dixon, John A., Lee M. Talbot, and Guy J. M. Le Moigne. 1989. *Dams and the Environment.* Technical Paper No. 110. Washington, D.C.: World Bank.

———. 1990. *Dams and the Environment.* Technical Paper No. 110. Washington, D.C.: World Bank.

Dogra, Bharat. 1985. "The Indian Experience with Large Dams." In *The Social and Environmental Effects of Large Dams,* Vol. II, edited by Edward Goldsmith and Nicholas Hildyard. Wadebridge, England: Wadebridge Ecological Centre.

Economic and Social Commission for Asia and the Pacific. 1985. *Environmental Impact Assessment: Guidelines for Planners and Decision Makers.* Bangkok, Thailand: UN.

Environmental Programme. 1988. *Environmental Impact Assessment: Basic Procedures for Developing Countries.* New York: UN.

Environmental Unit. 1987. *Environmental Guidelines for Selected Agricultural and Natural Resource Development Projects.* Manila, Philippines: ADB.

Fineman, Mark. 1990. "India's Gamble on the Holy Narmada." *Smithsonian* 21, no. 8 (November): 118–137.

Food and Agriculture Organization and United Nations Development Programme. 1981. *Volta Lake Research, Ghana: Interim Report.* Rome: FAO/UNDP.

Garzon, Camilo E. 1984. *Water Quality and Hydroelectric Projects.* Washington, D.C.: World Bank.

Goldsmith, Edward, and Nicholas Hildyard. 1984. *The Social and Environmental Effects of Large Dams.* San Francisco: Sierra Club Books.

Harrison, Paul. 1987. In *The Greening of Africa: Breaking Through in the Battle for Land and Food.* Washington, D.C.: Penguin Books.

Hart, David. 1980. *The Volta River Project: A Case Study of Politics and Technology.* Edinburgh: Scotland: Edinburgh Univ. Press.

Hillel, Daniel, 1987. *Efficient Use of Water in Irrigation.* Technical Paper No. 64. Washington, D.C.: World Bank.

Howe, Charles W. 1982. "Socially Efficient Development and Allocation of Water in Developing Countries: Roles for the Public and Private Sectors." In *Managing Renewable Natural Resources in Developing Countries,* edited by C. W. Howe. Boulder, Colo.: Westview Press.

Indian International Center. 1988. "Evaluating the Narmada Valley Projects." New Delhi, India: Indian International Center, 15 October.

Kalpavriksh et al. 1985. "The Narmada Valley Project: Development or Destruction?" In *The Social and Environmental Effects of Large Dams,* Vol. 2, edited by Edward Goldsmith and Nicholas Hildyard. Wadebridge, England: Wadebridge Ecological Centre.

Lohani, B. N. 1988. "Post Environmental Evaluation of the Nam Pong Project, 1979." *Environmental Impacts Analysis of Water Resources Project* (expert group workshop on River/Lake Basin Approach to Environmentally Sound Management of Water Resources). Mimeo. New York: United Nations Center for Regional Development, February.

Mikesell, Raymond F. 1987. "Resource Rent and the Valuation of Environmental Amenities." *Resources Policy* (June): 98–101.

Ochs, Walter J. 1987. "Salinity Management Issues." In *Sustainability in Agricultural Development* (proceedings of the Seventh Agriculture Sector Symposium), edited by T. J. Davis and I. A. Schmirer. Washington, D.C.: World Bank.

Olivares, Jose. 1987. "Options and Investment Priorities in Irrigation Development: Final Report." Mimeo. Washington, D.C.: World Bank and UNDP.

O'Mara, Gerald T. 1990. *Making Bank Irrigation Investments Sustainable.* Agricultural and Rural Development Department Working Paper. Washington, D.C.: World Bank, May.

Operations Evaluation Department. 1988. *Renewable Resource Management in Agriculture.* Report No. 7345. Washington, D.C.: World Bank, June.

Repetto, Robert. 1986. *Skimming the Water: Rent-Seeking and Performance of Public Irrigation Systems.* Research Report No. 4. New York: World Resources Institute, December.

_____. 1987. "Managing Natural Resources for Sustainability." In *Sustainability Issues in Agricultural Development,* edited by T. J. Davis and I. A. Schirmer. Washington, D.C.: World Bank.

Scudder, Thayer. 1980. "River Basin Development in African Savannahs." In *Human Ecology in Savannah Environments,* edited by D. R. Harris. London: Academic Press.

_____. 1988. *Cooperative Agreement on Settlement and Resource Systems Analysis: The African Experience with River Basin Development.* Worcester, Mass.: Clark Univ.

_____. 1989. "River Basin Projects in Africa." *Environment* 31, no. 2: 4–32.

Searle, Graham. 1987. *Major World Bank Projects: Their Impact on People, Society and the Environment.* Wadebridge, England: Wadebridge Ecological Centre.

Sierra Club. 1986. *Bankrolling Disasters: International Development Banks and the Global Environment.* San Francisco: Sierra Club.

Tillman, Robert E. 1981. *Environmental Guidelines for Irrigation.* Mimeo. Melbrook, N.Y.: New York Botannical Garden Cary Arboretum, June.

United States Agency for International Development. 1982a. *Sudan: The Rahad Irrigation Project.* Project Impact Evaluation Report No. 31. Washington, D.C.: USAID, March.

_____. 1982b. *The On-Farm Water Management Project in Pakistan.* Project Impact Evaluation Report No. 35. Washington, D.C.: USAID, June.

_____. 1988. *Renewable Resource Management in Agriculture.* Operations Evaluation Department, Report No. 7345. Washington, D.C.: World Bank, June.

Ward, Diane Raines. 1990. "In Anatolia, a Massive Dam Project Drowns Traces of an Ancient Past." *Smithsonian* 21, no. 5 (August), 28–40.

World Bank. 1989. *Annual Report 1989.* Washington, D.C.

CHAPTER 5

Forestry Policies and Resettlement Projects

MDBs and the Forests

Natural forests are an important resource for developing countries. They provide a raw material for the domestic wood-products industry, foreign exchange from logs and wood products, a self-contained economy for indigenous people, an ecosystem rich in wildlife, a recreation area for residents and tourists, and protection of the country's water systems. Forests should be used in a manner that will retain all these functions on a sustainable basis. Unfortunately, improper and wasteful use of forest resources and rates of deforestation incompatible with sustainability have occurred in most Third World countries. Much of the damage to tropical forests has been associated with resettlement projects, and MDBs have made loans to both forestry and resettlement projects.

Forests cover about 42 percent of the land in all tropical nations. They help to maintain soil quality, limit erosion, stabilize hillsides, modulate seasonal flooding, and protect waterways and marine resources. However, 10 to 20 million hectares of tropical forests are cleared each year. If present trends continue, an estimated 40 to 60 percent of the remaining tropical forests will be lost by the year 2000. The greatest impetus for forest destruction is the increasing demand for cropland. Rapid population growth is contributing to a rate of deforestation that is threatening the sustainability of agriculture in tropical countries. Decision makers face the problem of feeding an increasing population without irreparably damaging the natural resource base on which agricultural production depends (Ehui & Hertel 1989, 703).

Robert Repetto and Malcolm Gillis (1988, 2) estimate that the world's forested area has declined by about one-fifth from preagricultural time to the present. Prior to World War II, the largest cumulative losses occurred in the temperate forests of the industrialized countries. Tropical rainforests suffered the least attrition because, until recently, they were largely inaccessible and sparsely populated. In recent decades deforestation has shifted from the temperate to the tropic zones. Deforestation in the Third World now occurs at a rate of more than 11 million hectares per year, and that rate is accelerating. For some developing countries, forests will completely disappear within thirty years if these depletion rates continue. For other countries, such as Brazil and Indonesia, depletion is not imminent, but a continuation of current rates will have very serious global implications.

Tropical forests disappear primarily for two reasons: economic and demographic. In developing countries, growing populations invade the forests to survive. They clear forests for croplands and for fuel, while their governments promote timber harvesting as a source of foreign exchange. Under these circumstances, it is perhaps futile to ask developing countries to halt deforestation simply to make a contribution to global sustainability and their own survival. However, much of the current deforestation uses resources wastefully and uneconomically. As Repetto and Gillis state, "Economic and ecological losses go hand in hand" (1988, 15). Both governments and citizens of Third World countries should be educated about destructive policies that reduce the real incomes of both present and future generations.

Cumulative World Bank and IDA credits to forestry, as of 30 June 1989, totaled $1.7 billion, with smaller amounts provided by IADB, ADB, and USAID. USAID funding for a total of 146 forestry projects active in FY 1987 was $587 million (USAID 1988, 3). Forestry sector loans assisted in management of forests to achieve sustained production, develop tree plantations, and develop plant and animal management programs intended to protect and maintain biological diversity, among other things. In many cases, the forestry sector project is one component of a project designed mainly for another purpose, such as irrigation, water supply, tourism, or soil conservation. USAID has supported a number of agroforestry projects in which trees are planted beside crops to enrich the soil and protect it from erosion while also shading the crops. In some instances the forestry component is designed to compensate for deforestation associated with large development projects.

In the past, many MDB-supported projects have had adverse impacts on tropical forests. These projects have involved such things as highways, large dams, resettlements, and livestock. Recently, MDBs have made serious efforts to limit or prevent deforestation associated with the projects they support. Preventing harm to forests should be an important element in the EIA for any project.

The harmful consequences of improper forestry policies may be divided into two categories: (1) the reduced contribution of forest products in the form of raw materials and fuel to the real income of developing countries; and (2) the impact of forest destruction on domestic and world ecology through impairment of agricultural soils, water quality, ecological diversity, and the regional and global atmosphere. (Appendix 5-A details the adverse environmental impacts of forestry projects.) We may distinguish between natural resource policies that deliberately lead to the destruction of forests in favor of alternative uses of the land, and forest management policies that result in low productivity and nonsustainability of the industry. An example of the former is the Brazilian government's policy of allowing migrants to burn tropical rainforests to clear land for crops or cattle grazing; excessive tree cutting and inadequate reforestation exemplify the latter. Since we discuss the destruction of forests from nonforest projects in chapters about these projects, we discuss mostly government forestry policies here.

FOREST MANAGEMENT POLICIES

Natural resource production has long been regarded as an important source of both economic growth and exports. Therefore, development strategy has favored the promotion of timber production for domestic and foreign markets. Because the government owns a large share of forestland, its promotion of the timber industry has usually involved building roads and river transportation facilities and selling timber or contracting with private entities for harvest. Liberal credits and tax advantages to induce private firms to invest in timber and lumber production often supplement these actions (Repetto 1988; Repetto & Gillis 1988). Workers and lumber communities develop a vested interest in expanding logging as a source of jobs and income for all community members. Although the government may favor conservation and reforestation, the typical system is unlikely to result in sustainable yield. Moreover, virtually no government regards the depletion of virgin forests as "capital consumption" that should be offset by reinvestment.

Production and exports of tropical lumber by developing countries are both expected to decline sharply after the year 2005. Alan Grainger estimated that exports of logs and processed wood from the Asia-Pacific developing countries would peak in 1985 and fall to less than 15 percent of their 1985 level by 2020, while exports from Latin America and Africa are projected to peak in 2005, followed by a drastic decline in 2020 (1987a, 6–54). These projections suggest not only a sharp fall in export income from these products, but a radical adjustment in jobs and in the economies of the depleted forestlands. The fact that both production and export of timber by developing countries have risen sharply since 1980 but are projected to decline severalfold from the 1980 level by 2020 suggests that uneconomic as well as environmentally destructive forest management policies are being followed.

Good economic management policies require maximizing the present revenues from harvesting trees. This means that harvests need to take place at the proper time and that timber cannot be wasted. Economic management is not necessarily the same as sustainable forestry management, which requires maintaining revenues over time and avoiding ecological damage. Economic mismanagement occurs when the government sells timber to private contractors under short-term contracts. Private contractors simply maximize revenues by removing the most valuable trees without concern for future harvests. Governments may also be more interested in immediate revenues than in sustained timber production. Such practices have been common in developing countries. Another form of uneconomic management is the use of virgin timber for fuel wood rather than for commercial lumber, which would yield a much higher value. Reforestation programs should satisfy the demand for fuel wood with rapid-growth trees.

Even where forest management has been reasonably economic and maximized the present value of revenues from harvesting, excessive depletion of forest resources may cause environmental damage, destroy other valuable forest products, and fail to maintain the productivity of the forest resources for future generations. Excessive depletion of forest resources has occurred for the following reasons:

1. Both policymakers and the general public have consistently under-valued the continuing flow of benefits from intact natural forests.

2. The net benefits from forest exploitation and conversion have been overestimated, both because the direct and indirect economic benefits have been exaggerated and because many of the costs have been ignored.

3. Development planners have proceeded too boldly to exploit tropical forests for commodity production without adequate knowledge of their biological value or awareness of the adverse economic consequences of removal.

4. Policymakers have attempted — without much success — to draw on tropical forest resources to solve fiscal, economic, social, and political problems elsewhere in society.

5. National governments have undervalued traditional forest uses and the local traditions of protecting these uses through forest management.

MDBs that directly or indirectly assist the forestry industry have often ignored or tolerated the above mistakes. Early MDB-supported projects were designed largely to maximize foreign exchange earnings from timber exports. MDBs tended to encourage export industries, and natural resource products are the traditional exports of developing countries. Only in the past decade, in response to growing concern for the rapid disappearance of the world's tropical forests, have MDBs begun to take account of the potential damage associated with their loans.

SUSTAINABILITY OF TIMBER PRODUCTION FROM TROPICAL MOIST FORESTS

The debate over whether wood production from tropical moist forests can be sustainable hinges in part on the definition of sustainability as applied to a tropical forest. In the broadest sense, sustainability may apply to the ecosystem of the tropical forest, including the environmental services provided by the forest, the biodiversity values, the culture of the forest-dwelling people, and the extractable products (latex, oil, and nuts). For this concept, any intrusion of modern forestry activities is incompatible with sustainability. In the narrower sense — whether wood can be harvested from tropical moist forests on a sustainable basis — the answer is less clear. Some have argued that selective logging (as contrasted with clearcutting) with long rotation periods and extraction limited to a small number of tree species can be done on a sustainable basis. For 150 years the British

Navy selectively harvested teak forests in Burma. They used thirty-year rotations, taking only an annual increment and using nondamaging extraction methods such as elephant and river transport. However, such practices are rare today.

Some believe that tree plantations are the most promising tropical timber source for the future, but most plantations are still too young for their sustainability to be judged. The Jarí Project in Amazonia, initiated by Daniel Ludwig, a US investor, is designed to grow pine for pulpwood. The virgin tropical moist forest was cut and burned to make room for the plantation, but the project was a financial failure. Revenues did not cover even the annual operating costs, much less the huge investment. One reason was the disappointingly low timber yield, attributed to both poor tropical soils and insects that attacked plantation trees. (See Appendix 5-B for a case study of an Indian plantation project supported by MDBs.)

World Bank economist Robert Goodland (Goodland, et al. 1990, 28) concludes that sustainable forestry in tropical moist forests is possible only on a low-yield basis, with long rotations and very selective extraction. Governments would need to closely control harvesting, and expensive methods might be required to limit damage from felling and transporting trees. The Goodland paper points out that, under current management practices, the harvesting of tropical moist forests is unsustainable. Moreover, the environmental services of tropical forests and the biodiversity they harbor are declining at an alarming rate. Logging tropical moist forests benefits only a few people, while deforestation impoverishes millions, impairing local and global environmental services and exacerbating global environmental risks. The paper's authors conclude:

> We present the case for an urgent transition to sustainability by first, improving forest management at least to "best practice"; second, . . . deflection of logging from primary forests to secondary forests; and third, a phased transition to plantations, especially rehabilitating degraded lands. The transition should be rapid in those countries where forests are rapidly disappearing and where logging is one of the main causes (e.g., Ivory Coast, Nigeria, Ghana, Papua New Guinea). The transition is less urgent if there are any countries in which tropical moist forests are extensive and stable.

Some students of tropical forests have concluded that utilizing the bounty of the forests *without commercial logging* would yield a higher income on a sustainable basis. In addition to providing small plots for growing crops, the forest holds extractable products, such as oil and nuts, medicines, and animals for meat, the value of which would be greater than the revenue from logging (Stevens 1990, B5). Promoting development based on natural products would preserve the culture of native forest dwellers and give them a higher standard of living and at the same time preserve the biodiversity and other environmental values of the forest on a sustainable basis.

It is probably unrealistic to advise countries with abundant forests to cease all commercial logging. These countries should strive for optimum forest management on a sustainable basis. A great deal of research and experimentation is being done in this area, and the results are encouraging for many environments. Conceivably, profitable timber harvest could be combined with sustainability of supply, utilization of nonwood forest products, sustained food production and security for indigenous people, and increased fuel-wood output. Achieving these objectives will require applying the results of research and successful experiments that have been done on a variety of forest environments, including upland forests, tropical rainforests, and savannah woodlands. Various types of agroforestry— such as alley cropping (combining agricultural food crops with trees), maintaining tree cover, direct seeding (as opposed to raising stock in tree nurseries), and planting leguminous nitrogen-fixing trees—have been used with considerable success. Using these methodologies and supporting further research and experimentation are positive alternatives to traditional forestry projects supported by MDBs. Examples are given in Appendix 5-C.

THE IMPACT OF LOGGING
ON NONFOREST INDUSTRIES

Although logging will always have some adverse environmental effects, logging operations, conducted under proper management rules and with due regard to their environmental effects, can yield net social benefits. Under certain circumstances, however, the net social return (after labor and other costs) from logging may be negative after taking into account the damage to other activities. Logging in watersheds may cause erosion and stream sedimentation that impairs the value of the river water for fishing, household consumption, irrigation, and recreation. Whether the social cost to other industries is greater than the net return from logging cannot be determined by casual observation. The following case history illustrates the value of social benefit-cost analysis as a guide to policy decision making.

In recent years Bacuit Bay, on the island of Palawan in the Philippines, has become an important fishing area and has also attracted an increasing number of tourists and scuba divers to its clear water and coral. However, in January 1985 logging operations bordering Bacuit Bay commenced, only to be temporarily suspended the following year. The principal impact of logging was erosion, created by both disturbance of the soil and by road building in the area. Erosion resulted in a flow of sediment into the Manlag River, which drains into Bacuit Bay. Since Palawan has high annual rainfall, a large amount of sediment from logging operations now enters the bay, reducing the clarity of the water and destroying the coral. This reduces the water's attractiveness for divers and other tourists and has an adverse effect on the fish catch.

The conflict over the impact of logging on fishing and tourism led to a study by the East-West Center Environment and Policy Institute (Hudgson & Dixon 1988, 57). This study estimated the net present value of the revenues under two development options for the Bacuit Bay drainage basin: Option 1 — all logging banned in the Bacuit Bay drainage basin forest area; or Option 2 — logging continued within the Bacuit Bay drainage basin forest area. The analysis was done on a gross revenue basis for tourism, fisheries, and logging under the two options. Two discount rate assumptions were used to determine present values, namely, 10 percent and 15 percent. The resulting present value calculations are sensitive to the rate of discount used since revenue from logging is realized within a relatively short period of time, while revenues from fisheries and tourism have a lower annual average but continue indefinitely, with revenue from tourism expected to increase significantly over time.

The study found that the present value of gross revenues from tourist income and the fish catch for Option 1 (using a 10 percent discount rate) is almost double the gross revenue under Option 2. Since all logging under Option 2 occurs during the first five years, the effect of using a 15 percent discount rate on the present value of gross revenue generated from logging is relatively slight, but it does reduce the present value of the tourist and fishing revenue. However, even at the higher 15 percent discount rate, the total present value of gross revenue under Option 1 is 1.5 times higher than that under Option 2 (Hudgson & Dixon 1988, 58–59).

These calculations do not take account of intergenerational equity or sustainability of output. Once the trees are harvested, there are no further revenues from logging until new trees become available from reforestation. Furthermore, the next generation will experience a significant loss in tourist and fishery revenues. Therefore, the nonlogging option favors intergenerational equity and sustainability. In addition, a comprehensive analysis needs to take into account ecological consequences from logging, such as the loss of wildlife habitat and biological diversity.

NONFOREST POLICIES ENCOURAGING DEFORESTATION

Much of the deforestation in the Third World results from government policies that encourage alternative uses of forestlands. Our discussion of multipurpose dams and irrigation projects revealed large losses of forests associated with these projects. Deforestation has also occurred with settlement projects and with road construction in undeveloped forest areas. Some of the deforestation associated with development projects is the unintended result of settlers entering development project areas in search of jobs, with surplus labor moving into adjacent forested areas and clearing the land. Here the absence of conservation policies and land-use planning are to blame. Government taxation, land-use, and credit policies leading to deforestation are also sometimes to blame, as efforts of the Brazilian government to encourage the livestock industry in the Amazon illustrate (Binswanger 1989).

THE POLICIES OF SELECTED COUNTRIES

The following paragraphs summarize some of the policies followed by those countries experiencing the greatest depletion of tropical forests. In this discussion we shall be concerned with degradation that involves an uneconomic use of forest resources, not simply with deforestation. Much of this analysis is based on studies prepared by the MDBs and USAID.

Indonesian Policies

The forested areas in Indonesia are among the largest in the world; that country's annual deforestation in the first half of the 1980s is estimated at 600,000 hectares. The principal factors contributing to deforestation there during the post-World War II period have been (1) forest clearance for agriculture; (2) population resettlement programs; and (3) commercial logging. As in nearly all developing countries, Indonesia's government owns the vast bulk of the forests. Therefore, public policies — whether policies intended to affect forest utilization or nonforest policies having an impact on forest use but primarily intended to achieve nonforest objectives —

are in a sense responsible for the misuse of Indonesian forests. The effectiveness of public policies depends heavily on the economic, political, and social environment, and even the most enlightened policies may be thwarted by poverty, public ignorance, and the institutional framework. Thus, in dealing with any environmental problem in developing countries, simply changing government policies is not sufficient, since economic and social conditions and public awareness play an enormous role in the implementation of government policies.

Between the late 1960s and the late 1970s, the Indonesian government's forestry policy emphasized harvesting and exporting tropical hardwood. At the peak of Indonesia's timber boom in 1979, 25 million cubic meters of logs were harvested, ten times the average annual production during 1960–1965. Gross foreign exchange earnings from tropical hardwood rose from $100 million in 1970 to $2.1 billion in 1979, and in that year Indonesia was the world's leading exporter of tropical logs, with 41 percent of the market. Thereafter, log production declined, largely due to a shift in government policy. Not only were many government officials and various groups in Indonesia concerned about the rapid rate of forest depletion, but the government wanted to induce holders of timber concessions to invest in log processing, particularly in plywood mills. To achieve this objective, the government doubled the log export tax from 10 to 20 percent, and in May 1980 it announced a total ban on log exports by 1985, to be phased in gradually over five years. The government also imposed a reforestation deposit of $4 per cubic meter on all logs harvested by timber concessionaires in Kalimantan and Sumatra. As a result of these actions, timber export earnings dropped from more than $2 billion in 1979 to less than $1 billion in 1982, and Indonesia's share of the world market for tropical logs fell by half, to 21 percent.

Most Indonesian timber is produced by private firms that receive concessions from the government. The concessions tend to be quite large, averaging nearly 1,000 square kilometers; in most cases the duration is twenty years. Because of the long growing cycle for commercial tropical hardwoods, a second harvest should be delayed for twenty-five to thirty-five years after the initial cut. Given the short duration of the concessions, concessionaires have no interest in maintaining the long-run productivity of the forest, and have every incentive to reenter the stand to cut immature trees.

Although the Indonesian Forest Ministry has declared a policy of "sustained yield," the process of selective cutting combined with concessions of short duration has limited its implementation. Since the concession-aires have an incentive to cut immature trees, yields cannot be maintained. In addition, the major taxes are the *ad valorem* royalty and the export tax. The *ad valorem* royalty, a flat rate of 6 percent of the posted price for each tree species, is applied to all logs, regardless of merchantable size and condition. This provides a strong incentive for high grading, leaving uncut many commercial trees, that may die before they are harvested (Gillis 1988a, 64, & Appendix 5-A). The concessionaires have no incentive to maximize the yield for the concession area over time. These conditions promote deforestation, in part because the low yields from the areas under concession add pressure to develop unexploited forest areas.

The export ban on logs, designed to promote domestic processing, suc-ceeded in significantly reducing log production during 1981–1983, but expansion of the domestic plywood industry has increased the demand for logs. By 1988, according to estimates, the log cut was projected to be 2.7 times the 1982 level, and by 1998, 3.4 times the 1982 level. The country's reforestation program has not kept up with forest cutting.

Critics of Indonesia's forest policies have pointed out that the tax sys-tem has captured less than half the potential resource rents from the tim-ber concessions (Repetto & Gillis 1988, 84–98). This has implications for sustainable growth since government revenues from taxation should provide financing for investments equivalent to the natural resource deple-tion, either in the form of reforestation or through investment in other industries. In addition, the government's transmigration program has caused serious loss to Indonesia's forest resources (see Appendix 5-D).

The Brazilian Amazon
The Amazon is the world's largest contiguous tropical forest, embracing portions of nine countries. The Brazilian Amazon is estimated to contain up to 78 billion cubic meters of timber, enough to build a house for every person in the world (Browder 1988, 247). Although the Brazilian wood-products industry is large and growing, Amazonian timber accounted for less than 13 percent of the country's industrial output in 1980, and forest products accounted for less than 5 percent of its 1980 foreign exchange earnings (Browder 1988, 248). The increase in the number of government-licensed sawmills—from 194 in 1965 to 1,639 in 1981—indicates the rate of expansion of industrial wood production. Average annual output per mill increased from 2,000 cubic meters of saw wood in 1962 to 4,500 cubic meters in 1984. However, industrial cutting of the Brazilian Amazon's

tropical hardwood is limited to a few of the region's estimated fifteen hundred tree species; most exported tropical hardwoods are mahoganies. Thus, increased production reflects intensive cutting of only a few traditional varieties. This constitutes a barrier to economic forest management and conservation (Browder 1988, 250).

Adequate information on the rate of deforestation in the Brazilian Amazon is lacking. According to a Brazilian government survey based on LANDSAT (multispectral satellite scanning) reconnaissance, 14.8 million hectares of the Amazon forest—less than 3 percent of the region—have been deforested or altered. However, private forestry experts have estimated the actual damage at between 5 and 15 percent. It seems evident that the rate of deforestation is growing exponentially, and if this rate continues, much of the Brazilian Amazon region will be deforested or altered by the year 2000 (Browder 1988, 251).

The most important contributor to deforestation in the Amazon is not logging for industrial use but clearing for cattle ranching—estimated to account for more than 70 percent of the total deforested area. The second most important cause of tropical forest destruction since 1970 has been the settlement of small farmers, whose migration from other areas of Brazil has been encouraged by government colonization and land settlement programs such as the Polonoroeste Regional Development Program in the state of Rondônia and the National Integration Plan. Government power and mining projects, such as the Tucuruí hydroelectric project (which flooded 2,160 square kilometers of forestland) and the Carajás mineral and timber extraction project, have also heavily contributed to deforestation. The Brazilian government's colonization program has been accompanied by road building—the 2,300-mile Trans-Amazon Highway and the Cuiabá–Pôrto Velho Highway—financed in part by the World Bank. These projects have stimulated the migration of many thousands of small farmers and cattle ranchers into the Amazon.

It is perhaps understandable that the Brazilian government would seek to develop the vast Amazon region to provide employment and economic betterment for the country's poor and rapidly growing population. Encouraging migration to undeveloped land has been standard practice in all countries, including the United States and Canada. The harm has come through the economically and ecologically unsound practices that are destroying Brazil's natural resource base. The migration programs have involved huge expenditures of domestic and foreign capital. Financial returns have been low or negative, with little if any economic betterment to the migrants. Political considerations have heavily influenced the Brazilian government's policies. The major government programs that have wasted both natural and financial resources are summarized as follows:

1. Encouragement of forest conversion to pasture for cattle ranching. This low- or negative-yielding use of forestlands preempts utilizing the valuable wood and nonwood products on a sustainable basis.

2. Fiscal and land title policies that encourage the clearing of land.

3. Colonization programs undertaken without consideration of the soil's suitability for growing crops on a sustained basis. The highly subsidized programs have not been cost-effective in terms of the agricultural output generated.

4. Uneconomic cattle ranching and colonization programs that have destroyed or impaired important traditional industries, such as rubber tapping, and have disrupted the economies of the indigenous Indian population.

A number of tax, credit, and land-allocation policies have permitted implementation of these programs. The following paragraphs summarize these policies (Binswanger 1989):

1. Brazil's income tax laws virtually exempt agriculture so that agricultural land becomes a tax shelter. This increases demand for land by large investors and corporations that benefit most from the exemption. Corporate profits from other sources are taxed between 35 and 45 percent. Thus, private and corporate investors in high income brackets have an incentive to undertake projects in agriculture, even though the projects have a lower economic rate of return than nonagricultural projects. The result is an expansion of agriculture into frontier areas and the accumulation of large landholdings.

2. Brazil's rules of land allocation provide that a claimant who lives on the land may obtain a title for up to three times the area cleared of forest. Furthermore, a farm containing forest is taxed at a higher rate than one containing pasture or cropland, thus encouraging the conversion of forestland to pasture and cropland to reduce land tax and thereby providing an incentive for deforestation.

3. Corporate projects approved by the Superintendencia para o Desenvolvimento da Amazonia (SUDAM) or by the Grande Carajás Program receive special preferences for land titles and tax incentives for raising

livestock. The Instituto Brasileiro de Desenvolvimento Florestal provides a tax incentive to corporations that agree to undertake afforestation — but this incentive has apparently promoted little afforestation.

4. Subsidized credit is available for SUDAM-approved ranches.

John O. Browder prepared a benefit-cost analysis of Amazonia cattle ranching on the basis of a sample of twenty-one SUDAM-supported ranches surveyed over a five-year period (1988). Capital costs were approximately $242 per hectare of pasture, and five-year operating costs were $173 per hectare. The average revenue from cattle sales was $22.50 per hectare during a typical period (based on average 1984 prices). Hence, cattle sales did not even cover total operating costs in the absence of any subsidy. However, the SUDAM subsidies were sufficient to provide ample profits on the private financial investment. Thus, Brazilian policies are not only leading to destruction of the economic and ecological values contained in the Amazon forest, but wasting billions of dollars in financial capital that the country needs for economic development and debt service.

A World Bank study suggests the following changes in Brazil's land-allocation and tax rules (Binswanger 1989, 20–22):

1. Lower the ceiling on land that can be allocated to a single owner from three thousand hectares to one hundred or two hundred hectares.

2. Introduce a ceiling on corporate landholdings.

3. Change the definition of land use to include forest management for tax relief and government assistance purposes.

The Philippines
During the post-World War II period, the rate of deforestation in the Philippines has been higher than in any other large Third World country with a substantial tropical forest industry. The abundant virgin forests that once covered the archipelago have disappeared from the islands, and, except for a few park trees, will be virtually gone by the mid-1990s (Boado 1988, Ch. 4). The major causes of deforestation have been (1) the high rate of logging, with little regard for conservation or forest management, and (2) the influx of *kaingineros* (landless natives) who practice slash-and-burn cultivation. The latter have tended to inhabit logged-over areas, which prevents secondary growth. Timber harvest was 5 million cubic meters per year in the late 1950s and almost triple that amount between 1968 and 1974. Most of the timber harvesting has been done under concessions awarded to wealthy domestic individuals and firms and to multinational

corporations, such as Weyerhaeuser, Georgia Pacific, Boise Cascade, and International Paper. Between 1969 and 1971 most logs were exported, with exports averaging 8.6 million cubic meters per year between 1969 and 1971. Since 1974 the average percentage of the total production exported declined to 57 percent, contrasted with 77 percent in 1971. In 1984 only 22 percent of that year's production was exported. The decline in exports was partly in response to government efforts to promote the domestic wood-products industry.

Deforestation in the Philippines accelerated because the government opened public virgin forests to landless families, who converted an enormous area of forestland to agricultural land. Very often the shift in cultivation resulted in a waste of natural forest resources. A substantial number of *kaingineros* also entered the area illegally and occupied both virgin forests and logged-over areas. Most *kaingin* plots quickly lose fertility through erosion and depletion of soil after heavy rains and are abandoned after two or three crop seasons.

The government's practice of delegating forest management through a licensing system has resulted in overcutting and heavy damage to soil and vegetation by careless operations. There has been a shortage of personnel to supervise the licensees and little political support for conserving forest resources. The government's effort to expand agricultural acreage and to provide land for the landless was poorly planned; most of the deforested areas are unsuitable for sustained agricultural production and end up as pasture. Since government revenues from logging have been insufficient to fund forest management and afforestation, the capital represented by the vast forest resources has been largely lost to the Philippine economy.

West Africa

Commercial exploitation of West African forests dates from the last century and earlier, with much of the exports going to Europe. Four West African nations—Gabon, Ghana, Ivory Coast, and Liberia—produce nearly all of Africa's timber exports. In 1962 these countries had a 30 percent share of world tropical timber exports, but by 1984 this share was only 9.3 percent. The volume of productive tropical forests in the region is currently less than 1.5 percent of the world endowment. Since 1975 the rate of decline in productive forests of this area has been the highest in the world—nearly four times the average rate for all tropical countries.

The forest histories and public policies of each of these four countries are quite different. In Liberia, widespread shifting cultivation destroyed the primary forests more than a century ago, so that the country is now experiencing a second major deforestation. Logging, together with shifting cultivation in logged-over areas, is responsible for a rate of annual deforestation of about three times the average of all nations with tropical forest endowments.

Rapid depletion of Ghana's tropical forests has been taking place for many decades; by 1980 the virgin forests had all but vanished. Thus, the decline in deforestation since 1980 has been due mainly to the fact that there is little left to deforest (Gillis 1988b, 302). The principal sources of deforestation in Ghana have been shifting cultivation and the cutting of fuel wood. However, until the 1960s, the second most important cause was the conversion of closed forests to permanent tree crops, particularly cocoa. Logging has not been a significant factor in deforestation in Ghana in recent years.

The highest rate of tropical deforestation—estimated at 7.26 percent annually over the 1981–1985 period—is in Ivory Coast. Logging has been a major cause of deforestation there, with transnational firms carrying on much of it for export. Despite government efforts to create a domestic wood-products industry, in 1984 Ivory Coast still exported three-fourths of its log production. Shifting cultivation in logged-over areas and the creation of cocoa and coffee estates have also played a role in deforestation.

The story is quite different in Gabon, where much of the tropical forest (covering 77 percent of the land area) remains undisturbed and only 28 percent of the total forest area is under concession agreements. Deforestation rates here are less than 0.1 percent, among the lowest in the world. It is worth noting that foreign firms hold most of the forest area under concession agreements. Unlike the governments of many other major tropical timber producers, the government of Gabon has not promoted domestic log processing; as of 1984, 89 percent of licensed production was exported in log form (Gillis 1988b, 310). Gillis suggests that large foreign firms may provide better forest management than domestic firms, particularly where (as in Gabon) concession contracts are long enough to induce firms to consider the longer-term consequences of their operations.

Another reason for the low rate of deforestation in Gabon is that the government has set aside large forested areas as national parks. In addition, much of the forest is not accessible by road. As transportation improves, the forest may be subject to some of the same pressures from settlers or seekers of fuel as those in other countries (Gillis 1988b, 310).

THE TROPICAL FOREST ACTION PLAN (TFAP)

The FAO, World Bank, UNDP, and World Resources Institute (WRI) launched the TFAP in 1985 in response to the rapid pace and scale of tropical forest destruction. The TFAP's goal is to mobilize $8 billion from the international donor community for investment to protect tropical forests, and to benefit rural peoples and national economies (Winterbottom 1990). As of January 1990, seventy-four tropical developing countries and twenty government aid and multilateral lending agencies, including the World Bank, IADB, ADB, and the governments of the United States, Canada, Japan, Germany, France, the United Kingdom, and Italy, were involved. Although the Sierra Club and other conservation groups initially welcomed the TFAP, most environmental organizations have severely criticized its implementation. The major objection is that the forestry projects funded by the MDBs failed to include environmental safeguards and are contributing to actual or potential deforestation instead of promoting conservation and sustained yield management. Many MDB loans have supported the opening of new forest areas to commercial logging for export, financed roads into frontier areas and thereby facilitated migration, and financed wasteful destruction of forests and the invasion of lands inhabited by indigenous forest dwellers.

A World Resources Institute publication (Winterbottom 1990) recommended a restatement of the TFAP's goals and objectives to emphasize sustainable development of forestlands and avoidance of tropical forest destruction. It also proposed a new management structure, to replace the one currently housed in the FAO Forestry Department, and the establishment of a broadly representative international steering committee backed by a multidisciplinary staff independent of the current FAO structure. The steering committee would include experts from governments, aid agencies, NGOs, and the private sector. The publication also proposed policy and operational changes in the donor agencies, and the addition to their staffs of specialists in forestry and natural resource management, land-use planning, and biology. Competent personnel in these fields are believed necessary to properly carry out TFAP objectives in the lending process.

Recent World Bank Loans and Policies
The World Bank has recently made or has under consideration several forestry project loans to African governments, including loans to Ivory Coast, Zimbabwe, Kenya, and Cameroon, all within the framework of

the TFAP. Conservation groups have criticized the loans to Cameroon and Ivory Coast in particular on the following grounds: (1) the projects emphasize export markets and commercial logging; (2) they disregard the impact on indigenous peoples, their cultures, and physical survival; (3) they fail to involve local communities and NGOs; (4) they contribute to accelerated rates of deforestation and neglect sustainability principles; and (5) they open closed forests and thereby facilitate migration to the forest by those seeking land for crops and ranching. Officials of the Bank and conservation organizations, such as the World Wildlife Fund and the Environmental Defense Fund, have held discussions, and both groups have prepared a number of memoranda. World Bank officials have denied that their loans promote overexploitation and deforestation, although increased production from tropical forests for export is clearly one of the purposes of the loans. Bank representatives argue, among other things, that resource destruction is inevitable unless logging is properly managed and that the Bank's purpose is to promote well-managed use of forest resources on a sustainable basis. Bank representatives also point to the Bank's policy of protecting the traditional rights and customs of indigenous populations and avoiding involuntary resettlement. Regardless of the validity of the charges and countercharges, the controversy taking place during 1990 points to the need for a revised TFAP and an agreement that all MDB forestry projects will come under strong international community guidance and monitoring.

In response to criticisms of the Bank's forestry loans by NGOs and by members of its own board, the Bank recently circulated for comments from individuals and groups, both inside and outside the Bank, a forestry policy paper (World Bank 1991). The paper estimates the annual loss of tropical forests at nearly 20 million hectares and describes the implications of this deforestation for the earth's surviving plant and animal species, for global warming, and for sustainability in the Third World. The paper states that the Bank's goal will be to promote conservation and sustainable management of forest resources and to support: (1) expansion of protected areas for the preservation of forest ecosystems; (2) augmentation of forest resources to meet the demand for forest products; (3) the establishment of preconditions for sustainable use of forest resources; and (4) the development of programs for agriculture and rural development in densely populated areas adjacent to forests. The paper also states that the Bank will avoid financing commercial logging in primary tropical moist forests.

Although welcoming some portions of the draft paper, NGOs criticized the Bank's new approach to forestry lending in a letter to Mitchell J. Petit, director of the Agricultural and Rural Department of the World Bank, on the following grounds (EDP 1991):

1. The paper fails to deal adequately with the issue of "sustainable management of timber operations in primary tropical forests." Many forest specialists (including some in the World Bank) question whether sustainable commercial logging of primary tropical moist forests is feasible.

2. The paper does not fully take into account the rights and welfare of forest-dwelling and forest-dependent populations.

3. The paper does not set out a policy concerning the Bank's nonforest lending, such as for energy, transportation, and agriculture, that directly or indirectly affect tropical forests.

4. The paper fails to set forth specific priorities and guidelines for all future Bank lending affecting tropical forests.

It seems likely that the Bank staff will take account of these criticisms in preparing a new forest-policy statement. However, as is the case in other policy areas, only the Bank's loan operations in support of forestry projects and of projects that affect tropical forests will reveal its future policy.

CONCLUDING COMMENTS ON FORESTRY

Perhaps no economic activity in Third World countries has raised the ire of environmentalists as much as wasteful and extensive deforestation. This is true first because of its global consequences, and second because of its implications for the long-term viability of Third World countries. The fundamental forces behind wasteful destruction of Third World forests are the mutually reinforcing conditions of poverty and high population growth and the political imperative to relieve poverty. Major obstacles to dealing with poverty in an economic and ecologically sound manner are ignorance, misguided government policies, and poor administration. These characteristics define underdevelopment generally and explain the lack of progress in many Third World countries. For example, it is easier to allow poor landless peasants to enter and destroy the natural resource base than to adopt a sensible tax and land tenure system. By analogy, it is politically easier to deal with economic problems by printing money and thereby creating triple-digit inflation than by collecting taxes and allocating government revenue in a rational manner.

The answer to deforestation problems does not lie in inducing governments to lock up their forestlands and not utilize them. Both governments and the populace reject this out of hand. The answer lies in helping countries to find and pursue ways of developing their resources in a manner compatible with sustainable growth. One way to utilize tropical forests without destroying them is to cultivate edible fruits, cocoa, oils, rubber, and medicines within the forest reserve. A recent study by biologists shows that revenues generated by long-term harvesting of nontimber products in the Amazon forest can provide substantially greater net revenues than logging or clearing the forest for cattle pasture (Booth 1989, 1). Even animals native to tropical forests can be cultivated to yield economic benefits. For example, Dr. Dagmar Werner, director of the Green Iguana Foundation, found that if iguanas are reared in captivity and released into the wild, they can produce as much high-protein meat per acre as cattle. Iguana meat, which tastes like chicken, is a favorite food of people in the tropical forests and could be sold commercially. Farmers could also raise turtles and crocodiles in ponds and rivers, and deer and paca in open spaces in the forests ("A Plan to Save Iguanas" 1989, B7).

Ecologically and economically sound development will require careful consideration in providing transportation and other infrastructure in or near natural forest frontier areas. Building a highway into a virgin tropical forest requires land-use planning, limiting the number of settlers, and providing adequate job opportunities to avoid wasteful and destructive exploitation of the forest. This involves a host of social and political problems that external assistance agencies must take into account. Many of the technical problems with alternative uses of various types of forestlands require considerable research in Third World countries with the assistance of international agencies. Equally important is the need for social education, which will lead to popular demand for environmentally sound and sustainable practices. This is a major objective of conservation organizations.

Land Resettlement

Land resettlements may take three forms: (1) a government-sponsored movement of population from an area of high density to one of low density, accompanied by land ownership transfers and development projects in the new area; (2) an evacuation of people from areas where reservoirs or other projects incompatible with human residents are to be created; and (3) a spontaneous movement of workers and their families to new areas opened by roads or by some form of development that attracts workers to employment. (Appendices 5-D, 5-E, and 5-F are case studies of voluntary resettlement projects, while Appendix 5-G illustrates an involuntary project.) MDB loans have been associated with all three types of settlement, although in most cases their involvement has been supportive rather than direct. Nevertheless, where voluntary or involuntary resettlement is a consequence of projects supported by MDBs, the Bank has a responsibility for the impacts on both the settlers and the environment of the area to be settled. Thus, in the case of a large dam, the lending institution should carefully review government plans for involuntary evacuation. When a loan is made to finance a highway into a forested area or other area of sparse population, the lending institution should anticipate the spontaneous population movement and make sure that the government takes appropriate action to avoid environmental damage.

GOVERNMENT-SPONSORED SETTLEMENT IN NEW LANDS

Governments have promoted settlement of new lands for centuries, and substantial amounts of sparsely occupied land remain in Third World countries. Major environmental problems arise when underutilized land is in or near humid tropical forest areas. These areas are very vulnerable to permanent environmental damage from the destruction of trees and soil. This destruction may also have an impact on adjacent areas already under cultivation. For example, destruction of tropical forests may reduce rainfall in the region; there is evidence that large forested areas create their own rainfall from clouds formed by evaporation. New settlers in large, isolated forested areas may destroy the traditional economies of indigenous peoples, such as the Amerindians in Amazonia. Other areas of settlement are marginal lands that are vulnerable to environmental damage from cultivation and overgrazing. In the absence of a well-planned settlement program, spontaneous settlers are likely to occupy frontier lands and employ wasteful, resource-destroying practices.

MDBs have supported government-sponsored settlement programs in a number of Third World countries, and environmentalists have severely criticized many of these programs because of their adverse impacts on the land, the forests, or the indigenous peoples. The largest resettlement program in the world is the Indonesian Transmigration Program (ITMP), which is moving millions of people from the densely populated inner islands of Java and Bali to tropical forests in the sparsely settled outer islands—Kalimantan (Borneo), Sulawesi, and Irian Jaya (Western New Guinea). This program has been receiving World Bank assistance since 1976. Another World Bank–supported resettlement program is the Polonoroeste road project in Brazil, in which hundreds of thousands of migrants have been introduced to the state of Rondônia in northwestern Brazil, a region of rapidly depleting tropical forests. This project and the ITMP are two of the four projects that the Sierra Club publication *Bankrolling Disasters* (1986) criticized severely. Brief case studies of these projects are in Appendices 5-D and 5-E.

A government's motivation for sponsoring resettlement is often political. In many cases frontier areas extend across country borders that are uncontrolled and vaguely defined. One country may, therefore, be anxious to have its own citizens settle these areas to prevent takeover by an adjoining country—even when the land in the frontier area is poor and intensifying farming in already-occupied areas would be more economical. Opening frontier areas is often easier politically than land reform, which may threaten large, powerful landowners. In Latin American countries, large landowners often prefer to graze cattle on cultivatable land. Hence, so-called population pressure for settling frontier land is sometimes more a consequence of land misallocation than of a shortage of good-quality agricultural land (Ledec & Goodland 1989, 451–452).

In many cases it would be more economical and better for the environment to leave frontier areas in a natural state, particularly when they are moist tropical forest areas with poor soil. However, strong political pressures are likely to make developing these areas in some way inevitable. Ledec and Goodland (1989, 452) suggest several ways to modify the environmental impacts of developing frontier areas. One is to reduce the size of land parcels allocated to settlers; in the past, allocations have ranged from 100 to several hundred hectares. Titles to large areas encourage clear-cutting of the forest for grazing. Smaller plots of land might be cultivated intensively by terracing and by planting orchards and home gardens. Forest clearing should be minimized, and large forested areas should remain intact to preserve biological and ecological diversity and habitat for rare and endangered species. There should also be sustained yield management of forestlands; selected logging with care taken to minimize damage to the remaining forest; and adequate natural forest left for regeneration or replanting.

The requirements for a large land settlement program that will be economically advantageous and environmentally sound encompass the entire gamut of conditions for achieving sustainable development in Third World countries. They include the establishment of a new regional economy integrated with the rest of the national economy through trade and capital movements; transitional assistance to settlers (likely to cost $10,000 to $15,000 per family); a system of land distribution and tenure; infrastructure such as roads and water supply; local markets and access to external markets; agricultural extension for adapting methods suitable to the soil and the climate; plans for controlling spontaneous settlers outside the program; and community services, such as education, health clinics, and local government. Without comprehensive planning and competent implementation, a settlement program will face conflict, economic failure, and destruction of the environment. Planning and managing a large settlement program require the services of a number of national government departments, most of which will not have the experience and trained staff to guide such a program. For this reason it is usually best to conduct the program by phases and to learn through experience. An important sourcebook for experience with land settlement is the Indonesian Transmigration Program described in Appendix 5-D.

INVOLUNTARY RESETTLEMENT

Although involuntary resettlement may be a consequence of projects requiring substantial amounts of land, such as mines and plantations, extensive forced migrations are caused primarily by large dams associated with irrigation and hydroelectric projects. MDBs have been supporting large dam projects for decades, but only recently has there been a strong effort to see that people who are forced to migrate receive adequate compensation for the land and buildings submerged by the reservoirs created by dams, and that they get options for resettlement that enable them to live as well as they did before. Involuntary resettlement differs from voluntary in that the latter tends to involve working-age people who have an incentive to take advantage of new opportunities, while the former involves a total population, including retired persons who find moving from their ancestral homes a traumatic experience. Involuntary resettlement should be treated as an environmental problem and not simply one of shifting locations and employment of labor. Therefore, resettlement must be an integral part of the project plan and feasibility study and a part of the full social costs of the project.

Few if any large MDB-financed projects that have required mass migration have been accompanied by adequate resettlement plans and provisions for implementation. In some cases, little more was done than to provide compensation for the land and buildings rendered worthless by the project. This is surely not enough, even if compensation were equal to a fair value of the property lost. Opportunities for housing, employment, and infrastructure equal to or better than what was lost must be provided. Individuals to be resettled should also be given options such as individual land ownership, employment for wages in agriculture, or urban settlement and employment. Migrants should not be herded into temporary refugee camps pending employment or land occupation opportunities following forced displacement. The World Bank, ADB, and other MDBs have adopted guidelines for dealing with forced resettlement, but thus far the countries receiving the loans have not satisfactorily implemented them. (See the checklist at the end of this section.)

Involuntary resettlement may involve large numbers of people. For example, the Narmada Sardar Sarovar dam in Gujarat, India, will displace about 70,000 people (see Appendix 4-A), and the Cirata hydroenergy dam in Indonesia will displace about 55,000. An estimated forty projects approved for financing by the World Bank in agriculture and hydropower during 1979–1985 required relocating at least 600,000 people in twenty-seven countries. Compulsory resettlement has, according to a recent World Bank study, been "the most unsatisfactory component in the construction of dams throughout the world because it often impoverishes the people who are displaced, destroys productive assets, and disrupts the social fabric. Environmental degradation, including lost forests and grazing lands, is compounded if the site to which people are relocated cannot sustain both the population already living there and the new arrivals" (Cernea 1988b, 44).

A World Bank Technical Paper (Cernea 1988a, 9) states that past Bank-assisted projects were flawed by a lack of social planning and failed to restore the social and economic well-being of the displaced populations. We noted some of these criticisms in our discussion of large multipurpose dams in Chapter 4. Settlement plans have often been prepared after a project has been designed and a loan negotiated. This frequently causes delays in resettling the displaced population, and the government may lack the funds to carry out an adequate program. The resettlement plan should be an integral part of the project, with the full costs included in the financial feasibility analysis. When the full costs of an adequate resettlement program are included in the budget for a dam, the financial returns on the investment may not be sufficient to meet the Bank's 12 percent return-on-investment standard.

Michael Cernea identifies four key areas that need strengthening in the Bank's operations relating to projects involving resettlement (1988a, 11–12):

1. The borrower should improve the quality of planning for settlements with respect to economic, technical, sociological, and organizational content. Without comprehensive and detailed feasibility studies and a relocation design, little meaningful can be done at the time of the loan appraisal, and little can subsequently guide implementation on the effective path;

2. Increased attention should be given to economically and socially viable options for developing the productive capacity of displaced populations through project-financed strategies;

3. The Bank should exercise more regular, professional, and firm implementation of resettlement operations to help improve the performance of the agencies executing resettlement and insure that implementation adheres to loan agreements;

4. The special conditions and needs of tribal populations affected by displacement should be recognized. The implications of resettlement for the host population and the physical environment in the receiving area and the suitability of organizational arrangements for executing the relocation should be considered.

All of the above are supposed to constitute current World Bank policies. Cernea states that the first full-scale Bank project embodying this approach was the November 1987 Brazil-Itaparica resettlement and irrigation project. This project provides for the resettlement of forty-five thousand people being displaced by the flooding of the Itaparica reservoir on the border between Bahia and Pernambuco states. The Bank provided a loan of $132 million to support irrigation, housing, rural infrastructure, water supply, education, sanitation, health services, rural electrification, and urban resettlement for four affected townships. Another project that illustrates the new approach to relocation, according to Cernea, is the Narmada Sagar dam in Madhya Pradesh, India (1988b, 46). However, as we have noted, NGO criticisms of the Narmada Sagar project maintain that no matter what the Bank's provisions in the loan agreement, the Indian government is unlikely to provide satisfactory arrangements for those ousted.

SUGGESTED GUIDELINES FOR
INVOLUNTARY RESETTLEMENT PROGRAMS

Following is a checklist for appraising involuntary settlement programs associated with development projects (Cernea 1988a):

1. The project should include provision for fair and prompt compensation for property lost by those being settled. In the case of productive property, such as farms (including land, buildings, and equipment), forests, factories, power, and transportation systems, valuation should be based on the net present value of the income from the assets (that is, the discounted value of the net revenue from the assets). In the case of homes and personal property, replacement value might be used. All property valuations should provide for appeal by the owner to courts or arbitrators independent of the government.

2. Displaced individuals should be compensated for hardship, suffering, and psychological loss associated with resettlement. Although it is not possible to estimate monetary values, compensation in lump sum at least equal to the average annual income of those affected should be paid.

3. Transfer and disruption costs should be paid. Costs of migration, including removal of furniture, livestock, and so on, should be covered, plus the loss of income during the transition period until wage earners, farmers, shopkeepers, and so on are able to restore their incomes to at least the pre-relocation level.

4. Those being resettled should have an option as to where they will be relocated and as to their occupation. Preferences should be determined in advance of resettlement since this information needs to be used in designing the new settlements associated with a project. Work force, land ownership, irrigated areas, and creation of new towns will need to be considered. Where resettlement is to take place in areas with existing farming and urban life, information on the preferences of those being settled will be required for housing, infrastructure, land distribution, and urban business. For both new occupational areas and the expansion of existing areas, comprehensive redevelopment packages should be planned and implemented. These would include necessary improvements to the land (clearing, irrigation, leveling, and so on), housing, and provision for acquisition of inputs (seed, draft animals, tools, extension services, credit, and so on).

5. Adequate financing for all elements in the resettlement program should be provided before the project is initiated. All costs of resettlement should be included in the financial analysis contained in the feasibility study

of the project. Failure to provide for such financing in advance could lead to delays in compensation and in carrying out programs for rehabilitating those being resettled.

6. The value of community or public property lost by the project should be included as part of the project cost. Although compensation is ordinarily not made to resettled individuals for roads, schools, power facilities, public buildings, and so on, it will be necessary to provide an equivalent amount of investment in the resettlement area for these items, and this should be considered as replacement cost.

We understand that the Bank has adopted the above guidelines on resettlement for application to new loans. However, we are not aware of a case where they have been fully applied.

APPENDIX 5-A

Environmental Effects Commonly Associated with Forestry Projects

I. COMMERCIAL LOGGING
  A. *Project Siting*
    1. *Watershed Areas:* Is the proposed project area located in a critical watershed serving reservoirs, large population centers or industries? If so, what will be the likely effects on hydrology, siltation and water quality and how will they affect the various users?
    2. *Relation to Other Dedicated Land Uses:* Will the proposed project area infringe on other dedicated land uses such as parks and wildlife preservation zones, mining operations, etc.? Has the project duly considered including forestry as an integral part of development taking place in other sectors? How?
    3. *Traditional Forest Uses:* Have the different kinds and levels of traditional forest uses by local populations and the expected impacts of the project on these uses been adequately considered in the selection of project location?
    4. *Resettlement:* Will the proposed project entail resettlement of indigenous populations? If so, how will this be handled?
    5. *Relation to Regional/National Forestry Plans:* Has project siting taken into account the regional and/or national master plans for forest utilization/conservation? Does it contravene plans for conservation of minimum forest area/types that should be maintained for long-term regional welfare?

Source: Asian Development Bank, *Environmental Guidelines for Selected Agricultural and Natural Resources Development Projects* (Manila, Philippines: Environment Unit, ADB, 1987), Annex I–D.

6. *Critical Environmental Areas:* Is the project to be located in environmentally critical areas such as land with steep slopes and fragile soils? If so, what will be the effects on soil stability?

7. *Precious Ecology:* Does the selected site contain rare or useful species of wildlife, fish and plants? Will the project lead to serious depletion or loss of these resources as concerns their regional or national status? Are project "with project" (compared to "without project") depletion/loss of these and other precious ecological resources sufficiently high to warrant selection of an alternative site in order to preserve these resources? If not, will appropriate mitigation measures be provided?

B. *Planning and Design*

1. *Benefit/Cost Analysis:* Has a benefit/cost analysis been done that clearly addresses costs due to erosion/sedimentation; increased peak flows and flood flows; loss of recreational or tourism opportunities?

2. *Operation and Maintenance:* Does the fiscal setup ensure availability of necessary O&M funds, especially for erosion and sedimentation control and forest rehabilitation? Has training for the local labor force and/or foresters been included as an integral part of O&M plans as concerns technologies both at the logging site and at the processing site?

3. *Data Base for Decision Making:* Have the impacts of previous regional logging operations due to proper/improper planning and design been accounted for and modifications been made to the project based on this information? Will sufficient information be collected on timber stand density, species composition, terrain, logging conditions and the environmental effects of logging operations to provide the basis for long-term logging and road development plans? Has provision been made to store the above information in a data base of indicators that the Bank, government and others can use for planning and decision making for this and future projects? Is the data base defined/costed and how will the financing for monitoring be ensured?

4. *Road Network Design:* Has planning and design of roads adequately considered soil conditions, grades and curves, water drainage, proximity to waterways, and adequate drainage?

Will adequate monitoring be provided to ensure minimal erosion from road construction/operation? Has the road system been planned in advance, taking into account which areas are to be served first so that sites and directions of the proposed roads can be determined, thus reducing the area of soil disturbance and lowering construction/maintenance costs?

5. *Design of Logging Activities:* Does planning and design allow for minimal damage to the residual stand?

6. *Critical Environmental Areas:* Has due consideration been given to critical areas (i.e., those with extreme soil erodibility, rainfall erosivity and slope gradient/length) for erosion control measures?

7. *Precious Ecology:* Has planning and design taken into account the mitigation/protection/enhancement measures for rare or useful wildlife, fish and plant species, such as provision of buffer strips, of standing food trees, of newly created protected areas around the logging site? Selective logging can enhance habitat for several species of large mammals, including elephant, deer and others.

C. *Project Operations*

1. *Road Construction:*

   a) Will road construction be limited to the dry season and, if not, will there be added environmental dangers from wet season construction?

   b) Are drains spaced properly and has wise use been made of bridges, culverts and paved fords?

   c) Have up-and-down spur roads been avoided to the maximum extent possible?

   d) Have areas adjacent to logging roads been provided with vegetative cover, and have cut-and-fill areas been reseeded to minimize erosion?

2. *Felling:*

   a) Is the felling system employed optimal for minimizing loss of seed trees and residual stands?

   b) If wide-scale clear cutting (as opposed to selective cutting and shelterwood systems), can the following effects be expected: significantly accelerated erosion; increases in height of flood peaks; serious loss of wildlife habitat;

promotion of landslides? Clear cutting should be avoided, particularly in unstable areas. If clear cutting is being done, have adequate measures been taken to minimize the above impacts?

c) Is the felling system being monitored to check compliance with the concession contract as regards size and types of trees allowed to be logged and permissible area of operation?

d) Have precautions been taken not to disturb vegetation near waterways and to avoid blocking streams with logging debris?

3. *Log Conveyance and Allocation:*

a) Will the log conveyance system cause undue erosion and compaction? Erosion can be minimized by employing a suitable log conveyance system. Cable yarding in hilly regions will cause minimal damage compared to ground skidding, for example.

b) Is rational and profitable use being made of residues and will the logs be allocated to their most appropriate use so optimal benefits are gained from the logged area?

4. *Riparian Zones:*

a) Have the following values of riparian zones been recognized and measures taken to conserve these values: enhance the quality of habitat for aquatic resources; provide a "filtering" buffer zone, inhibit rises in stream temperature and provide bank/floodplain stability; provide important habitats for wildlife; and provide a focal point for many recreational activities? Defining riparian zones can be difficult and professional judgment must usually be employed, but immediate control over these areas will significantly reduce nonpoint pollution and provide sufficient time to later resolve competing use demands.

b) Have the following general rules for logging vis-a-vis riparian zones been adhered to: keep wheeled and tracked vehicles out of these zones; keep roads and trails as far away as possible; carry out all silvicultural and logging operations by hand or from the outside edge of the riparian zone; avoid burning that would leave the riparian zone exposed during periods of high-intensity rainfall; keep tracers for firebreaks as far uphill as possible?

5. *Socioeconomics:*
   a) Does the project include close involvement of local leaders to avoid future problems from disgruntled villagers due to loss of traditional forest uses?
   b) Is manual labor involved to the maximum extent possible and are local people given special employment considerations to provide maximum benefits to locals?
   c) Will the project provide compensation to local people for loss of forest use, such as provision of planting stock and adequate training to enable production of multipurpose species?

D. *Post Project*
   1. *Rehabilitation and Conservation:* Does the project provide for silvicultural treatment of logged-over stands and protection against encroachment and fire after the operation has ceased? If so, has adequate monitoring of such activities been provided? For selectively-logged areas, has consideration been given to incorporating the logged-over area as a multiple-use zone within a larger conservation unit including nature reserves?
   2. *Road Shutdown:* Has provision been made to "put to bed" temporary roads such as spur roads after completion of the operation?

II. REFORESTATION

A. *Project Siting*
   1. *History of Forest Abuse:* Does the proposed project site have a history of forest degradation and, if so, has an O&M plan been prepared which can realistically ensure protection of the new forest? If not, can the new forest be expected to survive or should alternative sites be considered?
   2. *Relation to Other Dedicated Land Uses:* Will the project interfere with other established land uses? Has the project duly considered potentials for reclaiming for forest those areas dedicated to other uses that have not been sustainable or profitable, such as unsustainable agriculture? Does it fit in with regional/national plans for forest utilization/conservation?

Are there opportunities for enhancing existing conservation areas?

3. *Resettlement:* Will the proposed project entail resettlement of local populations and, if so, how will this be handled?

4. *Siting in Degraded Forest:* If reforestation is to be done by clearing existing degraded forest, has due consideration been given to alternate siting in adjacent areas, thereby taking pressure off the existing forest and promoting its conservation?

B. *Planning and Design*

1. *Benefit/Cost Analysis:* Has a benefit/cost analysis been done that clearly delineates specific benefits to result from the project, for example erosion control; savings in downstream flooding hazard; decreases in sedimentation and turbidity in streams/estuaries/nearshore marine waters, including protection of fisheries and beaches; enhanced opportunities for recreation and tourism; increased fuel sources; enhanced employment opportunities?

2. *Selection of Tree Species:* Is the selection of tree species optimal to meet project objectives, and are sufficient seed supplies available? The use of monoculture planting in extensive areas should be avoided; mixed crops provide greater safety against damage from pests and diseases. Have the physical and environmental site characteristics been adequately studied to help determine which tree species will best adapt to the site? In some cases attempting to reforest extremely steep and shallow soils may result in less environmental gains than leaving the area in grass/shrub cover.

3. *Precious Ecology:* Have opportunities been recognized for enhancing environmental parameters such as wildlife habitat, species diversity and soil/water conservation through selection of multipurpose species and appropriate harvesting schedules? Has the project been planned so that it complements existing forests in providing critical ecological benefits?

4. *Allocation of Benefits to Locals:* Has it been identified who is to benefit from the project and how? Does the overall plan include provisions for local job employment and other incentives for local people (such as intercropping) so they will protect the new forest? Has appropriate training of locals and/or foresters been included in the O&M plans? If the new

forest has potential to attract recreation/tourism activities, will villagers be supported to meet this demand through training as guides, establishment of handicraft centers and the like? Have local needs and traditional forest uses been considered in project planning/design, especially the use of forests as sources of protein, edible and medicinal plants, and recreation?

5. *Operation and Maintenance:* Does the fiscal setup ensure regular availability of necessary O&M funds, especially for weeding, fire protection, watering and protection from encroachment?

6. *Data Base for Decision Making:* Does the cited literature contain all salient, pertinent references? Have the impacts (both beneficial and adverse) of previous reforestation efforts due to proper/improper planning and design been accounted for and modifications made to the proposed project based on this information? Does the project include a data base system (see I.B.3.)? Has provision been made for systematic data gathering on such parameters as before and after impacts on groundwater supplies, stream flow, wildlife use, soil building and socioeconomics to provide a basis for future decision making?

7. *Project Financing and Reservoirs:* If a major reservoir project is to be developed in the region, has the potential been explored to finance the reforestation project as a component of the reservoir project?

8. *Appropriate Technology:* Is the technology to be used appropriate for developing countries in tropical monsoon areas or is it copied from possibly inappropriate western models?

9. *Relation to Other Dedicated Land Uses:* Have efforts been made to incorporate the project into existing land use practices and has significant modification of land use been minimized to the extent possible? If not, what are the expected social effects?

10. *Road Network Design:* Has sufficient consideration been given to the impacts of road siting to minimize erosion (see I.C.1.)?

11. *Use of Grasslands:* Has the use of grass cover instead of trees been considered in areas where sufficient downstream water supply is a critical concern?

C. *Project Operations*

1. *Commercial Logging:* If the plantation is to be harvested, guidelines as presented in Section I, Commercial Logging, will need to be followed to minimize increased erosion and sedimentation rates. Will there be proper replanting to maintain a sustainable yield?

2. *Reduced Water Supplies:* Have project impacts on downstream water supplies been identified? Large reforestation projects may reduce supplies of water to downstream users and reservoirs as the trees mature due to increased evapotranspiration rates. Mitigation measures such as shorter harvesting rotations or retaining grassland areas may be needed where sufficient water supply is a critical consideration.

3. *Chemicals and Fertilizers:* Will suitable controls be used when applying chemicals and pesticides to protect young plants; burning slash; and applying fertilizers near waterways to avoid or minimize detrimental effects on fish and other aquatic life?

4. *First Year Operations:* Has due consideration been given to erosion mitigation measures during the plantation's initial year, such as leaving unplowed strips or bunding? A combination of vegetative (reforestation) and mechanical (engineering) control of erosion and overland flow can provide the most effective technique for erosion and water problems in depleted watersheds.

5. *Soil Conservation Benefits:* Soil conservation is perhaps the most profound environmental result of reforestation. Have the following beneficial impacts been identified/maximized: erosion protection; decreased sedimentation that can affect reservoir life, water quality and aquatic/marine/estuarine systems; promotion of improved soil capacity, soil surface moisture and soil nutrients?

6. *Socioeconomic Benefits:* Have the following beneficial impacts been identified/maximized: provision of alternative employment opportunities; increased fuelwood supplies; increased fisheries (particularly in the case of mangrove plantations); and enhancement of recreational and tourism potentials?

7. *Water Resources Benefits:* Have the project's beneficial effects on reducing overland flows and flood peaks been identified/

maximized? Reforestation's beneficial/adverse effects on groundwater and periodicity of stream flow remains a topic of much debate, thus the need for a usable data base system as part of Bank-supported projects as mentioned in II.B.6.

III. COMMUNITY FORESTRY

Considerations for siting, planning/design and project operations as presented in the section on reforestation are, by and large, applicable to community forestry projects. Presented below are additional considerations as well as some parameters already discussed in previous sections but deserving emphasis when dealing with community forestry projects. It is assumed that the main goals of most community forestry projects are timber and fuel production and that most projects involve afforestation, not the use of existing forests.

A. *Project Siting*

1. *Siting in Well Defined Areas:* Will the project be located in a well defined area such as a watershed or a group of villages?

2. *Historical Patterns of Illegal Land Use:* Has special emphasis been placed on understanding historical patterns of illegal land use? Can these problems realistically be overcome? For instance, lands that have a history of prior illegal use for grazing may need to be ruled out because of the hazard that these users would try to maintain their "rights" by eliminating the new forest through fire and grazing. Conversely, well sited and designed projects can serve as an intervention to illegal use of nearby forests by offering similar products without the risk of arrest.

3. *Critical Environmental Area:* What effects will project harvesting rates have on soil and water? Highly unstable lands may need to be avoided because a "working" community forest can require frequent soil-disturbing harvests. Such areas may also significantly affect expected benefit/cost ratios due to sub-optimal tree production.

4. *Essential Surveys:* Have the following been surveyed prior to site selection: climate, soil and land use characteristics; past/present types and uses of existing forests including gathering of non-wood products; wood use and needs; market prospects; community social systems; land tenure and other legalities; population characteristics?

5. *Relation to Other Dedicated Land Uses:* See II.A.2.
6. *Resettlement:* See II.A.3.
7. *Siting in Degraded Forest:* See II.A.4.

B. *Planning and Design*

1. *Relation to Overall Development:* Has the project been included as an integral part of intersectoral development?
2. *Operation and Maintenance:* Effective handling of threats to the new forest is a requisite for success. Does the O&M plan provide realistic and adequately funded mechanisms to prevent encroachment and fire? Does it provide for sufficient weeding, watering and other essential maintenance?
3. *Selection of Tree Species:* Will single-species or multispecies planting be done? Single-species forestry over large areas should be avoided as it can be particularly susceptible to pests and diseases with potential for loss of the entire crop. For similar reasons, indigenous species should be used whenever possible. Multispecies planting can provide greater yields due to more efficient site utilization. In selection of tree species, has consideration been given to the potentials to improve local environmental / ecological conditions such as limited wildlife habitat, soil conservation, water conservation and nutrient enhancement (particularly through use of nitrogen-fixers)?
4. *Precious Ecology:* See II.B.3.
5. *Data Base for Decision Making:* See II.B.6.
6. *Appropriate Technology:* See II.B.8.
7. *Relation to Other Dedicated Land Uses:* See II.B.9.

C. *Project Operations:* See II.C.

D. *Socioeconomic Factors*

Past projects have shown socioeconomic considerations to be of paramount importance in achieving full benefits from community forestry. Major considerations are presented below.

1. *Including Villagers in Decision Making:* Have community members, particularly village leaders, been included in decision making at all project stages?
2. *Accelerated Benefit Flow:* The time scale of most community forestry projects is bound to conflict with priorities of poor rural people. Because many villagers are hard-pressed to meet everyday needs, have mechanisms been included to accelerate the flow of tangible benefits to the villagers? This

could include growing multiple-use species; intercropping; and introducing additional sources of income as an adjunct to the forestry project.

3. *Operation and Maintenance:* Have provisions been made for training villagers and forestry officers responsible for community forestry projects? Forestry officers should be trained in social as well as technical skills. Will new local institutions such as forest cooperatives be required in order to ensure project success?

4. *Key Social Factors:* Have the following key social factors been considered: cultural knowledge and values regarding forestry; availability of resources—land, capital, materials and labor; social constraints on resource management; social competition and conflict over resource use?

5. *Economic Inequities:* Will the project increase the gap between rich and poor members of the community? Would changes in project design or operation help bridge existing economic differences among villagers?

6. *Nutrition and Health:* What likely effects will the change in land use patterns caused by the project have on nutrition and health? For example, malnutrition has been found in many Malaysian rubber plantations because, although income has soared, local markets have few fruits and vegetables as all efforts stress industrial crops.

7. *Reliance on Markets:* Will the project result in heavy reliance on markets? Community forestry projects that emphasize cash crops may suffer from significant price instability and thus increase local dependency on national/international markets.

APPENDIX 5-B

Case Study: The Bastar Wood Pulp and Paper Project

This short case study concerns a project designed to produce pulp and paper in the Bastar district in the southeast corner of the state of Madhya Pradesh, central India. Tropical moist forests cover about 57 percent of Bastar and include about one hundred species, mostly teak, sal, and laurel, with the balance (about 20 percent) consisting of bamboo. The Bastar Project emerged from a number of government studies and reports prepared during India's third Five-Year Plan from 1961 to 1966. The World Bank's appraisal mission in Bastar in 1964 recommended a 100,000-ton-per-year pulp mill for Bastar (Anderson and Huber 1988, 55).

Between 1964 and 1968 the UNDP and the government of India conducted a number of joint studies on the Bastar Project. In 1970 the Marketing and Research Corporation of India identified Bastar as a prime source of exports. Other studies, including those reviewed by the World Bank, concluded that reforestation of the area with fast-growing industrial species would yield 10,000 to 15,000 hectares per year of marketable wood, about five times the growth rate of the Bastar forest's natural regeneration (IDA 1975, 10). In 1975 IDA made a $4 million loan to the Indian government for technical assistance to determine the feasibility of a commercial pulp and paper mill in Bastar. The government of India provided $3.5 million and the Madhya Pradesh Forestry Development Corporation provided $660,000, for a total of some $8.2 million for the project. The project included pilot plantations, a feasibility study, pilot logging, research trials, and a study of tribal peoples in the area (IDA 1975, 8). The Indian government and the World Bank anticipated a larger loan if the project appeared to be profitable, and it was also expected that a substantial amount of private funding would be invested. The native forest would be clearcut and replanted with Carolina pine to provide wood for the pulp and paper mill.

Fortunately, this project was terminated in 1981. Had it gone forward with the aid of a large loan from the World Bank and with a further commitment by the Indian government and private investors, it would have resulted in substantial financial loss and embarrassment to the World Bank. There were many problems. One had to do with the feasibility of growing pine on poor tropical soil following the harvest of native timber. Concerned people were undoubtedly aware of the failure of the Jarí Project in Amazonia. Only one crop rotation had been completed at Jarí, but studies showed that all of the potassium in the soil would be depleted following the second harvest. Yields were poor and cultivation costs higher than for other species. The species used at Jarí were the Caribbean pine and the gmelina, a tree native to India. Other questions related to the choice of the best place to establish a pulp and paper industry within India. Finally, tribal people opposed the project. A 1981 census showed the population of Bastar to be 1.8 million, of which 98 percent were rural and 70 percent tribal. Tribal people carry on subsistence agriculture and earn income from forest products such as oil, seeds, honey, and bamboo. Despite efforts of the project promoters to interest the tribal leaders by providing employment and a form of tribal ownership, the majority of the people opposed the project and had no interest in working there. They were concerned that it would destroy their life-style and their culture, and they did not want to become wage earners.

In light of subsequent tribal demonstrations against the project in 1981 and 1982, there is some doubt whether the Bank would have made a loan to support construction of the mill even if the project had been viable on economic grounds (Anderson & Huber 1988, 95). The Bank may have turned down a large loan for the Bastar Project because it conflicted with the Bank's policy on tribal peoples in forested areas, announced in 1978 (Goodland, 1982).

APPENDIX 5 - C

Examples of Beneficial MDB- and USAID-Financed Forestry Projects

Rwanda: Second Integrated Forestry, 25 June 1987
The World Bank supported a project whose main objectives were to protect and conserve Rwanda's remaining natural forest and increase fuelwood supplies by promoting agroforestry. This included creating plantations; strengthening the government's afforestation program; developing an integrated approach to livestock and forest management; and applying research on plantation development and agroforestry (Ledec and Goodland 1988, 110).

*Philippines: Watershed Management
and Erosion Control, 4 August 1980*
This World Bank–supported project includes reforestation of 321 square kilometers of denuded land with fast-growing species, the construction and maintenance of forest roads, and pilot programs for ecologically sound agroforestry (Ledec and Goodland 1988, 118).

Niger: Forestry and Land-use Planning, 1980
In 1980 USAID began a seven-year $4.2 million forestry land-use planning project in Niger that included reforestation and watershed management. Test sites were chosen to demonstrate sound rehabilitation and resource management practices. The main goals at the test sites were to stop degradation and to restore the forest to a balanced, stable condition so that vegetative resources used each year did not exceed annual growth. Project planners also sought to provide a continued source of forest products for local users and markets. Small, valuable crops and pasture plants were grown on the newly improved land before the trees grew large enough to protect the land. The project demonstrated that natural forest management can be both economically and ecologically viable. Local users were provided with forest products, the land was restored, and wildlife returned to the protected areas (USAID 1988, Ch. 2).

Senegal: Reforestation and Soil Conservation, 1986
The Senegal Reforestation and Soil Conservation project supported by
USAID aims to motivate large-scale participation in tree planting. Reforestation is an important step in stemming the trend toward desertification. Forest service personnel and extension agents will be trained in
forestry techniques and in ways to motivate farmers, community leaders,
and the private sector to plant trees (USAID 1988, Ch. 2).

Peru: Central Selva Resource Management Project, 1982
USAID made a $22 million loan to support the Central Selva Resource
Management Project, which was designed to test whether natural forest
can be managed on a self-sustaining basis to provide long-term economic
and social benefits to local people. The project involved an improved
agricultural system and natural forest management for the existing ten
thousand to fifteen thousand inhabitants, including Amuesha Indians. The
Amuesha will continue to hunt, fish, and forage in the protected forest
and will carry out sustained-yield forestry activities based on natural
regeneration. Timber is harvested in thirty-year rotations from long narrow strips bordered by intact forests, the source of seed for natural regeneration. Every sixth strip is left as a permanent reserve of primary forest
(USAID 1988, Ch. 2).

Indonesia: Timber Estates Development Project, 1989
The ADB made a loan of $50 million for planting cutover forestland with
the objective of producing timber and developing a financially viable system for operating the timber estates. Since the timber estates are located
on watersheds, this project will have a significant positive environmental
effect.

APPENDIX 5-D

Case Study: The Indonesian Transmigration Program[1]

The Indonesian Transmigration Program (ITMP) began under Dutch colonial administration but was not launched on a large scale until 1969. During the past twenty years, more than 2 million people have resettled on the outer islands of Sumatra, Kalimantan, Sulawesi, and Irian Jaya, transmigrating from the densely populated rural areas of Java, Madura, Bali, and Lombok. Sponsored migrants received a small house on village land and 0.75 to 1.0 hectare of cleared land outside the settled areas, with additional land (averaging 1.0 to 2.0 hectares) reserved for future development. The facilities, including schools and clinics, are located in the village center. The program provides subsistence supplies for one year while the transmigrants till the land and establish crops. Most settlers also receive planting materials and small livestock such as chickens and goats (World Bank 1988, 18–21).

The World Bank has been involved in the Indonesian program since 1976. As of 1986 it had committed about $560 million for transmigration and swamp relocation, and another $680 million for smallholder cattle development and tree-crop and cash-crop development. In the latter projects, existing public estates receive technical and financial support to establish their own holdings and to develop adjacent areas for smallholders, who may be indigenous people, existing transmigrants, or new settlers.

On the basis of a 1986 review of the ITMP, the Bank imposed a temporary moratorium on its loans because of the enormous environmental and social problems the program was creating. But some environmental groups report that the Bank has now released payments under an earlier loan and is planning new loans to finance additional migration (NRDC/WALHI 1990, 7–9). As of December 1990, the Bank was considering a loan of $140 million to finance the second stage of the ITMP.

TABLE 5-D-1

SPONSORED TRANSMIGRATION PROGRAM, 1950–1984

YEAR	Five-Year Plan	Total Families Moved	Local Families[a]	Resettled Families[b]	Total Families Settled	Total People
1950–54		21,037	0	1,280	22,317	87,000
1955–59		32,114	0	128	32,242	134,000
1960–64		26,456	0	0	26,456	111,000
1965–69		21,633	0	0	21,633	92,000
1969–74	(Repelita I)	39,436	0	75	39,511	240,000
1974–79	(Repelita II)	44,484	7,600	0	52,084	465,000
SUBTOTAL		185,160	7,600	1,483	194,243	1,129,000
1979–84	(Repelita III)	301,279	22,284	42,414	365,977[c]	1,492,000
TOTAL		486,439	29,884	43,897	560,220	2,621,000

[a] Indigenous families settled in transmigration sites.
[b] Resettlement of sponsored or spontaneous migrants within the province.
[c] In addition, 170,000 identified families moved spontaneously.
Source: World Bank, *Indonesia: The Transmigration Program in Perspective* (Washington, D.C.: Country Study, 1988), xxi.

Table 5-D-1 shows the numbers of families moved and settled during successive five-year programs from 1950 to 1984. In addition to families moved from the more densely populated inner islands, some local families on the outer islands elected to join the transmigration settlements, and a number of spontaneous migrant families also resettled in the program. During 1979–1984, 301,000 families moved and 366,000 settled; this was seven or eight times the corresponding number for any five-year period during the 1970s. About 80 percent of all families settled in rainfed sites, based mainly on food-crop production; 18 percent in swamp reclamation areas where rice was the main crop; and 2 percent on tree-crop farms. The total cost of the 1979–1984 program was $2.3 billion, of which the World Bank contributed $107 million (5 percent). The ADB, USAID, and bilateral agencies of other countries have also provided funds for resettlement, and the UNDP, FAO, and other agencies have provided technical assistance.

The first Bank-assisted transmigration project was approved in 1976 and completed in 1983. It consisted of two pilot schemes in southern

Sumatra: the rehabilitation of an existing settlement of 12,000 families and the settlement of 4,500 families. It also provided funds for research on cropping systems and for long-term evaluation. In one area new settlers received 5.0 hectares, which included 1.25 hectare of land cleared for food crops and 1.0 hectare of rubber trees. To promote food crops, farmers received cattle for draft power and free agricultural inputs (seed, fertilizer, pesticide) for three years. Settlers also received a house and one year of subsistence supplies (World Bank 1988, 159–161).

A second bank-assisted project approved in 1979 was intended to settle 30,000 families. In addition to financing the settlement of migrants, the Bank provided technical assistance in site selection and evaluation, staff training and agricultural research, and technical assistance to the Ministry of Population and Environment to monitor and improve the environmental soundness of the project. The Bank also made loans to support swamp reclamation projects, smallholder cattle development projects, and public estate smallholder projects concerned with tree-crop and cash-crop development.

IMPACT ON INDIGENOUS PEOPLE

Of about 6 million people in the outer islands in 1986, about 1.5 million are regarded as isolated or native tribal people, most of whom live in areas with marginal soils and practice some form of shifting cultivation. However, some, such as the tribal people in the highlands of Irian Jaya, have complex sedentary farming operations and high population densities. Protecting the rights and the way of life of these people has given rise to the greatest problems. A few of the local people have been integrated into the ITMP and received land. Some sell their lots to spontaneous migrants and return to their villages. Local people outside the ITMP have benefited from some parallel development of infrastructure, wells, and supplementary agricultural inputs, but this parallel development has received insufficient attention. Moreover, these people have not received compensation for land relinquished for transmigration purposes except for tree crops in areas to be used for settlements. This has given rise to disputes over land and compensation (World Bank 1988, Ch. 5).

The greatest criticism of the ITMP and of the World Bank's involvement has concerned treatment of the native tribal peoples in the outlying islands, particularly in Irian Jaya. Conservation groups and Indonesian NGOs have charged that the government displaced indigenous people in

Irian Jaya to make way for transmigrants and that some of these people have fled to neighboring Papua New Guinea (Sierra Club 1987, 7). The Indonesian government has also been charged with planning to force Irian Jaya's entire indigenous population of 800,000 tribal people to move from their traditional homesteads and villages into resettlement sites by 1998 (Hancock 1989, 134).

The World Bank's review of the treatment of resettled indigenous peoples hints that their rights may not have been satisfactorily protected in the past, but that the Bank's policies will be carried out in future migration programs. These policies include recognizing and protecting areas containing resources required to sustain traditional means of livelihood; providing appropriate social services, including protection against new diseases; maintaining cultural integrity; and allowing local people to participate in decisions affecting them (World Bank 1988, 95).

IMPACT ON THE ENVIRONMENT

Environmental concern has focused on the areas where settlement has reduced forest cover and put pressure on conservation areas and wildlife habitat. Between 30 and 50 percent of land cleared for the ITMP in the 1979–1984 program was forested. Less than 1 percent of the forested area was used for sponsored settlements on the outer islands and less than 5 percent of total conversion forest was cleared. (Conversion forest is land that can be converted to agricultural or other uses; areas classified as protected forest and nature reserves cannot be used for sponsored transmigration.) Land cleared by the spontaneous migrants nearly doubles these figures. To reduce the adverse environmental impact, preference was given to the development of grasslands and secondary forest areas. During the five-year period 1979–1984, official settlement diminished forest cover by about 500,000 hectares. Assuming spontaneous migrants occupy an equal area, up to 1 million hectares of forested land have been brought into agricultural production in the five-year period ending 1984. This is an important loss of tropical rainforest. The World Bank review of the ITMP states that, ideally, no forest areas would be used for development, but that past experience indicates that preventing the conversion of some forestland to agricultural purposes will be virtually impossible. For this reason the ITMP should concentrate on protecting land unsuited to agriculture (World Bank 1988, 99–100). The World Bank review states that indigenous cultivators rather than transmigrants are responsible for most degraded land.

Critics of the Indonesian program have linked destruction of the tropical rainforest to shifting cultivation practices of spontaneous migrants. The World Bank report (1988) states that this is incorrect. Javanese migrants, whether settled under the sponsored program or moved spontaneously, rarely engage in shifting cultivation on a large scale. They do encroach on forest areas, occupying 1 or 2 hectares per family, but they do not ordinarily use land for production on a temporary basis. Indigenous peoples practice shifting cultivation on low-fertility soils (World Bank 1988, 100); hence, the report states, most degraded land is the result of practices of indigenous cultivators. Critics have also charged that programs for settling transmigrants in swamps irreversibly damage wetlands and the streams and rivers associated with them. The World Bank report minimizes this point but does state that further study is needed. The report also points out that the problem of encroachment on natural wildlife habitats needs to be dealt with.

While stating that environmental destruction and mistreatment of indigenous peoples have not been as great as the critics charge, the report nevertheless admits that the Indonesian government needs to improve its program. For example, the report admits the need for a culturally appropriate "parallel development" that will provide comparable services to local people who do not want to live in transmigration settlements. It also suggests that there is a need for better presettlement planning, adequate supervision of land-clearing contracts to assure adherence to land-clearing instructions, prevention of wasted forest resources and close coordination of land clearing and commercial logging, and the development of an extension service to create public awareness and appreciation of conservation values (World Bank 1988, 95–100).

Since 1980 Indonesia's government has moved about 500,000 families, and it may move 500,000 more by the end of the century. Spontaneous migrants may put an equal land area into production. If 50 percent of this land were forested, this could mean a loss of 2 million hectares of forested land by the year 2000, which is equivalent to about 10 percent of the conversion forest and 2 percent of the forested area of the outer islands. Loss of the forest area must be weighed against economic and employment benefits. According to the report, the World Bank apparently sees no way to avoid this loss, but it does see that strong programs are needed to protect areas unsuited for cultivation, to protect wildlife and biotic reserves, and to bring spontaneous migrants into the planning process to reduce their encroachment on protected land. The plan also requires a program to upgrade indigenous agriculture and reduce shifting cultivation. In addition, the land purchase and registration programs should be improved to enable migrants to acquire land already under cultivation without robbing the indigenous population.

The report should have attempted a benefit-cost analysis, however crude and inexact, to determine whether better cultivation methods and changes in land tenure in the inner islands might provide greater benefits than resettling families on the marginal lands and tropical forest areas of the outer islands. Such an analysis might have reached the conclusion that all or a major portion of the transmigration program is not cost-effective. But without this study, we cannot provide an economic justification for this conclusion.

EXTERNAL CRITICISMS

Investigators both in and outside Indonesia have made a number of highly critical reviews of the ITMP; some have been assembled by Graham Searle (1987, Ch. 6). The *Ecologist* published a special report in 1986 containing six papers dealing with settlement performance, the environment, and the ITMP's impact on indigenous peoples, and including an open letter to outgoing World Bank President Clausen and incoming President Conable urging that the Bank halt funding for the program until it is implemented in line with the Bank's Guidelines for the Development of Tropical Forest Regions and Areas Inhabited by Tribal Peoples, so that it will not lead to the destruction of the environment (Searle 1987, 149).

One of the articles in the *Ecologist*'s special report points out that many resettlement sites are located on land unsuitable for agriculture. In addition, the resettlement sites lack roads and other infrastructure, and settler families can survive only if they take on outside work. Another article refers to 11,000 transmigrants who face starvation because their land is incapable of producing most types of food. Still another states that migrants in the Merauke region in Irian Jaya have abandoned the site to find work elsewhere. Searle states that "at the end of third five-year plan, it is clear that the present settlement policy has been a disastrous failure. By promoting the same pattern of subsistence agriculture found in Java, the government is simply recreating the same set of problems from which the transmigrants were supposed to have been rescued. The result is what many observers have described as the transfer of Javanese poverty" (1987, 152).

Marcus Colchester (1986) states in his *Ecologist* report that the project has violated the Bank's guidelines for such projects and accuses the Bank of ignoring these violations. Also, he writes, the loan agreements did not include provisions to guarantee the rights of tribal peoples in their traditional lands. Colchester is especially critical of the treatment of the indigenous population in Irian Jaya, where the people have been forcibly resettled and subjected to various kinds of pressures from the migrants, causing thousands to flee across the border to Papua New Guinea.

In another *Ecologist* paper, Charles Secrett of the Friends of the Earth draws on reviews by Indonesian government officials who condemn forest destruction associated with the ITMP. Secrett points out that the ITMP has made serious mistakes in selecting settlement sites, from the standpoints of both utilizing viable farming areas and protecting the environment. Too much resettlement has been in tropical forest areas with poor soils for farming. Site selection has not been based on a knowledge of climate and soils, a criticism made by Indonesian government specialists. Secrett denies the argument in the World Bank study that the indigenous population has caused most of the forest destruction with its traditional agricultural practices and that newcomers using slash-and-burn methods are not responsible. Finally, Secrett questions the entire policy of moving populations from a high-density area to frontier areas in the outer islands. He cites the Indonesian Department of Agriculture's view that more intensive farming on Java could double food production: "By controlling siltation, including watershed management and increasing irrigation, the Department believes that agricultural productivity may be able to keep pace easily with population growth" (*Ecologist* 1986, 60).

As far as we are aware, the World Bank has never provided a detailed response to the outside criticisms of the ITMP. In its Project Performance Audit Report on Transmigration I (1976–1983), the Bank concluded that the project was successful in terms of food production and family income. However, it did point out that yields were lower than projected and that reserve land had not been put into food-crop production on the scale expected (1988, 161–162). The Bank's review of the Transmigration II project pointed to the need for better site selection and evaluation, institution and staff training, and better resource utilization through development of grasslands and timber in forested areas. The recommendations in the 1988 World Bank report suggest that they were prompted by the finding of shortcomings in the existing program.

A June 1990 report by the NRDC and the Indonesian Environmental Forum (an Indonesian NGO) is highly critical of ITMP settlements in the wetlands. Draining wetlands and cutting down coastal mangrove have damaged both the economy and the ecology, the report states, and neither the crops (mainly rice) nor the settlers are suited to soil, water, and other conditions in the settlement area. The report also advises that the World Bank should not fund any new transmigration until (1) existing social and economic problems of the migrants are alleviated and an adequate level of living achieved; and (2) a comprehensive EIA of each wetland transmigration site is completed. The report says that the Bank's own resettlement guidelines are being violated and concludes as follows (NRDC/WAHLI 1990, 13).

> Two decades of experience [have] demonstrated that the drainage of Indonesia's wetlands for settlement carried out under the transmigration program has been largely unsuccessful. Agricultural and economic returns have fallen far short of expectations. Acidic soils, inadequate drainage and irrigation systems, and outbreaks of agricultural pests and diseases have undercut agricultural productivity. Desperate transmigrants have been forced to seek a living in Indonesia's forests, resulting in wholesale clearance of vast areas. Ecosystems, such as mangroves, which are important for economic as well as biological reasons, have been severely damaged.
>
> Given this history, the continued involvement of the World Bank in transmigration is of great concern. The World Bank should move forward with support of the transmigration program only if specific procedures are adopted that will prevent the mistakes of the past from repeating themselves.

APPENDIX 5-E

Case Study: Polonoroeste Resettlement Project in Rondônia, Brazil

Beginning in 1982 the Brazilian government launched a gigantic colonization and resettlement scheme—the Polonoroeste Project in the state of Rondônia in the Amazon area of northwestern Brazil. The opening of Highway 364 facilitated the project, which was designed to attract and support hundreds of thousands of migrants to unpopulated regions of Rondônia. Also provided were agricultural credits and urban centers. The World Bank made loans totaling nearly half a billion dollars to the project between 1982 and 1985. The loans supported rural activities of the project and the paving of Highway 364.

The program was seriously flawed. Most of the poor, landless peasants lured to the area with the promise of free land and higher income found only hardship and disappointment. Most of the small farms have failed, leaving the migrants destitute. The devastation created by the project has made it one of the world's biggest environmental disasters. Large areas of the tropical Amazon forest have been destroyed and the land rendered useless. Cattle ranchers, land speculators, loggers, and miners invaded the protected areas of Amerindian reservations, causing widespread violence. Following the clearing of the land, on which little timber was recovered, the soil was found unsuitable for agriculture, at least with the methods used. Because the Brazilian government did not honor its agreements with the World Bank for dealing with the migrants and protecting the Amerindians, in 1985 the Bank imposed a temporary halt on disbursements of the undistributed balance of the loans. Disbursements were renewed after the Brazilian government gave additional guarantees that the rights of the tribal peoples in Rondônia would be respected, but complaints about the management of the project persisted.

By 1987 the World Bank admitted the shortcomings of the project. In a public speech, Bank President Barber B. Conable characterized Polonoroeste as a "sobering example of an environmentally sound effort which went wrong. The Bank misread the human, institutional and physical realities of the jungle and the frontier . . . protective measures to shelter fragile land and tribal people were included; they were not, however, carefully timed or adequately monitored" (Conable 1987).

PROPOSED NEW LOAN FOR THE POLONOROESTE PROJECT

In late 1989 the World Bank was considering a $167 million loan to Brazil for the Rondônia Natural Resources Management Project, which is designed to address some of the environmental and other impacts of the original program. However, major conservation organizations in the United States and other industrial countries, in consultation with Brazilian NGOs, found serious flaws in the design and implementation of the project. A letter to E. Patrick Coady, US executive director of the World Bank, was accompanied by a detailed memorandum of the principal findings and recommendations. In summary, the memorandum noted the following (Environmental Defense Fund 1990):

1. The Bank should insist that the Brazilian authorities legally regularize the Amerindian Reserves and protected natural areas whose legal regularization and protection were a condition of the 1981–1983 Polonoroeste loans.

2. NGOs, local unions, and indigenous and community groups in Rondônia maintain that, contrary to Bank claims, there has been little or no substantive consultation with and participation of groups representing the target populations and beneficiaries of the project: Amerindians, rubber tappers, and agricultural colonists. The Bank should ensure that indigenous, environmental, and landless peasant NGOs have full access to information on the project and participate in its planning. More than most Bank loans, this project is being justified on its prospective environmental and social benefits to these peoples; their active involvement and participation as the constituency for the project is indispensable for its success.

3. Disbursements should be linked to a schedule set forth in the loan agreement to physically establish the integrity of the seventeen Amerindian reserves and four protected natural areas that should have been established under the first Polonoroeste project. Of particular concern is the situation in the Guapore Biological Reserve, whose establishment was a specific condition of the 1981 Polonoroeste loan. The reserve has not been

protected from illegal logging, land speculation, illegal colonization, and mining encroachments.

4. Loan disbursements should be linked to the establishment of the physical integrity of the other agro-ecological zones. Areas designed as agro-ecological zones are suffering from ongoing road construction, government-endorsed land claims, illegal logging, land speculation, and forest clearing.

5. Although the project acknowledges that access to credit for smallholder agriculturalists is absolutely essential for its success, its agricultural credit component is gravely flawed and inadequate. It should be reformulated to include analysis of smallholder cultivation of perennial crops.

6. Greater attention needs to be given to the environmental and health problems caused by gold mining along the Madeira River and its tributaries. Studies indicate that the entire food chain of the Madeira is showing signs of toxic contamination from mercury used in gold-mining activities. There is little analysis of its impacts on the project area, nor are effective measures proposed to address its impacts.

At the time of writing, negotiations on the proposed loan were still in progress, and the project had not yet been presented to the Bank's Board for approval.

APPENDIX 5-F

Case Study: The San Julian
Settlement Project in Eastern Bolivia

The San Julian Settlement Project in eastern Bolivia was established in 1972 with USAID support. Although it suffers from some of the general problems associated with new settlements in tropical forests, careful planning and innovative design features made it a success in contrast to most settlement efforts (Painter & Partridge 1989, Ch. 11). As of 1984, there were 5,436 people in 1,661 households in the project, and an additional 2,518 households settled spontaneously around the area officially belonging to the San Julian Project. About 90 percent of the settlers have migrated to the region from the highland and Andean valley regions of Bolivia.

Painter and Partridge cite three features of the project as contributing to its relative success: (1) a three-month orientation program for new settlers that included training, provision of communal shelter, and food aid until housing could be constructed and the first crop harvested; (2) a nucleus settlement in which forty households were established around a central clearing with 50-hectare farm parcels radiating outward, a design that facilitated the distribution of essential services, encouraged the establishment of business, and facilitated community organization; and (3) a settler selection program that discouraged potentially unsuccessful migrants. San Julian communities manage their own affairs, including building schools, maintaining roads, and assuring land rights. USAID provided funds for construction of two hundred deep wells, but as of 1985 only forty had been dug, and most communities have inadequate and/or poor-quality water supply.

The most important agricultural crops are rice and corn, produced for both subsistence and cash. However, both products are subject to chronic overproduction, and revenues have not been sufficient for investment in processing and other off-farm economic activity. Poor transportation has hampered diversification into vegetables and fruits, and the growth of urban business has been slow because low farm revenues do not generate sufficient demand. As Painter and Partridge state, "San Julian teaches us that no matter how well conceived a settlement project may be, it will not experience sustained economic growth unless all design and implementation occur at the level of the project itself. Success in this area demands creation of economic linkages that will join the settler population to regional and national markets" (1989, 369–370).

APPENDIX 5-G

Case Study: Involuntary Resettlement Associated with the Manantali Dam in Mali[2]

Some ten thousand persons in western Mali were resettled largely in a sparsely populated area downstream from the Manantali Dam after its creation flooded their villages and productive lands in 1986. The dam, which was completed in 1988, is intended to irrigate 375,000 hectares; give landlocked Mali direct access to the sea; and generate 800 gigawatt-hours of electricity annually, provided priority is given to energy production. A consortium of Arab states, the Islamic Development Bank, the AfDB, Canada, the UNDP, and European country donors loaned $500 million for the infrastructure. USAID agreed to fund the Manantali resettlement for approximately $18 million, with an additional $5 million from the World Food Program and $3 million from the government of Mali. The empoundment reservoir at Manantali extends some 70 kilometers south of the dam and has forced the evacuation of twenty-one villages, of which the largest had 900 inhabitants and the average had about 350. Most villagers opposed being agglomerated with people from other villages in new settlements, and no preexisting village opted to join with any other.

Households received new farmland based on the number of persons aged eight years and older. Prominent villagers with large families or the ability to hire labor staked out claims for unallocated bushlands in close proximity to the villages, leaving others either with inadequate lands for the full cropping-fallow cycle of about fourteen years or with the need to travel considerable distance from village to field. USAID explicitly decided not to introduce any development programs during resettlement. The underlying objectives were simply to replace existing resources and to duplicate the previous standard of living. The project addressed the availability of land and water for the reestablishment of the production system but gave much less attention to other resources. Project villages meet domestic water needs directly from the river or from shallow-dug wells. Newly located villages downstream from the dam are at some distance from the river. These villages are provided with boreholes and hand pumps; they will also receive cisterns for water storage during times when pumps are inoperable. Because no development project promotes new crops or agricultural technology, there are no formal constraints on farming. Farmers retain a good deal of autonomy; women retain their rights to plots for groundnuts, maize, and vegetables.

Before displacement, villagers supplemented agriculture and herding with hunting and foraging in the bush. Wild game and indigenous plants are apparently less available in the resettlement area, which may reduce village income. Also, increased population density in the resettlement area and the pressure to clear land for farms and pastures will reduce wild game and plants. The dam construction has, however, led to increased fish in the reservoir. But the resettlement area will remain isolated, and high transportation costs will make marketing fresh fish and vegetables outside the area infeasible.

Infrastructure adequate for economic development is largely absent in the resettlement area. The benefits of the dam — irrigation, navigation, and hydropower — will accrue to areas far downstream, such as Dakar, which are entirely outside the region. No residents are likely to receive electricity. In the absence of possible important mineral discoveries, the prospects for development in the Manantali region are remote. According to an Institute for Developmental Anthropology report the "losses endured by the people involuntarily resettled from the reservoir area of the Manantali dam appear unlikely, at present, ever to be made up" (Koenig & Horowitz 1988, 11).

The project was concerned with the living conditions in the new villages, but little attention has been paid to conditions for economic production. In general, settlers were given little opportunity to participate in the decision making and in the project's implementation. People might have been given more responsibility for building their own houses. The report also faults the project for "the lack of a coherent development program that would compensate for lost resources and improve the income and conditions of life of the largest number of settlers, both host and relocatees" (Koenig & Horowitz 1988, 14).

NOTES

1. This discussion is based largely on a World Bank staff study of the Indonesian Transmigration Program (1988).
2. This brief study is based on a report prepared at the Institute for Developmental Anthropology in Binghampton, New York, funded by USAID (1988).

REFERENCES

Anderson, Robert S., and Walter Huber. 1988. *The Hour of the Fox: Tropical Forests, The World Bank, and Indigenous People.* Seattle, Wash.: Univ. of Washington Press.

Asian Development Bank. 1987. *Environmental Guidelines for Selected Agricultural and Natural Resources Development Projects.* Manila, Philippines: Environment Unit, ADB.

Binswanger, Hans P. 1989. *Brazilian Policies that Encourage Deforestation in the Amazon.* Environment Department Working Paper No. 16. Washington, D.C.: World Bank, April.

Boado, E. F. 1988. "Incentive Policies and Forest Use in the Philippines." In *Public Policies,* by Robert Repetto and Malcolm Gillis. Cambridge, UK: Cambridge University Press.

Booth, William. 1989. "Saving Rainforests by Using Them." *The Washington Post,* 29 June.

Browder, John O. 1988. "Public Policy and Deforestation in the Brazilian Amazon." In *Public Policies,* by Robert Repetto and Malcolm Gillis. Cambridge, UK: Cambridge University Press.

Cernea, Michael. 1988a. "Involuntary Resettlement in Development Projects: Policy Guidelines in World Bank-Financed Projects." Technical Paper No. 80. Washington, D.C.: World Bank, July.

———. 1988b. "Environmental Resettlement and Development." *Finance and Development* (September).

Colchester, Marcus. 1986. "Banking on Disaster." *Ecologist* 16, no. 213: 61–70.

Conable, Barber. 1987. Speech before the World Resources Institute. Washington, D.C.: World Bank, 5 May.

Ecologist. 1986. "Indonesia's Transmigration Programme: A Special Report in Collaboration with Survival International and TAPOL," 16, no. 2/3: 58–117.

Ehui, Simeon K., and Thomas W. Hertel. 1989. "Deforestation and Agricultural Productivity in the Cote d'Ivoire." *American Journal of Agricultural Economics* (August): 703–711.

Environmental Defense Fund. 1990. Letter to E. Patrick Coady, and memorandum entitled "Issues that Need to Be Addressed and Resolved in the Rondônia Natural Resources Management Project," mimeo. Washington, D.C.: EDF, 9 January.

_____. 1991. Letter to Mitchell J. Petit, World Bank. Signed by representatives from the Environmental Defense Fund, the Sierra Club, NRDC, and other conservation organizations. Washington, D.C.: EDF, 2 April.

Financial Times. 1986. London, 31 October.

Gillis, Malcolm. 1988a. "Indonesia: Public Policies, Resource Management, and the Tropical Forest." In *Deforestation and Government Policy,* by Malcolm Gillis and Robert Repetto. Cambridge, UK: Cambridge Univ. Press.

_____. 1988b. "West Africa: Resource Management Policies and the Tropical Forests." In *Deforestation and Government Policy,* by Malcolm Gillis and Robert Repetto. Cambridge, UK: Cambridge Univ. Press.

Gillis, Malcolm, and Robert Repetto. 1988. *Deforestation and Government Policy.* Cambridge, UK: Cambridge Univ. Press.

Goodland, Robert. 1982. *Tribal Peoples and Economic Development: Human Ecological Considerations.* Washington, D.C.: World Bank.

Goodland, Robert, E.O.A. Asibey, J. C. Post, and M. D. Dyson. 1990. *Tropical Moist Forest Management: The Urgent Transition to Sustainability.* Washington, D.C.: World Bank, April.

Grainger, Alan. 1987a. "The State of the World's Tropical Forests." *The Ecologist* 10:1.

_____. 1987b. "Tropical Moist Forests." Unpublished paper. Washington, D.C.: Resources for the Future, May.

Hancock, Graham. 1989. *Lords of Poverty.* New York: Atlantic Monthly Press.

Hudgson, Gregor, and John A. Dixon. 1988. *Logging Versus Fisheries and Tourism in Palawan: An Environmental and Economic Analysis.* Honolulu: Univ. of Hawaii, East-West Center.

International Development Association. 1975. *Report and Recommendations of the President to the Executive Directors on the Proposed Credit to India for the Madhya Pradesh Technical Assistance Forestry Project.* Washington, D.C.: World Bank, 16 December.

Koenig, Delores, and Michael M. Horowitz. 1988. *Lessons of Manantali: A Preliminary Assessment of Involuntary Relocation in Mali.* Binghampton, N.Y.: Institute for Development Anthropology, October.

Ledec, George, and Robert Goodland. 1988. *Wildlands: Their Protection and Management in Economic Development.* Washington, D.C.: World Bank.

_____. 1989. "Epilogue: An Environmental Perspective on Tropical Land Settlement." In *Human Ecology of Tropical Land in Latin America,* edited by D. A. Schumann and W. L. Partridge. Boulder, Colo.: Westview Press.

Natural Resources Defense Council and the Indonesian Environmental Forum. 1990. *Bogged Down: the Tragic Legacy of the World Bank and Wetlands Transmigration in Indonesia.* Washington, D.C.: NRDC, June.

Painter, M., and W. L. Partridge. 1989. "Lowland Settlement in San Julian, Bolivia—Project Success and Regional Underdevelopment." In *Human Ecology of Tropical Land Settlement,* edited by D. A. Schumann and W. L. Partridge. Boulder, Colo.: Westview Press.

"A Plan to Save Iguanas and the Rainforest in the Bargain." 1989. *New York Times,* 22 August.

Reed, David, and Jennifer Smith. 1990. *A Review of World Bank Forestry Sector Projects in the Republic of Cote d'Ivoire.* Washington, D.C.: World Wildlife Fund, 20 March.

Repetto, Robert. 1985. *Paying the Price: Pesticide Subsidies in Developing Countries.* Washington, D.C.: World Resources Institute, December.

———. 1988. *The Forests for the Trees?: Government Policies and the Misuse of Forest Resources.* Washington, D.C.: World Resources Institute, May.

Repetto, Robert, and Malcolm Gillis, eds. 1988. *Public Policies and the Misuse of Forest Resources.* Cambridge, UK: Cambridge Univ. Press.

Searle, Graham. 1987. *Major World Bank Projects.* Wadebridge, England: Wadebridge Ecological Centre.

Secrett, Charles. 1986. "The Environmental Impact of Transmigration." *Ecologist* 16, no. 2/3: 77–88.

Sierra Club. 1986. *Bankrolling Disasters.* San Francisco: Sierra Club.

Spears, John. 1988. *Containing Tropical Deforestation: A Review of Priority Areas for Technological and Policy Research.* Environment Department Working Paper No. 10. Washington, D.C.: World Bank, October.

Stevens, William. 1990. "Research in 'Virgin' Amazon Uncovers Complex Farming." *New York Times,* 3 April.

United States Agency for International Development. 1988. *Progress in Conserving Tropical Forests and Biological Diversity in Developing Countries.* Washington, D.C.: USAID, June.

Weatherly, W. Paul. 1983. "Insect Pest Outbreaks." In *Natural Systems for Development: What Planners Need to Know,* edited by Richard A. Carpenter. New York: Macmillan.

Winterbottom, R. 1990. *Taking Stock: The TFAP After Five Years.* Washington, D.C.: World Resources Institute, June.

———. 1991. "The World Bank Forest Policy Paper." Mimeo. Washington, D.C.: World Bank, 1 April.

World Bank. 1988. *Indonesia: The Transmigration Program in Perspective.* World Bank Country Study. Washington, D.C.: World Bank.

CHAPTER 6

Other Agricultural and Land-use Environmental Problems

In this chapter we deal with livestock projects, fertilizer and pesticides, wildlife protection, agricultural credit, and other issues having to do with sustainable agriculture. We also raise the question of how effective MDBs have been in promoting sustainable agriculture, and consider what approaches they should take in the future. Much of the discussion in this chapter is based on studies prepared by World Bank staff.

Livestock Projects

Grazing antedates crop production as an agricultural pursuit. Livestock production is important for domestic food and exports, and, in the form of animal traction and manure fertilizer, as a complement to crop production. Nevertheless, the design and implementation of livestock projects can contribute to a number of adverse environmental impacts. These include soil degradation, deforestation, runoff detrimental to aquatic ecosystems and fisheries, health hazards from pesticides, increases in disease habitats, destruction of wildlife, and diversion of land and water needed for food production for optimal regional balance. Since livestock projects often promote large-scale commercial ranching at the expense of subsistence farming and tribal grazing, they may have adverse social, cultural, and distributional impacts on existing indigenous populations. MDBs need to take account of these impacts, including how government agencies and private livestock owners will manage them, when evaluating livestock projects.

Livestock projects benefiting from external support include the purchase of new breeding stock, pasture improvement, irrigation, technical assistance for livestock management, meat and hide processing, marketing, and the construction of fencing and of facilities for veterinary care. The success of a livestock project depends heavily on how it relates to the existing system of livestock production, and on whether the project is designed to correct or to perpetuate practices that make the industry environmentally destructive and less efficient.

ENVIRONMENTAL IMPACTS

The major environmental impacts of livestock projects are deforestation, wildlife destruction, and range degradation. (Appendix 6-A lists environmental guidelines for livestock projects.)

Deforestation
Because cattle grazing often provides foreign exchange earnings, governments frequently give incentives to the industry, such as tax benefits and titles to frontier land. Forests are sometimes cleared to create pastureland — as has occurred on an enormous scale in the Brazilian Amazon and to a lesser extent in Central America — often with direct or indirect support from MDBs. Cattle ranching contributed more than any other activity to deforestation in the Brazilian Amazon, accounting for an estimated 72 percent of total deforestation. The Brazilian government has provided tax incentives, mainly in the forms of tax exemptions and loans at subsidized rates of interest. Between 1966 and 1983, investment tax credits and subsidized loan disbursements to the livestock sector in the Amazon totaled an estimated $731 million. The larger projects were promoted by the Superintendencia para o Desenvolvimento da Amazonia (SUDAM). The average area of a typical SUDAM-supported ranch is 23,600 hectares, as contrasted with 9,600 hectares for a non-SUDAM property (Bonfiglioli 1988). In a financial survey, Bonfiglioli shows that these cattle ranches do not generate a positive return from livestock production. The only profits to the owners come from government tax and credit subsidies. Bonfiglioli shows

that cattle sales during a typical five-year period (based on the average 1984 price of steers) failed to cover operating costs, leaving no profit to justify the capital investment. Nevertheless, because the investor can defer a personal equity contribution and use tax credits and government loans instead, the investor receives a high rate of return on the equity investment. Inflation enables borrowers to repay in depreciated money, thus enhancing the effective subsidy even more.

In addition to the large losses the government has incurred by subsidizing the Amazon livestock industry, the country has lost much by clearing the forested areas. Bonfiglioli estimates that during 1966–1983 only 18 percent of the SUDAM-subsidized ranches recovered any sellable timber when clearing forests. The SUDAM-subsidized landowners cleared the forests quickly, often by burning, salvaging little timber. However, 42 percent of the non-SUDAM- subsidized ranches marketed the timber. Bonfiglioli estimates the cost of timber destroyed in the process of creating cattle ranches at $1 to $2 billion over the 1966–1983 period (Bonfiglioli 1988). It is impossible to justify these losses by the potential social gains. In Amazonian Brazil, each $63,000 invested in cattle ranching creates only one job. This is the lowest employment expenditure ratio for virtually any type of development project in Brazil (Ledec & Goodland 1988, 49). Development projects that promote cattle ranching in tropical forest regions should improve pasture management and animal husbandry to raise productivity on existing pastureland, rather than expand pasture at the expense of forests.

The Central American cattle industry has also been expanding rapidly. Before 1980 the countries there exported an increasing percentage of beef (about 40 percent in the 1970s), but exports declined in the 1980s. Most of the capital invested in the agricultural sector has gone into livestock; about half the agricultural credits provided by governments were used to support the livestock industry. Most of the region's cattle production is on medium to large ranches whose main activity is cattle grazing. Such ranches tend to range in size from about 45 hectares up to more than a thousand hectares, and herds may include more than ten thousand animals.

The forests harbor poor-quality soils subject to erosion. Colonists tend to clear more and more land to compensate for the declining fertility of land already exploited. When lands cleared for growing crops are abandoned, cattle ranchers move in. The loss of fertility from overexploitation and mismanagement leads to the abandonment of land after only a few seasons. Some land returns to brush and secondary forests, but much is left exposed to erosion that sets in when the soil is badly compacted or loses its nutrients.

Some of the Central American countries follow the familiar pattern of building roads to forested frontier areas and bringing in unemployed and landless peasants to clear the land for crops. As land degradation occurs, colonists push further down the road, leaving the lands to secondary growth or erosion and gullying. Much of the timber felled in Central America is not commercially harvested because of lack of transportation. For example, an estimated $300 million worth of commercial timber is squandered annually in this way in Honduras.

Wildlife Destruction
Another environmental problem is the destruction of wildlife arising from loss of habitat and hunting. Especially serious is the loss of habitat for migratory birds that breed in North America and spend the nonbreeding season in Central America. Studies have shown that about one-third of the fifty-three species spending the winter in Central America have been declining in population (Leonard 1987, Ch. 4).

Degradation of Rangeland
Raising livestock has been a major occupation in Africa for centuries, often in combination with crop growing. Recent decades have seen substantial degradation of pastureland, which has contributed to low productivity and desertification. Three developments have been cited as being responsible for these conditions in the Sahelian and Sudanian zones of West Africa: (1) the "colonization of pasturelands" through expansion of crop production; (2) the annexation of rangelands by the West African states; and (3) the shift of ownership and control of herds from traditional pastoralists to absentee owners (wealthy farmers, businesspeople, and bureaucrats) (Bonfiglioli 1988, Ch. 3).

Colonization of pastureland results in reduced fallow and the disappearance of grazing lands. A decrease in available manure reduces crop yields and leads to a further expansion of cultivated lands. The result, according to Bonfiglioli (1988, Ch. 3), has been declining productivity in Sahelian pastoral lands and agropastoral systems.

Since the independence of African countries from colonial rule after World War II, states have annexed substantial amounts of rangeland. This has fundamentally altered resource management by canceling pastoral groups' traditional rights to water, land, and grazing. Pastoralists maintain fewer herds, and absentee owners have more animals. In some cases the government assumes management for parastatal livestock development projects. Also, according to Bonfiglioli, these changes constitute separation of ownership from management of livestock and have subjected pastoral land to speculation, hoarding, and investment by the wealthy minority. The former pastoralists simply become hired workers and have no motivation to improve the management of the rangeland. This has led to larger herds, which are less mobile and more concentrated around wells, towns, and markets, leading to consequent degradation of rangeland.

Agricultural experts do not agree regarding optimum ownership and managerial arrangements for the livestock industry in Africa, nor do they agree on the major problems that call for a change in traditional arrangements. One traditional arrangement still in widespread use is "subsistence pastoralism." Under this system pastoralists consume the livestock and its products (meat, leather, and dairy goods). While livestock is sometimes sold, it is not specifically produced for market. Livestock and the cultivation of crops using cattle for both manure and draft animals are closely related in this arrangement. An individual herder does not own the pastoral land, but groups associated with particular villages provide a certain amount of management and cooperation.

In a second system, called "open range ranching," individuals or families own the herds but the livestock is produced for market rather than for consumption by herders. Commercial pastoralists producing for the market seek a healthy crop of animals for sale at an age that maximizes their revenue, while subsistence pastoralists prolong the useful life of an animal to extract the maximum amount of replenishable animal products. For example, commercial pastoralists allow young animals to suckle rather than maximizing milk production for consumption. A third system, "fenced ranching," requires larger herds, capital for improvements, and exclusive rights of land ownership by an individual herder. This system may be accompanied by absentee ownership. An important advantage of fenced ranching is that it provides a way of keeping squatters off the land.

Each of these three arrangements has advantages and disadvantages from the standpoints of productive efficiency and pastureland health, but what is optimum depends heavily on the social and economic environment and on the social goals of the government. Subsistence pastoralism is well suited to a noncommercial herding society with abundant land and no outside group of herders or cultivators to compete for land traditionally used by a village or group of villages. But where land is scarce and available to all, and where there are no grazing fees or quotas, individual herders have an incentive to maximize the number of animals to maximize marketing revenues. There is little incentive to protect the commons by avoiding overgrazing, or to make investments to prevent degradation. This is known as "the tragedy of the commons." Some argue that the only way to avoid land degradation is to give each herder exclusive rights and title to a certain area. To protect these rights, the herder is then induced to fence the area. However, individual ranch owners must provide their own infrastructure in the form of water sources and other facilities. Those opposed to fenced ranching argue that the system is not economical or even feasible for herders with a small number of animals. For such herders, some form of cooperative arrangement is necessary. Also, ranching may not be feasible in areas of highly variable rainfall patterns because such areas are useable only for a limited time each season. In such cases each herder would need to hold exclusive rights to land in several areas. This would require unfenced corridors so that herds could be moved from one area to another.

The literature on the livestock industry in tropical environments does not provide agreed upon guidelines by which to judge livestock projects from the standpoints of efficiency and environmental protection. What is appropriate in one physical and social environment may not be appropriate in another. Nor is there agreement on the relationship between certain livestock practices and the degradation of soil and loss of vegetation. For example, in a study published for the Overseas Development Institute, Steven Standford (1983) argues against what he calls "the mainstream view" that most of the world's rangelands are suffering from overgrazing. Nor does he regard the communal grazing system as necessarily giving rise to overgrazing and desertification. He further states that, although range degradation does take place after some level of stocking, few agricultural specialists agree on the right level of stocking. Standford does not accept the mainstream view that open ranges inevitably lead to "the tragedy of the commons" or that pastoral societies are unable to regulate the size of member herds (1983, 14–15). He believes that one of the consequences of the mainstream view has been the hasty introduction of private range management systems sponsored by MDBs. In criticizing efforts to promote private over communal land ownership, he points to cases in Africa where environmental degradation was worse on private commercial ranches than under the traditional communal system (Angola and Botswana, for example). Finally, he is critical of programs that assign the government—instead of existing pastoral institutions—a key role in managing pastures. Given the sorry record of developing-country governments for corruption and abuse of power, there is a strong case for minimizing government control.

Standford's approach, which has many adherents among African livestock specialists, is in sharp contrast to the ideals of the Botswana Land Management and Livestock Program, which the World Bank supported. The Botswana Livestock Program and the controversy regarding it illustrates the conflict over livestock management in Africa.

THE BOTSWANA LIVESTOCK PROGRAM

Botswana has long been a cattle-raising country, combining that industry with agriculture. Originally, tribal chiefs controlled land for both crops and grazing on tribal lands covering large areas. Plots for plowed fields were allocated near the villages, while open-range grazing areas were designated beyond the agricultural fields. The availability of water determined grazing areas, and herds were often moved to a new area when water became scarce or when overgrazing affected cattle production. With the advent of mechanically drilled boreholes in the 1920s and 1930s, grazing was oriented to boreholes bringing groundwater from below the Kalahari Desert, and seasonal movements of people and cattle became less frequent. Tribal grazing perimeters are seldom more than 30 kilometers. Increased dependence on boreholes resulted in de facto control of communal tribal land by those who could afford to drill, equip, and operate boreholes. Normally, the only restriction that a tribal chief imposed on drilling was that sites be no closer than 8 kilometers. Those with small herds unable to afford their own boreholes made arrangements to buy water from borehole owners. The emerging pattern was increased overgrazing of communally managed land and de facto control of large areas of land by those who owned boreholes.

After independence in 1966, the Botswana government attempted to control this process through legislation, removing responsibility for land allocation from the tribal chief and giving it to a tribal land board that included the chief and five members appointed by district and central government authorities. Although this achieved some democratization of land allocation, it did little to solve the problem of overgrazing. In the early 1970s, the government of Botswana initiated a program to revise land tenure and livestock management. Its fundamental approach was outlined in the Tribal Grazing Land Policy White Paper of 1975. The goals were (1) to stop overgrazing and degradation of the land; (2) to promote greater equality of income; and (3) to allow growth and commercialization of the livestock industry on a sustainable basis. In the communal areas, the policy was to safeguard the welfare of small livestock owners by promising each tribesman as much land as needed to sustain himself and his family. Viable groups of smallholders were to be assisted in improving their agricultural production. A major component of the program was the creation of fenced ranches on an individual or group basis. Fencing was regarded as necessary to improve range management by replacing the commons system that encouraged overstocking and land degradation. Other elements of the program were access to land under long-term leases tantamount to ownership; technical assistance and training; and human resources development

A World Bank loan financed the First Livestock Development Project (LP 1) in 1972. It was designed to encourage individuals who owned large herds to withdraw them from overgrazed communal areas and relocate them on leased fenced and paddocked ranches on state land located in remote areas of the country. The project was poorly managed and suffered from a number of design flaws. For one thing, it did not benefit those living in the communal areas from which the cattle were withdrawn; rather it helped relatively large livestock owners with sufficient resources to participate in the scheme. Second, the project never worked closely with local institutions or with residents of nearby villages. Third, inadequate ecological information resulted in fences being erected on land traversed by tens of thousands of migrating wildebeests and other wildlife. This resulted not only in damage to fences and competition with the cattle for the grazing land, but in the destruction of wildebeests trying to cross the rangeland during migration. Finally, the project failed to reduce overstocking, either in the commons or in the fenced ranges.

Botswana's Second Livestock Development Project (LP 2), financed by a World Bank loan approved in 1977, emphasized training ranch managers and providing supervised agricultural credit to stockholders. It also provided for technical and managerial services to blocks of ranches on a shared-cost basis, and for the development of livestock marketing facilities. Several fully developed ranches and some experimental grazing units in communal areas were to be established. By the time the project ended in 1984, it was generally rated a failure. Livestock owners showed little interest in obtaining ranches, and those who did were relatively unconcerned about management and reluctant to invest in improvements. Cattle production did not increase significantly, and only two of the fourteen proposed communal grazing units were completed.

A World Bank loan approved in 1985 financed the Third Livestock Development Project (LP 3). It contains many of the elements of LP 1 and LP 2 and emphasizes the provision of credit to stimulate commercial development. Like its predecessors, it is premised on the assumption that large cattle holders would move to virgin territory and thereby relieve pressure on the communal areas — and that the answer to overgrazing is private landholding. A substantial portion of the $17.8 million loan was to be used to establish 130 fenced lease-hold ranches. Benefits from the fenced ranches and the commercial ranch credits would accrue to only a few large-scale, politically powerful cattle ranchers.

LP 3 came under intense criticism from conservation groups in both the United States and Botswana, and from leading agricultural specialists familiar with the African livestock industry. The USAID Mission in Botswana also criticized it. As a consequence of adverse reports on LP 3 prepared by US conservation organizations, including the NRDC and the Sierra Club, in August 1986 Secretary of the Treasury James A. Baker III issued instructions to the US executive director on the Bank's board to seek specific changes in the Botswana project, including redirecting financing away from ranches and toward small-scale farmers. Subsequently, the Bank suspended disbursement of funds, in part because of the widespread failure of ranches financed by previous projects.

The World Bank's promotion of commercial ranches was in line with the Botswana government's 1975 White Paper, which attributed overgrazing mainly to communal ranges. The promotion of commercial ranching was also based on the presumption that most Botswana herders are reluctant to sell their cattle and, therefore, hold cattle on the commons well beyond the optimum marketing age, thus contributing to overgrazing. Those opposing this position have argued that herders on communal ranges will abide by rules that avoid overgrazing if local associations organize and manage them properly. The critics also deny that the majority of the cattlemen are subsistence pastoralists whose traditional values prevent them from selling their cattle. They maintain that the herders are unwilling to lease land and establish ranches because of the high costs of ranching (requiring fencing and creating water facilities) and the high risks of operating in a semiarid environment. Finally, critics argued that loan assistance, rather than benefiting a handful of large cattle ranchers, should be made available for improved management of small herds in combination with crop production, and for small-scale enterprise, such as dairies for processing milk. US conservation groups were also concerned that the proposed new ranches — requiring an average of 60 kilometers of fencing each — would further hinder wildlife migration and continue to kill thousands of animals each year.

Although the Botswana livestock projects illustrate the shortcomings of livestock projects financed by the World Bank, this experience has not provided a satisfactory answer to the major problems that the livestock industries in Africa and other tropical countries face. These problems include overgrazing, lack of efficiency in the industry, few opportunities for small herders, and competition between the wildlife and domestic cattle. No one model would be appropriate for the conditions in every African country, and it will be necessary to experiment with several pilot projects before proceeding with one on a national scale in any country.

REVIEW OF WORLD BANK LIVESTOCK PROJECTS

Donor-supported livestock project failures have been high. During fiscal years 1974–1979 the World Bank made loans for twenty-seven livestock projects that were audited, of which eleven, or 41 percent, were rated as project failures (World Bank 1988a, Annex 6). For the eight evaluated projects financed by the World Bank in 1986, the weighted average rate of return was only 7 percent, as contrasted with 16 percent for all projects reviewed (World Bank 1988b, 27–28). For the period 1980–1984 the success rate for audited livestock projects was only 47 percent, and for 1985 it was only 33 percent, as contrasted with an average of about 70 percent for all audited projects that year (World Bank 1987, 159). (The Bank's criterion for financial success is a rate of return of 12 percent on the total investment in the project.) USAID's results in financing livestock development have also been relatively poor.

Over the twenty-five-year period 1962–1987, the World Bank provided $7.7 billion (in constant 1983 dollars) for livestock development projects, including $1.3 billion for livestock projects in Sub-Saharan Africa. The Bank's Operations Evaluation Department (OED) audited 125 livestock projects, half designed to encourage incorporating livestock into smallholder farming systems.[1] The OED audit concluded that livestock projects performed poorly in Sub-Saharan Africa and that 71 percent had economic rates of return of less than 10 percent.

Lack of economic incentives to farmers to adopt new technology were a major cause of the project failures. In large part this resulted from government marketing monopolies and price controls. Some of the projects for pasture improvement failed because the land tenure system did not protect herders' investments in pastureland. Pastures improved when outsiders were kept out and smallholders could obtain title to the land. However, urban citizens abused the opportunity to gain title to land, in some cases by engaging in absentee-owner ranching. For instance, in Rwanda the civil servants—not the smallholders—captured the benefits.

The promotion of fodder crops was not successful in the vicinity of urban areas, since fodder crops compete with cash crops such as fruits and vegetables that can be sold in nearby urban centers. Fodder crops were successfully promoted in relatively remote areas with poor market access conditions. Stall-feeding schemes were complete failures, largely because of additional labor requirements for transporting and storing forage.

The greatest success was with projects administered by pastoral associations, or by farm or village groups operating collective fields, grain banks, and fodder banks. Where donor assistance was channeled to parastatal organizations, performance was poor. The success rate for technology transfer within pastoral associations or village groups was also considerably higher than that without cooperative-group involvement. A final finding was that subsidized credits or input subsidies did not promote success for the livestock projects. Civil servants instead of farmers absorbed the subsidies in several projects.

CONCLUSIONS ON LIVESTOCK PROJECTS

Improving the productivity of rangelands in dry regions is principally a question of improving the utilization of moisture, the scarcest resource (Standford 1983, 106). This can be accomplished by contour furrowing and range pitting to impede surface runoff of rainfall and to increase infiltration; bush clearing and haymaking; planting and seeding; rotating grazing; and adjusting grazing pressure in terms of the number of livestock and the way they move and congregate (Standford 1983, Ch. 5). These same activities are required for sustainable livestock production. They should be integrated with the managerial arrangement, whether individual land ownership, cooperative ownership and control of rangeland, or subsistence pastoralism. Agricultural specialists generally do not seem to recommend a single system of pastoral organization and management for

all types of societies and physical environments. A successful pastoral program often depends upon participation by the pastoralists, especially participation that provides representation for different interests.

These requirements for rangeland productivity and sustainability constitute a substantial investment and necessitate integrated management of
all pastoral activities. Since pastoralists own their own herds, they must
participate in policy formulation and in the selection of managerial arrangements. Investments in the rangelands, which will in large measure
represent the labor of the pastoralists themselves, are unlikely to be made
without strong incentives, especially security of land tenure. The conclusions from the review of the Bank's livestock loan projects suggest that
adequate incentives can exist for pastoral associations. The fenced ranching
program under the World Bank's Botswana loans failed because individual
pastoralists were unwilling or unable to make the necessary investments.
No single system will succeed in all physical, economic, and sociocultural
environments. Pilot projects must be used to experiment with different
arrangements to determine which will be successful where.

Agricultural Credit Loans

Government-sponsored agricultural credit institutions have long been
popular in Third World countries, just as they have been in industrial countries. The rationale for them is that small farmers are unable to borrow
at commercial banks in the urban centers, and private moneylenders charge
exorbitant rates of interest that few farmers can afford to pay. The cost
of extending credit to small farmers is so high that agricultural credit must
be subsidized by rates less than those necessary to cover the full cost of
the loans, including the risk of nonrepayment. Governments have, therefore, sought loans from MDBs and bilateral assistance agencies to finance
agricultural credit assistance. External loans are made in foreign currencies
and converted into local currency for relending to farmers. Governments
can afford to lend these funds at rates below the free or noninstitutional
market rates and still cover their lending costs. This is true in part because most developing-country currencies are overvalued in terms of foreign exchange at the official rate. When the government loans domestic
currency to farmers, that currency is actually worth less than the foreign
exchange value of the loan when converted into domestic currency at the

official rate.[2] In addition, MDBs nearly always charge interest rates lower than domestic interest rates.

Since MDBs are generally anxious to channel their assistance to the agricultural sector but are unable to make loans to individual farmers, loans to government agricultural credit institutions have been popular. The World Bank and IDA alone made nearly $10 billion in agricultural credit loans from the beginning of operations to 30 June 1990 (World Bank 1990, 177).

CRITICISMS OF AGRICULTURAL CREDIT LOANS

Agricultural economists have made several criticisms of subsidized credit loans. First, these loans give rise to distortions in financial markets. Second, subsidized interest rates do not provide a true measure of the cost of money, and the loans may be used for purposes that are not justified in terms of the return on the investment. Third, regulated low-interest rates discourage private financial institutions from serving rural markets. Subsidized interest rates impair the ability of private financial institutions to mobilize domestic savings, since these institutions must offer rural depositors low rates of interest in order to compete with government-sponsored credit. Not only is this a disincentive to saving, but it leads rural savers to channel their savings to metropolitan centers where they can earn a higher return, thereby drawing capital out of the agricultural sector. The general consensus among development economists is that external loans for financing subsidized agricultural credit tend to discourage the development of credit institutions for mobilizing rural savings, which could then be reinvested in agriculture rather than in the industrial and urban sectors (Bon Prischke 1984, 284–297; Krueger, Michalopolous, & Ruttan 1989, 162–167).

A recent article published by the IADB (Zavaleta 1990, 4) also criticizes subsidized credit—a dominant feature of Latin American agricultural credit banks, which in turn have borrowed heavily from MDBs. The article points out that setting interest rates below market levels generates an excess demand for credit, which can only be resolved through some form of nonmarketing rationing procedure. Rationing is likely to favor large borrowers who use the funds to grow cash crops, thus exacerbating the inequitable distribution of wealth and income. Subsidized credit is unlikely to be directed to the most efficient use and is often used to sustain current consumption levels, to invest in consumer durables, or to invest in land. Subsidized credit programs may not be related to promoting agricultural practices and technologies specifically designed for efficiency and sustainable agriculture. In fact, they sometimes give the wrong signals. The use of agricultural credit to clear tropical forests in Amazonia for inefficient agriculture and cattle ranching illustrates this point.

These criticisms are not meant to discourage the establishment of agricultural credit institutions designed both to mobilize savings and to channel those savings into productive investment. MDBs can play a role in providing technical assistance and working capital for such institutions, but they should not provide a continual flow of external funds at subsidized rates of interest.

Agricultural Mechanization

Agricultural mechanization is frequently blamed for degradation of humid tropical soils, particularly in sub-Saharan Africa (World Bank 1989, 97). Most soils in the humid tropics are not suited to intensive production of field crops. Continuous cultivation leads to leaching, acidification, and erosion. Attempts to establish permanent field crops on these soils with mechanized clearing and land preparations have often led to progressive soil degradation and eventual abandonment. Early experiments with mechanization in tropical Africa were carried out by the Belgian colonial administration in Zaire in 1960, and later in the humid zones of Ivory Coast, Nigeria, and Ghana; in all cases the projects produced extremely low returns on the investments and very high levels of environmental degradation (Pingali, Bigot, & Binswanger 1987, 173). Mechanized tilling to clear the forests had disastrous results in the Brazilian Amazon. According to Fauck (1977, 192), mechanization can be combined with anti-erosive techniques, such as contouring and terracing, strip cropping, mulching, and restricting tilling to the seeding row on some humid tropic soils. Mechanization has been successful in Asia, where it has followed long periods of animal-drawn plowing and has been used only for specific tasks, with other tasks performed by hand.

Following independence, several Sub-Saharan African countries adopted the use of tractors in areas where animal traction had not been established. After 1961, the Tanzanian government promoted mechanized block-cultivation schemes under which groups of farms were managed and operated as a single unit, and equipment was available for multifarm use through tractor-hire programs. Large private farmers could also get tractors on favorable credit terms. The mechanization schemes adopted by Zimbabwe, Kenya, Zambia, Malawi, Tanzania, Ethiopia, Guinea, and Ivory Coast, among others, turned out to be fiascos. Some of these mechanization schemes were supported by MDB loans. By the mid-1980s, few tractors from the earlier period remained in operation. Those still in use were usually associated with rice cultivation and were privately owned. During the 1980s, governments encouraged the use of improved hand tools and animal-drawn equipment (Pingali, Bigot, and Binswanger 1987, Ch. 6).

Early mechanization failed because of soil erosion but also because spare parts were difficult to find and repair facilities were few. Pingali, Bigot, and Binswanger point out that rapid agricultural development through technological change cannot be viewed as the replacement of an entire set of traditional activities by modern ones. Certain tasks are mechanized first, followed by others, depending upon profitability, soil conditions, inputs (such as fertilizers), and the nature of the crops. Often tractors have been introduced in areas of bush-fallow agriculture where costs of clearing land and sustaining tractor operations were extremely high. These programs failed because they were inappropriate (1987, 181).

Pesticides and Fertilizers

MDBs and national foreign assistance agencies, such as USAID, have provided billions of dollars to governments of developing countries for pesticides and fertilizers, either directly through agricultural development loans or indirectly through support of agricultural credit programs. This assistance has encouraged governments to subsidize the sale of these commodities to local farmers. Both pesticides and fertilizers can make a contribution to farm output, but they may also have harmful environmental effects.

PESTICIDES

Toxic pesticides expose humans to health hazards through residues in foods and water and may destroy fish and birds. Subsidies tend to encourage overuse in the sense that the additional benefits from increased output are less than the additional costs of pesticides at nonsubsidized prices. Much use also increases the risk of harmful health effects. Moreover, pesticide use may be self-defeating since insects develop a resistance to the pesticide. Finally, pesticide subsidies may impede the adoption of more economically efficient and less harmful alternatives.

The Integrated Pest Management (IPM) program is an alternative method of pest control that depends less on chemicals and more on other inputs (Weatherly 1983, Ch. 6). IPM does not reject the use of chemical pesticides, but applies various techniques. It is based on a thorough understanding of physical and biological conditions and on the adoption of pesticides, fertilizers, and farming methods suitable to these conditions. IPM includes biological control techniques, such as introducing a pest's natural enemies, using resistant varieties of seeds, trapping flying insects, and timing pesticide applications carefully. It takes into account environmental impacts and the relationship between the benefits and the costs of control (Repetto 1985, 15). Since research is necessary to discover the most efficient IPM program for a particular pest infestation problem, MDBs might well shift their emphasis from providing pesticides to providing research assistance and training for the development of IPM programs.

Although the World Bank, IADB, ADB, and USAID continue to provide pesticides, they have adopted guidelines governing pesticide use in the projects they finance (see Appendix 6-B). The guidelines recognize the risk of excessive reliance on chemicals and advocate sound pest management to reduce dependence on chemicals in favor of alternatives. However, they have neither ruled out pesticide subsidies nor recognized that these subsidies encourage overuse (Repetto 1985, 2).

FERTILIZERS

Chemical fertilizers also contribute to environmental pollution of rivers, lakes, and wetlands. Some critics argue that sustainability requires the elimination of *all* chemicals in agriculture, although most agricultural specialists reject this extreme position. All agree, however, that the mineral nutrients extracted from the soil must somehow be replaced. It is possible to avoid all chemical fertilizers by using prepared compost or manure, or through some form of multiple cropping that includes legumes. Wholly organic farming may increase costs, and some use of chemical fertilizer is likely to be more efficient for certain types of soils and crops. The problem is not so much whether to use *any* chemical fertilizer, but whether farmers use *too much* fertilizer. Exceeding the optimum amount may mean that additional fertilizer inputs yield additional value less than the incremental cost of the fertilizer, as well as exacerbating environmental problems. Foreign aid programs providing fertilizers at low or no cost may promote overuse. Again, as with pesticides, foreign aid money might be better spent on research and pilot projects to determine the types and amounts of fertilizers that are beneficial and the most efficient alternatives to chemical fertilizers.

Export Agriculture

Environmental groups frequently criticize MDBs for emphasizing export crop production at the expense of both food output for local consumption and soil quality. They argue that export agriculture tends to be monocrop and chemical and energy intensive, and that loans for such programs benefit large farms and plantations while actually making a negative contribution to alleviating poverty.

Although one can find cases where export agriculture has been socially and ecologically harmful and may have constituted a misallocation of government funds and national resources, a general condemnation of export agriculture not only is unwarranted, but may be harmful to sustainable development. As Robert Repetto, one of the world's leading environmental economists, points out, the argument that developing countries overemphasize export-crop production at the expense of basic food crops is mistaken: "Most developing countries underemphasize export commodity production, and export crops tend to be, if anything, less dangerous to soils than basic food crops. Many export crops grow on trees and bushes that provide continuous root structure and canopy cover: coffee, cocoa, rubber, palm oil, bananas, tea, spices and so on. Such crops are quite suitable for the hilly terrain where they are often grown" (1988, 6). Many Third World countries have combined export price controls with overvalued exchange rates and tariffs on imported agricultural inputs to effectively tax export crops by 50 percent or more.

Studies counter the argument that export agriculture benefits mainly large farms and plantations and show that small farmers who have an opportunity to market export crops can significantly raise their incomes. They also show that production for export will not take place at the expense of food production for the local economy if farmers own their land. To quote from a recent study by the International Food Policy Research

Institute: "Export cropping can significantly raise the incomes of small-holder farms. The government needs first to make a conscientious effort to encourage export cropping by smallholders, by providing credit and knowhow through extension and by actively promoting their access to processing and marketing facilities where necessary" (Bouis & Haddad 1990, 10).

Exports are essential for development. A nation that does not export is doomed to a no-growth subsistence economy and low productivity, since it will not be able to acquire modern technology. Providing incentives for export is not necessarily inconsistent with either sound environmental policy and sustainability on the one hand, or economic improvement for the poorer classes of society on the other.

Wildlife

MDB loans have supported wildlife in components of two types of projects: those designed to promote tourism and those designed to modify or compensate for damage from irrigation or other development projects. Appendix 6-C gives examples of both types.

Development constitutes the greatest threat to wildlife when farms, cities, airports, roads, and golf courses take over their natural habitats. Most wildlife species diminish for lack of natural foods and specialized breeding environments. In addition, many birds, animals, and fish fall victim to the toxins distributed by humans in the air, water, and land. Only a few species, such as deer, raccoon, and the English sparrow, are able to survive alongside dense human populations.

Development does not require the extinction of species or the diminution of birds and animals to the point where people can see them only in zoos. Wildlife is valuable enough in any society to justify maintaining preserves. The best farmland has already been developed in most countries, so the remaining animals tend to be concentrated in semiarid mountains, desert regions, or tropical rainforests where the soil is too poor for crop cultivation. Wetlands are important for both birds and animals and are of great value for fisheries and for maintaining the purity of rivers and coastal waters. Since it is costly to drain wetlands for other uses, their social value as wildlife reserves tends to be greater than their social value for farming and urban structures.

Much wildlife can be accommodated and preserved alongside farms, livestock pastures, and rivers and coastal areas subject to commercial use. This is especially true for birds—provided that wetlands are maintained, pesticides containing highly toxic chemicals are not used, and rivers and lakes are not polluted. Wildlife can also live in forested areas near farms and pastures if fences do not inhibit their movement and interfere with seasonal migration and access to water. Development projects need to be designed with a view toward accommodating wildlife. Appendix 6-D lists guidelines for wildlife protection.

TYPES OF DEVELOPMENT PROJECTS THAT MAY HAVE ADVERSE EFFECTS ON WILDLIFE

In the following paragraphs we review the major types of development projects that may have adverse impacts on wildlife. These projects could be modified to avoid or mitigate these adverse impacts.

Water Development Projects
Dams for hydroelectric power, irrigation, or other purposes that convert free-flowing rivers and streams into reservoirs fundamentally transform the aquatic environment, change species composition, and reduce biological diversity. Some reservoirs have inundated enormous areas of land: The Akosombo Dam in Ghana flooded 8,482 square kilometers, and the Aswân High Dam in Egypt inundated nearly half that amount. The diversion or impoundment of water may reduce downstream supplies for aquatic life and for terrestrial wildlife. Dams can severely affect fish and other aquatic species by reducing river nutrients. For example, declining nutrient loads in the Nile River from construction of the Aswân High Dam have virtually eliminated the sardine fisheries. Extensive damming and diversion of the Colorado River in the United States have caused the decline of sea bass, shrimp, and shark fisheries because of the cutoff of nutrient flow into the Gulf of California.

Draining and reclaiming wetlands for agricultural or industrial development, or other purposes can severely impair biological diversity, fisheries, birds, and terrestrial animals. For example, the Drainage and Land Reclamation Project in Sri Lanka, which the World Bank financed, reduced fish catches because the control of tidal action impeded the free flowing and mixing of seawater with fresh water and limited access to the flooded marshy areas. Urban sewage disposal projects can adversely affect water quality in areas important to local fisheries. Sewage settling ponds sometimes involve the conversion of marshes, or other wetlands, which are important fish nurseries and migratory bird habitats.

Wildlife losses need to be considered in calculating the net benefits of all water projects. In some cases projects can be designed to minimize these impacts by reducing areas inundated by dams; in other cases provision can be made for compensatory wildlife preserves.

Agriculture and Land Settlement

Agriculture or land settlement projects that expand cultivated areas by clearing wildlands for crops and livestock are responsible for perhaps the most significant loss of birds and terrestrial wildlife. A large irrigation canal can block movement of wildlife unless it is properly situated and has appropriate crossings. Fertilizer and pesticide runoff from irrigated areas may harm downstream aquatic life.

Highways

Highways affect wildlife when they penetrate previously remote areas, mainly because they provide access for slash-and-burn cultivators, spontaneous settlers, timber cutters, and hunters. Building a road into a forest encourages spontaneous human migration, often resulting in the clearing of natural vegetation, followed by soil degradation, water-supply disruption, loss of biological diversity, and the destruction of wild animals and birds. Humans have not inhabited existing wildlands in many developing countries largely because soil conditions and other environmental factors have made them unsuitable for farming. Nevertheless, wildlands have great value as habitat and as watersheds; unplanned migration promoted by roads destroys these values. Where planned development of forested areas is economical, some of the area should be left in a natural state without penetration by roads.

Industry and Mining

Some industrial development projects destroy or degrade wildlands. Aquatic and marine areas are vulnerable to industrial pollutants discharged in lakes and rivers. Mining projects often cover large areas that previously contained unique vegetation and animal species. Mines damage wildlife even more because of their discharge of toxic materials into rivers and lakes, and because of the large amounts of waste materials from them that cause sedimentation.

MEASURING THE VALUE OF WILDLIFE
AND OTHER WILDLAND BENEFITS[3]

An important prerequisite for incorporating wildlife protection in the design of development projects is a comprehensive measurement of the social values of wildlife. This is true because project designers tend to use benefit-cost analysis in allocating expenditures for achieving a variety of project goals. If they employ only market benefits and costs, they are likely to neglect or give only perfunctory attention to nonmarket benefits, such as those provided by wildlife. During the past thirty years environmental economists have developed methods for the quantitative valuation of various forms of outdoor recreation, including fishing, hunting, bird-watching, and being able to enjoy animals as a part of the wilderness experience. These valuations are important for comparing the monetary cost of alterations in project design that will protect wildlife (or the reduction in market benefits that may occur from an alteration) with the nonmarket social benefits of wildlife preservation.

In developing methods for estimating benefits from wildlife resources, environmental economists have sought to determine how much consumers are willing to pay for recreation associated with fishing, hunting, or simply viewing wildlife. These methods include surveying visitors and estimating travel time and expenditures to visit wildlife areas. US Fish and Wildlife Service economists used such investigations to design and analyze the 1980 and 1985 National Surveys. The US Water Resources Council has also adopted methodologies for the valuation of recreation benefits in federal water resources projects.[4]

The social value of wildlife is considerably greater than the amounts that those actively engaged in fishing, hunting, and viewing would be willing to pay. Social values include *option* and *existence* values. Potential users of goods or services are willing to pay something to retain the option of using them sometime in the future, and nonusers are willing to pay something to insure the continuing existence of a resource. Thus, many people who never expect to see the great caribou herds in the Alaska Wildlife Refuge are, nevertheless, willing to pay something to preserve them. What they are willing to pay might conceivably be a somewhat higher price for petroleum, if this is a consequence of keeping a wildlife refuge closed to petroleum exploration.

For many developing countries, wildlife preservation has a direct monetary value from tourism; it is important to establish this value to encourage preservation. (Without tourism, it is doubtful whether many of the African wildlife parks would still be in existence.) However, since wildlife is valued by an amount much greater than the actual expenditures that tourists make when visiting wildlife parks, both those who actually visit the parks and those who realize option and existence values might be willing to make voluntary contributions to the maintenance of wildlife parks. It is desirable on economic grounds that MDBs assist developing countries in maintaining the parks and protecting the wildlife.

The social value of wildlife is a part of the complex of benefits provided by the wildlands where wildlife exists. Certain wildlife species require wildlands with specific attributes. Some birds and animals exist only in tropical rainforests; others require a semiarid environment; still others need a specialized aquatic habitat. For example, greater flamingoes need shallow alkaline lakes containing small organisms such as mollusks and crustaceans, while the trumpeter swan requires remote arctic lakes for breeding. But each category of wildlife habitat provides other benefits, such as the waste assimilation and ecological continuity provided by wetlands. Thus, wildlands provide a complex of interdependent benefits, some contributing to the production of marketable goods, such as fish, and others constituting nonmarketable recreational amenities.

MDBs recognize the value of wildlife in the guidelines they have prepared for taking account of environmental impacts of development projects (see Appendix 6-D). The EIAs' borrowers are required to prepare for projects supported by MDB loans are also supposed to take the impact on wildlife into account. Thus far, however, we have found little evidence that appropriate attention has been given to wildlife preservation in MDB-supported projects, largely because governments of borrowing countries often ignore the provisions of loan agreements that deal with wildlife.

Halting Land Degradation

Degradation of agricultural land is taking place all over the world in both developed countries (as in the US Midwest) and in the Third World (MacNeill 1989). It is regarded as a primary threat to sustainable development, especially in areas with high population growth and limited agricultural land. Governments and MDBs often face the dilemma of promoting expansion in agricultural output by measures that destroy the soil, on the one hand, or promoting sustainable development by more traditional methods that limit output growth, on the other.

Land degradation does not usually occur in farm communities that have been operating for centuries without changing crops or methods of production. Over time, farmers have learned to deal with soil erosiion, loss of nutrients and moisture, and even cyclical changes in rainfall and temperatures. The traditional systems may provide sustained yields, but they are often characterized by low productivity and inflexibility in the face of changing market conditions and new available technology. Land degradation can, of course, occur from secular changes in rainfall and temperature unrelated to human activities and institutions in a given region.

We may recognize two general sources of land degradation. First, increased population pressures and other social developments that disturb traditional farming and livestock grazing practices may lead to ecological changes such as deforestation, soil erosion, and a lowering of the water table. Second, new technology, agricultural systems, or products may replace traditional practices and may also lead to land degradation. This may occur as a result of government programs for new irrigation systems, farm mechanization, large resettlement programs, livestock programs, farm credit programs, changes in land tenure, or substitution of plantation for traditional peasant agriculture, all frequently financed or assisted by MDBs. Changes in traditional agricultural systems may, of course, be necessary to increase productivity, or to meet national objectives, such as increased foreign exchange income. But some of these programs have contributed to the degradation of agricultural resources so that the long-run social costs exceed the social benefits. Frequently, the problem lies in the specific nature of the programs rather than in the general desirability of the changes introduced.

Environmentalists sometimes regard certain types of agricultural innovations financed by MDBs as sources of environmental problems and inconsistent with sustainable development. These include shifts from traditional subsistence and local market production to the production of export crops, farm mechanization; large-scale irrigation; cattle ranching; or commercial forestry—all of which have contributed to soil degradation and ecological destruction. However, the adverse environmental impacts of these innovations may be avoided or significantly mitigated by the way in which they are introduced. Sound environmental planning and project design may avoid the adverse environmental impacts of projects and programs necessary to raise agricultural productivity and to promote desirable economic objectives. For example, many export crops—particularly tea, palm oil, and cocoa—if grown in the right soil are ecologically beneficial and can earn substantial income for thousands of smallholders in developing countries. Economic progress requires structural changes in agriculture, industry, and services. The goal is to promote changes that are consistent with environmental conservation. Accomplishing this often requires conducting research, including pilot projects, and applying knowledge gained from similar projects in comparable environments. We discuss the role of MDBs in promoting sustainable agriculture in the following section.

Have MDBs Made a Difference in Promoting Sustainable Agriculture?

Since 1950 MDBs have made hundreds of billions of dollars in loans to more than one hundred developing countries for promoting a wide variety of economic objectives. MDBs have shifted their dominant policies from time to time. Initially, they provided a source of external funds for "bankable" projects. Then they followed a policy of promoting a high rate of per capita GNP. Later, the announced dominant objective was elimination of abject poverty. More recently the major objective has been to achieve sustainable development.

Priorities given to economic sectors have changed with shifting policy goals, beginning with an emphasis on infrastructure. This was followed by the promotion of industrialization, which was succeeded by agriculture and rural development as the highest-priority sector. More recently nonproject loans for structural adjustment through public policy reform have received major attention. Within the industrial and agricultural sectors, emphasis has shifted between promoting exports and providing for domestic demand. Most developing countries did not sustain the rapid externally financed growth of the late 1960s and 1970s in the 1980s and early 1990s, and many of the Sub-Saharan African countries experienced very low or negative rates of per capita GNP growth in the 1970s and 1980s. Few developing countries have yet achieved the fundamental conditions for sustainable development. The reasons for this are complex, but they include disastrous governmental policies, high population growth rates, and a seriously degraded resource base.

We cannot blame the MDBs for the failure of developing countries to achieve sustainable development, but we can question whether the MDBs have made a difference. Their loans represent only a fraction of the external capital flows to developing countries, and an even smaller fraction of the total investment outlays of these countries: Governments have largely determined Third World development policies. By and large, the MDBs have made loans for public projects, or for projects and programs under government control. They simply have not been in a position to directly support the private sector in countries whose economies are dominated by governments. Some critics charge that making loans to public agencies helps to perpetuate government control and thereby prevents the establishment of a private free enterprise economy. There is something to this argument, but a policy of loaning only to the private sector and bypassing government agencies would mean a small flow of external assistance. It is beyond the scope of this book to comprehensively deal with the causes of poor performance of developing countries, especially since the reasons differ greatly among countries and among regions. However, we can discuss what the MDBs have accomplished in the agricultural sector and how they might make a greater contribution.

THE MADIA STUDIES

The following discussion of the role of MDBs in promoting sustainable development is based on the findings of the World Bank's study program, Managing Agricultural Development in Africa (MADIA), covering six Sub-Saharan African countries: Cameroon, Kenya, Malawi, Nigeria, Senegal, and Tanzania. The Bank has published the results of this study in a series of discussion papers.[5] The efforts of the MDBs and other donors to promote sustainable development in Sub-Saharan Africa may not be representative of their performance in other regions and in other economic sectors, but the lessons from their experience have considerable relevance for understanding overall donor performance. The single most important conclusion of the MADIA discussion papers is that there is little connection between where donor assistance has gone and where growth has occurred in the six countries.[6] Thus, MADIA Discussion Paper 1 acknowledges "the relative[ly] small role that donor assistance has played in the growth that has occurred in MADIA countries. Large amounts of aid have been allocated with the best of intentions, but to types of activities that have had little effect on growth" (Lele 1989a, 41).

A MADIA discussion paper that deals with agricultural performance in East Africa (Lele and Meyers 1989, 6) states that—except for small-holder tea, coffee, and dairying in Kenya—there appears to be relatively little connection between growth in the agricultural sectors of Kenya, Tanzania, and Malawi and World Bank agricultural project assistance totaling nearly $1 billion. The World Bank financed sixty-eight agricultural projects in these three countries between 1965 and 1986. Of twenty-four agricultural projects completed involving total investments of $266 million, only fourteen had positive rates of return. This record suggests that the countries would have been better off had they not borrowed from the Bank for many of the activities funded.

Between 1971 and 1988 the World Bank made loans to Nigerian agriculture totaling $1.7 billion, of which $1.1 billion went to support smallholder rain-fed food-crop development. The Bank's strategy was to make a visible impact on smallholder agriculture in the shortest possible time. By and large the results have been disappointing (Lele et al. 1989). Of the fifteen projects for which ex post evaluations were completed, six had negative rates of return; rates of return for most others were well under those expected. For example, the agricultural growth rate in Nigeria was only 2.3 percent per annum between 1970 and 1986, while population probably increased by 3 percent per annum. The self-sufficiency food ratio declined from 97.7 percent in 1970 to 90.8 percent in 1985. Soil has deteriorated substantially because of reduced fallow periods, and desertification affects more than 10 percent of the land area in the northern part of the country. The forested area has declined by more than 2 million hectares during the 1975–1984 decade alone. This has contributed to the decline in soil fertility, and there is urgent need for tree planting.

Although the reasons for the donors' seeming failure to make a difference vary from country to country, a common factor has been the failure to create internal capacity for sustained agricultural growth, in contrast to visible immediate results through investing in infrastructure. Such internal capacity requires investment in human and institutional capital, and the support of local research and analytical capability. The need for this type of assistance arises not only from a lack of understanding of which agricultural policies and technologies work best in varying social and physical environments of the African countries, but also from the lack of trained nationals for developing and implementing effective policies.

The MADIA papers are critical of the shifts in donor strategies and corresponding forms of assistance, which have not only failed to deal with basic long-term problems for raising agricultural production, but have tended to divert attention from them. In the 1970s, donors tended to concentrate on alleviating poverty quickly, giving priority to low-income regions and to raising food-crop production, mainly to meet growing urban demand. In the mid-1980s emphasis was on correcting price distortions and providing price incentives to raise production, particularly for exports. More recently, interest has revived in food security. Donor projects designed to help the poor tend to depend on raising farm output in marginal areas where there has not been any suitable technology for raising productivity. Donor-supported investment has favored extensive farming and rural infrastructure in areas of low productive potential and high transport cost. Transport development in the MADIA countries has emphasized creating truck routes, rather than maintaining existing rural feeder routes.

The MADIA studies recommend agricultural intensification, combined with measures to protect soil fertility through changes in farming methods and soil management techniques (such as growing trees that retain soil and moisture). They also favor more use of fertilizer and high-yield seeds. The studies point out that average per hectare use of fertilizer on arable land in Africa is the lowest in the world, despite an increase in foreign aid there. This is due to irregular donor support for fertilizer imports and lack of knowledge about fertilizer application in specific locations. More attention needs to go toward raising productivity in the agricultural sector rather than toward expanding cultivation in marginal areas. The effort to achieve a rapid increase in food output has often led to "soil mining," (producing food without restoring soil conditions for future production) and to deforestation (Lele & Stone 1989, 8–10).

The authors of the MADIA studies advocate donor support for broadly based sustainable agricultural growth. Such policies would encourage (1) a balance of food and export crops; (2) greater use of African institutional and human capacity; (3) human capital and institutional development; (4) soil management and integration of cropping with livestock and forestry; and (5) research tailored to the needs of small farmers. All of this requires a longer-term perspective—fifteen to twenty years—for sequencing an agricultural development strategy for a given country (Lele & Meyers 1989, 59–60).

The findings of the MADIA studies are supported in other World Bank reports (World Bank 1989; Repetto 1988; Barnes & Olivares 1988; Davis & Schirmer 1987). Past lending policies of the MDBs have not promoted sustainable agriculture because the elements of sustainability have not been an integral part of the programs financed. Moreover, without field research and experimentation, we do not know what will work in many environments. Sustainable development in agriculture is not simply avoiding the wrong things—it is knowing and doing the right things.

APPENDIX 6-A

Guidelines for Livestock and Animal Health Projects

A. *General*
1. Will the project result in the need for major additional infrastructural projects (highways, community facilities)?
2. Will the project be in conflict or competition with other development projects for water, energy, space, etc.?
3. If the response to 1. or 2. is "yes", will the cumulative environmental impact be assessed?
4. Are agencies actively involved with the project responsible for enforcement of laws or regulations applying to:
    a) soil conservation?
    b) water quality?
    c) pesticide use?
    d) protection of valuable ecosystems, flora and fauna (indicate if non-involvement is acceptable or unacceptable)?
5. If the area is susceptible to erosion, have adequate measures been planned to minimize erosion?
6. Will rainfall and cropping practices result in high rates of loss of existing nutrients and applied fertilizer to leaching or runoff?
7. Will erosion result in siltation causing:
    a) loss of aquatic system productivity?
    b) raising of river beds and resultant flooding?
    c) siltation of downstream reservoirs?
8. Has adequate consideration been given to the cost and impact of maintaining pasture in humid climates where weed invasion is a serious problem?

Source: Inter-American Development Bank, *Environmental Checklist for Livestock Reports* (Washington, D.C.: IADB, n.d.), 15–17.

B. *Hydrology and Water Quality*
    9. Will land clearing result in accelerated runoff?
  10. Will runoff contain organic matter or nutrients in quantities detrimental to aquatic ecosystems and fisheries?
  11. If well will supply irrigation water, does withdrawal rate exceed replenishment?

C. *Ecological Values*
  12. Will the project be located in an area of extensive natural vegetation?
  13. Are natural ecosystem services recognized and adequately incorporated in the regional plan, such as:
    a) biological reduction of wastes in aquatic systems?
    b) regulating water flow and controlling erosion?
    c) source of food and possibly saleable products such as timber?
    d) source of recreation?
    e) natural laboratory for scientific research?
    f) habitat for endangered species?
  14. Where livestock compete with wildlife for pasture previously inhabited only by wildlife, what will be the consequences for wildlife survival? Will herdsmen destroy wildlife to protect their livestock?
  15. Will fences and other obstructions provided by the project interfere with wildlife migration or with routes to water? What provision is made to avoid or relieve this interference?
  16. Will "integrated pest management" (combination of biological and chemical controls of pests) be adequately incorporated in the project?
  17. Will the project promote the proliferation of livestock beyond the ability of the natural range to sustain them—resulting in long term productivity losses?
  18. Will improvements in animal health result in accelerated deterioration of natural range quality due to increased livestock populations?

D. *Agricultural Practices*
  19. Does this project contribute to an optimal regional land use balance among:
    a) local food production?
    b) production of livestock or crops?
    c) natural system services including fuel, wood, watershed protection, waste treatment and recreation?

E. *Health Hazards*
   20. Are the following health hazards adequately addressed:
       a) pesticide use?
       b) increase in disease vector habitat?
       c) lack of disease resistance among pre-project population?
       d) introduction of colonists without disease resistance or preventive education to guard against disease?
F. *Social and Cultural Factors*
   21. Are existing indigenous populations in the project area adequately considered in the following areas:
       a) physical displacement by engineering works and new people?
       b) technologically displaced by introduced practices?
       c) loss of cultural integrity and economic status as new people move in?
       d) concentration of land ownership?
   22. Will the people become less adapted to their environment and more dependent on imported materials and technology?
G. *Follow through*
   23. Has an adequate monitoring program been designed to measure the success of environmental protection efforts?
   24. Are specific agencies responsible for project monitoring?

A P P E N D I X   6 - B

World Bank Guidelines
For the Use of Pesticides

1. A pesticides component is now very often incorporated in Bank agricultural projects. As a consequence, this Office has received several requests for advice on the toxicity and the use of certain pesticides.

2. In some cases, the answer given was not complete because the name mentioned was a trade name unknown in the US. To prevent this, sponsors should be asked to supply the chemical name and the common name generally used in the pesticides trade. For instance, if the sponsor decides to use RAVYON, there is no way here to identify the material. The sponsor should give the generally accepted common name CARBARYL, the chemical name 1-naphtyl methyl carbamate, and if possible the chemical formula, or even the US trade name. In this case SEVIN.

Choice of Pesticide

3. The criteria for choosing pesticides should be based on the following factors:

> Biodegradability
> Toxicity to Mammals and Fish
> Risks of Application
> Price

4. Biodegradability should be the most important criterion as stable chemicals will accumulate, and this accumulation can be magnified into the food chain. This is why chlorinated hydrocarbons which are very stable, chemically speaking, should be avoided and why the US Environmental

Source: Environment Department, *Environmental Guidelines* (Washington, D.C.: World Bank, September 1988), 331–336.

Protection Agency banned the following products: DDT, Aldrin, Chlordane, and Heptachlor.

5. Using these products in Bank projects should be avoided if at all possible. If they are absolutely required, the detailed reason should be given; price differential is not a sufficient reason.

6. Depending on when the chemical is used and where it will end up, toxicity for mammals and/or fish should then be taken into account.

7. Toxicity figures show the relative toxicity of the product to laboratory animals (white rats unless otherwise specified). LD_{50} is the dose that kills half of the experimental animals in any test expressed in milligrams of the chemical per kilogram of animal weight. The higher the LD_{50} value, the lower the toxicity. Toxicity can be oral (mouth ingestion), dermal (skin absorption), or inhalation dusts. Special measures should be taken when handling products with high dermal toxicity.

8. Risks of application depend in part on the toxicity but also on the physical properties of the material and the way it is applied. The product can be sold as a concentrate, a solution, an emulsifiable concentrate, a wettable powder, or a dust. It is for instance safer to apply a solution on the ground than a dust, but it may not be always possible to do so. Aerial spraying is potentially the most damaging.

9. Price as an element of choice between two pesticides should only be considered after the other criteria have been decided.

Application of Pesticides
10. Even the safest among pesticides will probably involve some health risks. To avoid any serious accident, the appraisal mission should make sure that the people going to handle or be in contact with the product (dealers — formulators — applicators — farmers) have been properly trained in its use and know about the hazards of handling it. The product should be shipped in adequate containers with labels, clearly identifiable, showing how to use it, how to avoid any problems, and how to give first aid in case of an emergency.

11. The use of casual (migrant) workers for applying pesticides is widespread but should be avoided for the following reasons: These workers

do not have the knowledge or the experience necessary for safe application and they will have a tendency to disregard the safety rules.

12. If these workers must be employed, they must be educated and trained, keeping in mind that their schooling is most of the time inadequate or nonexistent. Secondly, they must work under experienced supervisors doing nothing but supervising the pesticide application.

13. Disposal of containers should not be overlooked. In 1967, 16 people died in Mexico from eating flour and sugar stored in Parathion drums.

14. Common transportation of pesticides and food in the same vehicle should be forbidden. In Colombia 63 people died and 165 became seriously ill from eating flour contaminated with Parathion during transport by truck.

15. For additional details see UNIDO's [the United Nations Industrial Development Organization's] book "Industrial Production and Formulation of Pesticides in Developing Countries" — 2 volumes — UN — New York, 1972.

16. Tables 6-B-1 and 6-B-2 show the acceptable substitutes for EPA-banned pesticides.

17. The following pesticides should not be used: DDT, Aldrin, Dieldrin, Chlordane, Heptachlor, 2,4,5T (2,4,5 Trichlorophenoxyacetic Acid), EBDC (Ethylenebisdithiocarbamate), all mercury compounds, all arsenic compounds, MIREX (Dechlorane), and DBCP (Dibromochloro Propane).

18. The product Phosvel (leptophos), an organo phosphate made but not sold in the United States, should also be banned for its long range effects. Chronic neurological disorders, paralysis, and sometimes death are associated with this chemical believed to eat away myelin, the sheathing around the nerves. The pesticide EDB (Ethylene Dibromide) is a proven carcinogen.

19. The following pesticides are suspect of long-range chronic effects and should be avoided: endrin, toxaphene, strobane, 1080, strychnine, kepone, lindane, cadmium, DECP, BHC, dimethoate, diallates, triallates, chlorobenzilate, ethylene oxide, EPN, carbaryl, aramite, PCP, creosote, chloranil, monourea, benomyl, DDVP, chloroform, (SST) DFF, piperonyl butoxide, rotenone, perthane, safrole, promide and merphos.

TABLE 6-B-1

INSECTICIDES

PRODUCT	DDT	Aldrin	SUBSTITUTE FOR Dieldrin	Chlordane	Heptachlor
Phorate	•	•		•	•
Demeton	•				
Methyl parathion	•				
Parathion	•	•		•	•
Guthion	•				
Aldicarb	•				
Azodrin	•				
Diazionon	•	•		•	•
Dimethoate	•				
Fenthion	•				
Methomyl	•				
Crotoxyphos	•				
Chlorpyrifos	•	•		•	•
Bux		•		•	•
Carbofuran	•	•		•	•
Counter		•		•	•
Dasanit	•	•		•	•
Disulfoton	•	•		•	•
Dyfonate	•	•		•	•
Landrin		•		•	•
Trichlorfon	•	•		•	•
Dacthal				•	
Aspon	•	•	•	•	
Siduron				•	
Ethion	•	•	•	•	
Propoxur	•	•	•	•	•
Acephate	•		•	•	
Methoxychlor	•		•	•	
Endosulfan	•	•	•	•	•

TABLE 6-B-2

HERBICIDES AND INSECTICIDES

	SUBSTITUTE FOR	
HERBICIDES	*2,4,5-T*	*EBDC*
Bromacil	•	
MSCA/DSMA	•	
Cacodylic acid	•	
Dinoseb (DNBP)	•	
Dicamba	•	
Monuron	•	
Simazine	•	
Trifluralin	•	
FUNGICIDES		
Captan		•
PCNB		•
Folpet		•

20. The use of DBCP and EDB should be restricted to cases where no substitutes exist for the considered application. The use of MIREX should be restricted to compounds where it is mixed with products enhancing its photodegradability.

21. In view of the added potential damages to the environment and of the Bank's official policy favoring "Intermediate Technologies," aerial spraying of pesticides should be discouraged whenever it can be replaced by ground spraying.

22. Ultra low volume application (ULV). ULV techniques with quantities habitually below 5 liters per hectare are now well proven and should be promoted in Bank projects either for aerial or ground spraying. To be effective this technique requires proven equipment, strict control of the spray droplets diameter . . . and experienced supervision to take into account the weather conditions. The main pesticides manufacturers will supply technical bulletins on ULV and also trained supervisors.

ADDENDUM

1. The pesticide MIREX (Dechlorane) has been forbidden by the EPA and the same Organization has suspended the use of the pesticide DBCP (Dibromochloro Propane).

2. The pesticide EDB (Ethylene Dibromide) is a proven carcinogen. EPA has cancelled all major uses of EDB and the "largest volume use has been emergency suspended" (an action taken only once before against a pesticide in the entire history of EPA).

3. The use of DBCP and EDB should be restricted to cases where no substitutes exist for the considered application.

A P P E N D I X   6 - C

Selected Wildland Projects Supported by the World Bank

Sri Lanka: Mahaweli Ganga Development III, November 1981
This power, clearing, and irrigation project cost $202 million, 3.4 pecent of which was for the wildland component. The wildland portion was designed to minimize or mitigate damage to the wild elephants and other endangered species affected by the project. It included wildlife corridors and reserves to be created in areas set aside under the project. The program has also been funded by USAID ($5 million) and the Sri Lanka government ($1.9 million).

Cyprus: Limassol Sewerage and Drainage Project, May 1984
This project, costing $37 million, was to provide sewerage service for the city of Limassol. The government proposed a treatment plant to be sited near the edge of the Akrotiri Salt Lake. The wildland component was designed to protect the lake, the habitat for 50 million birds that migrate between Europe and Africa. Problems developed regarding the proposed site, and as of 1987 there was a question as to whether any funds would actually be dispersed.

Brazil: Northwest Agricultural Development
and Environmental Protection, December 1983
This $200 million project (9 percent of which was for the wildland component) provided for agricultural development and land settlement, including access roads, village infrastructure, and agricultural extension services. The wildland component consisted of establishing a national park

Source: George Ledec & Robert Goodland, *Wildlands: Their Protection and Management in Economic Development* (Washington, D.C.: World Bank, 1988), Appendix A.

and biological reserves, which encompass about 15,000 square kilometers of natural ecosystems, largely rainforest. Implementation of the wildlife component lagged behind the other components, so that disbursements were suspended for several months in 1985 until progress on the environmental components improved. Unless unplanned settlement and illegal timber cutting are effectively controlled, the long-term integrity of wildlife management areas is in doubt.

Brazil: Carajás Iron Ore, August 1982
The total cost of the project was $4.5 billion, of which $20 million was to protect the environment and $14 million was to protect Amerindians. The project was for iron ore mining in the Carajás region of the Amazon Basin, a railroad, and port facilities. The wildland component provided for environmental personnel and management of several wildland units, and for the rehabilitation of mined land. A 1983 supervision report indicated that the main problem in implementing the wildland and Amerindian components has been inadequate control of illegal settlement in the vicinity of the mine and railroad.

Brazil: Northeast Rural Development VII Project, July 1987
Of the $191 million total cost for this project, 2.2 percent was for the wildland component. It provided for development of water resources, five small irrigation schemes, 253 simple water supply systems, two fish hatcheries, rural credit, and agricultural extension. The wildlife component provided for Mirador State Park, a watershed of the Itapecuru River.

Colombia: Guavio Hydro Power, May 1981
This was a $1 billion project, $0.3 million of which was for the wildland component. The wildland component consisted of watershed management plans including the protection of existing natural forests and wildlife. In 1985 the Bogota Electric Power Company created a unit to implement the plan.

Colombia: Upper Magdalena Pilot
Watershed Management, April 1982
The project was for watershed management to reduce flooding, soil erosion, and siltation of hydroelectric and irrigation works, and to maintain a regular water supply for irrigation and domestic use. The wildlife component provided for the equipment and operating costs to protect the

natural forest areas, including two national parks. The World Wildlife Fund was to provide technical assistance in developing the national parks component. However, as of December 1986, total project expenditures were only about 20 percent and the wildland component was not completed.

Kenya: Bura Irrigation Settlement, June 1977
This $98 million project, of which 0.3 percent was for the wildland component, provided for resettlement of 5,150 landless families; a canal for irrigation; and the construction of roads, housing, schools, medical facilities, and tree plantations for firewood. The wildland component included measures to protect the area's riverine forest; antipoaching measures; development of alternative watering areas for wildlife away from populated areas; and canal crossings for wildlife. The project has not been successful, and the wildlife component has suffered from poor implementation. For example, the forest is being cut for charcoal production and fuel wood.

Tanzania: Tourism Rehabilitation, January 1979
A project costing $19.5 million, 3.2 percent of which was for the wildland component, provided for rehabilitated hotels and other facilities to attract tourists. The wildland component provided for antipoaching equipment and the monitoring of wildlife populations in the Serengeti National Park. Reports indicate the implementation of the wildland component to be highly satisfactory.

Zambia: Kafue Hydroelectric II, July 1973
The project, costing $138 million, provided for the construction of a hydroelectric dam and power-generating and -transmitting facilities. The wildlife component provided for periodic water releases from the reservoir to replicate the natural seasonal flooding of the Kafue Flats, an important area for cattle and wildlife. However, water releases have not replicated natural flooding conditions as well as was hoped.

The Philippines: Watershed Management
and Erosion Control, August 1980
This $75 million project, 14 percent of which was for wildlands, provided for reforestation of denuded lands with fast-growing species, construction and maintenance of forest roads, and construction of charcoal ovens. The wildland component provided for equipment and vehicles for fire

prevention, protection of natural forests, and resettlement of cultivators. A 1985 supervisory report noted that the program for forest protection and range management showed little progress owing to insufficient commitment on the part of the government.

Sri-Lanka: Tree Crop Diversification, July 1978
The total cost of this project was $6.5 million, of which 0.3 percent was for the wildland component. It provided for agricultural diversification of marginal lands, shrub areas, and degraded forests; the establishment of small farms; soil conservation; and social infrastructure. The wildland component provided for preservation of 21 square kilometers of steep land in conservation areas. There were problems with the resettlement and transfer of workers.

APPENDIX 6-D

Guidelines for Wildlife and Wildland Protection in the Design and Location of Development Projects

1. Wildlife and wildlands impacted by a project should be identified and adverse impacts avoided or mitigated in the project design, with the cost incorporated into the budget.

2. Projects should not be located in areas containing existing or proposed protected areas; known endangered species; important breeding, feeding, or staging areas for wildlife or fish; or important water catchments.

3. Wildlife management goals should be identified and translated into specific measures, with a budget for implementing them. These measures include the hiring and training of personnel; provision of infrastructure and equipment; and the policy environment—legal, economic, and institutional—that supports the objectives. For example, in the Alto Turi land settlement projects, the World Bank's appraisal report specified conservation of two forest blocks containing 1,000 square kilometers, but this measure was never translated into an actual wildlife component with the necessary budget for implementation.

4. When development of wildlands is justified, less valuable rather than more valuable wildlands should be converted, and the loss of wildlands should be offset by a compensatory wildlife management component that supports preservation of a similar ecological area.

5. Wildlife management areas (WMAs) must be large enough to conserve biological diversity, safeguard evolutionary processes, and provide extensive environmental services.

Source: George Ledec and Robert Goodland, *Wildlands: Their Protection and Management in Economic Development* (Washington, D.C.: World Bank, 1988), Appendices C and D.

6. The government must have sufficient commitment and ability to establish and maintain the WMAs and other wildland components of a project. This includes financing for the components. In many cases, it is preferable for the MDB to provide the financing.

7. Carrying out wildland components may be contingent upon the support of the local people who are affected. Such support often depends on including the locals in WMA planning and benefits, and on rural development investments that provide an alternative to encroachment.

8. Agricultural or land settlement projects that expand a cultivated area by clearing wildlands should not be based on wildlands that are of the greatest value for biological conservation or environmental services. Any projects converting sizable wildland areas should routinely support the establishment or improved management of a compensatory WMA in an ecologically similar area.

9. Unique arid wildlands with high biological value should not be irrigated. A few square kilometers in desert and semidesert areas may harbor the entire world population of a highly endemic plant species. Care should also be taken to prevent excessive water diversion and the runoff of fertilizers and biocides from significantly harming downstream aquatic life. Large irrigation canals can block movement of wildlife unless properly situated with appropriate crossings provided.

10. Cattle and other livestock may displace wildlife and may degrade and desertify grazing lands. Hence, livestock development loans should be contingent on sound stocking densities that do not lead to overgrazing. Since livestock fences may impede wildlife migration routes, or even kill animals that become entangled, their use should be avoided in areas with important wildlife resources.

11. Certain wildlands sustain important species of fish, crustaceans, and mollusks. These areas include freshwater swamp forests, freshwater and saltwater marshes, mangroves, estuaries, coral reefs, and other wetland and coastal shallows. These should be protected in all fishery projects, including credit, marketing, processing facilities, boat building, and ports.

12. Water development projects can reduce fishery productivity by harming aquatic wildlands. Pollution from agriculture and industry can jeopardize the survival of valuable fish species or affect their marketability because of concentrations of toxic substances.

13. An important cause of species extinction is the introduction of nonnative species that prey on or out-compete native species. For example,

the introduction of common carp in Brazil has led to muddy waters and losses of vegetation, thereby threatening the survival of native species. Non-native species should not be introduced into natural lakes and rivers unless scientific assessments of the risks from ecological disruption have been completed.

14. Highways and rural roads imperil wildlife when they penetrate previously remote wildland areas. The main problem is that they provide access for slash-and-burn cultivators, spontaneous settlers, timber cutters, and hunters.

15. Coral reefs constitute an important form of wildlife and should be protected.

NOTES

1. This material is based on an unpublished review of the audit for 125 livestock projects and projects with significant livestock components. It was prepared by the Operations Evaluation Department of the World Bank.
2. Assume the official rate is ten pesos per dollar, but the free market rate is fifteen pesos per dollar. The peso value of each dollar borrowed is ten pesos at the official rate, but the government loans pesos to farmers that are only two-thirds as valuable on the free market. If the government borrows $1 million from an MDB, it will loan 10 million pesos to farmers, but at the free market rate (which tends to reflect the true value of the peso in dollars) the government lends the peso equivalent of only $667,000.
3. For a more detailed discussion, see George Ledec and Robert Goodland (1988, Ch. 4).
4. For a discussion of the methodologies for measuring the economic value of wildlife, see Daniel J. Decker and Gary R. Goff (1987) and G. L. Peterson and A. Randall (1984).
5. The MADIA Discussion Papers from which the analysis in this section is based are Uma Lele (1989a & 1989b); Lele and L. Richard Meyers (1989); Lele and Steven W. Stone (1989); Lele, Robert Christiansen, and Kundhabi Kadiresan (1989); Lele and Rahul Jain (1989); and Lele et al. (1989).
6. Donor agencies are the World Bank, USAID, UK Overseas Development Administration, Swedish International Development Authority, Danish International Development Agency, the European Community, and the Governments of France and West Germany.

REFERENCES

Barnes, Douglas F., and Jose Olivares. 1988. *Sustainable Resource Management in Agriculture and Rural Development Projects: A Review of Bank Policies, Procedures and Results.* Environmental Department Working Paper No. 5. Washington, D.C.: World Bank, June.

Bonfiglioli, A. M. 1988. "Management of the Pastoral Production in the Sahel: Constraints and Options." In *Desertification Control and Renewable Resource Management in the Sahelian and Sudanian Zones of West Africa,* Technical Paper No. 70, edited by F. Falloux and A. Mukendi. Washington, D.C.: World Bank.

Bon Prischke, J. D. 1984. "Improving Donor Intervention in Rural Finance." In *Undermining Rural Development with Cheap Credit,* edited by Dale W. Adams. Boulder, Colo.: Westview Press.

Bouis, R. D., and Lawrence J. Haddad. 1990. *Effects of Agricultural Commercialization on Land Tenure, Household Resource Allocation, and Nutrition in the Philippines.* Washington, D.C.: International Food Policy Research Institute, January.

Davis, Ted J., and Isabel A. Schirmer, eds. 1987. *Sustainability Issues in Agricultural Development: Proceedings of the Seventh Agriculture Sector Symposium.* Washington, D.C.: World Bank, November.

Decker, Daniel J., and Gary R. Goff, eds. 1987. *Valuing Wildlife: Economic and Social Perspectives.* Boulder, Colo.: Westview Press.

Environment Department. 1988. *Environmental Guidelines.* Washington, D.C.: World Bank, September.

Fauck, R. 1977. "Erosion and Mechanization." In *Soil Conservation and Management in the Humid Tropics,* edited by D. J. Greeland and R. Lal. New York: Wiley and Sons.

Krueger, Anne O., Constantine Michalopolous, and Vernon W. Ruttan. 1989. *Aid and Development.* Baltimore: Johns Hopkins Univ. Press.

Ledec, George, and Robert Goodland. 1988. *Wildlands: Their Protection and Management in Economic Development.* Washington, D.C.: World Bank.

Lele, Uma. 1989a. *Agricultural Growth, Domestic Policies, the External Environment, Assistance to Africa: Lessons of a Quarter Century.* MADIA Discussion Paper No. 1. Washington, D.C.: World Bank.

_____, ed. 1989b. *Managing Agricultural Development in Africa: Three Articles on Lessons from Experience.* MADIA Discussion Paper No. 2. Washington, D.C.: World Bank.

Lele, Uma, and L. Richard Meyers. 1989. *Growth and Structural Change in East Africa: Domestic Policies, Agriculture Performance, and World Bank Assistance, 1963–86, Parts I and II.* MADIA Discussion Paper No. 3. Washington, D.C.: World Bank.

Lele, Uma, and Steven W. Stone. 1989. *Population Pressure, the Environment and Agriculture Intensification.* MADIA Discussion Paper No. 4. Washington, D.C.: World Bank.

Lele, Uma, Robert Christiansen, and Kundhabi Kadiresan. 1989. *Fertilizer Policy in Africa.* MADIA Discussion Paper No. 5. Washington, D.C.: World Bank.

Lele, Uma, and Rahul Jain, 1989. *Aid to African Agriculture: Lessons from Two Decades of Donor Experience: A Synthesis.* Washington, D.C.: World Bank.

Lele, Uma et al. 1989. "Nigeria's Economic Development, Agriculture's Role, and World Bank Assistance, 1961–88: Lessons for the Future." Mimeo. Washington, D.C.: World Bank.

Leonard, H. J. 1987. *Natural Resources and Economic Development in Central*

America: A Regional Environmental Profile. Washington, D.C.: International Institute for Environment and Development.

MacNeill, J. 1989. "Strategies for Sustainable Economic Development." *Scientific American* 261, no. 3 (September), 154–165.

Peterson, G. L., and A. Randall, eds. 1984. *Valuation of Wildlands Resource Benefits.* Boulder, Colo: Westview Press.

Pingali, Prabhu, Yves Bigot, and Hans P. Binswanger. 1987. *Agricultural Mechanization and the Pollution of Farming Systems in Sub-Saharan Africa.* Baltimore: Johns Hopkins Univ. Press for the World Bank.

Repetto, Robert. 1985. *Paying the Price: Pesticide Subsidies in Developing Countries.* Washington, D.C.: World Resources Institute, December.

_____. 1988. *Economic Policy Reform for Natural Resource Conservation.* Environmental Department Working Paper No. 4. Washington, D.C.: World Bank, May.

Standford, Stephen. 1983. *Management of Pastoral Development in the Third World.* New York: Wiley and Sons for Overseas Development Institute.

Weatherly, W. Paul. 1983. "Insect Pest Outbreaks." In *Natural Systems for Development: What Planners Need to Know,* edited by Richard A. Carpenter. New York: Macmillan.

World Bank. 1987. *Twelfth Annual Review of Project Performance Results.* Washington, D.C.: World Bnak.

_____. 1988a. *Rural Development: World Bank Experience 1965–1986.* Washington, D.C.: World Bank.

_____. 1988b. *Project Performance Results for 1986.* Washington, D.C.: World Bank.

_____. 1989. *Sub-Saharan Africa from Crisis to Sustainable Growth: A Long-Term Perspective Study.* Washington, D.C.: World Bank, November.

_____. 1990. *Annual Report 1989.* Washington, D.C.: World Bank.

Zavaleta, Luis. 1990. "The Paradox of Subsidized Credit." In *The IDB.* Washington, D.C.: Inter-American Development Bank, 4 March, 4–7.

CHAPTER 7

Infrastructure and the Extractive Industries

Power

MDBs have helped finance hundreds of power projects, beginning with the World Bank's loan for a power project in Chile in 1948. About 18 percent of all World Bank loans, 20 percent of ADB loans, and 25 percent of IADB loans go for power. Approximately half of the World Bank-financed power generation has been for hydro and the other half has been for thermal (oil-gas and coal). Half of all power loans have been for transmission and distribution. MDBs have favored the power sector for a number of reasons: (1) Power generation is highly capital-intensive, with a substantial foreign exchange component. Hence, large capital transfers can be made in a single package, thus reducing administrative costs. (2) Power projects generally involve large contracts with international engineering and construction companies to build all or large sections of the project, thereby simplifying administration. (3) Virtually all power projects in developing countries are in the public sector, so the government is the borrower. (4) Power projects satisfy the traditional MDB preference for infrastructure lending. (5) Power projects are popular with governments, especially those dominated by urban industrial and political leaders. They often serve as a means of transferring resources from the agricultural sector to the urban economy. Moreover, development has traditionally been associated with rapid industrial growth and with the creation of modern urban centers with power-intensive facilities. Many hydropower projects contribute to both irrigated agriculture and industrial-urban development.

We discussed the environmental impacts of hydroelectric power generation in Chapter 4. Dams are often located in prime forest areas open to destruction by the reservoirs and by the roads built to haul equipment and workers. The dam sites may also attract migrants who clear the forest for agricultural use. Since the power-generating facilities are often located hundreds of miles from the cities and factories using the power, transmission lines cross large areas of forest or agricultural land. (Power generated by fossil fuels in the industrial and urban areas may give rise to air pollution, but it destroys less land and rivers.) Hydropower is generally lower in cost per kilowatt-hour than power produced from oil or coal, which is its principal attraction, but its cost in social terms is not included in a country's energy budget.

Traditionally, proponents of low-cost power in developing countries have argued that it promotes industry, which is often improperly identified with development. Actually, the availability of low-cost power does not in itself attract industry, either domestic or foreign. Many other conditions—such as the availability of raw materials at world market prices, government investment policies, wage rates and labor union practices, and the availability of markets—are more important than the cost of power. Although certain industries are energy-intensive, manufacturing industries suitable for poor countries tend to be labor-intensive. In such industries, power may represent less than 5 percent of total production costs. Moreover, the generation of power at a source hundreds of miles from where it is consumed may cost only one-third of the *total* power cost, which also includes transmission and distribution. Large hydroelectric facilities hundreds of miles from where power is to be consumed, then, may have relatively little cost advantage over the use of fossil fuel in the cities. The monetary savings may not be sufficient to offset the social costs of building a huge hydroelectric complex on a river.

We are not arguing that MDBs should never finance power generation. The point we are making is that planners should take into account the social costs of environmentally harmful projects, such as the hydroelectric power complexes financed by MDBs throughout the Third World, when making comparisons with alternative sources of energy and with energy conservation. In most countries, conservation could eliminate the need to increase energy-producing capacity over the next decade or more—and at a much lower cost.

CONSERVATION

Governments could encourage energy conservation by requiring both industrial and household consumers to pay the full social cost of the energy they use and by promoting the use of energy-efficient equipment. Instead, they have tended to sell power to household users and to industry at *subsidized* rates; in fact, utility rates of all kinds—power, telephone, water, and so on—are so politicized that governments often fear raising rates in line with inflation. Power subsidies not only encourage a broader use of power but also discourage conservation. Even if rates approximate the full monetary costs of power production and distribution, they rarely include full social costs. If they did, rates would be significantly higher and conservation and alternative sources of energy would be more attractive.

Energy specialists have suggested that Brazil, India, Costa Rica, and many other developing countries could cut their need for expanded power-generating capacity by 30 percent or more by investing in more energy-efficient industrial equipment, lighting systems, air-conditioners, and other appliances. The cost of this type of energy-saving investment is often a third or a quarter the cost of an investment to produce the equivalent amount of new power from new generating facilities (Rich 1990, 11). US and Brazilian engineers have estimated that Brazilians could eliminate about two-thirds of the projected need for increased electricity consumption in their country over the next decade just by increasing efficiency in their use of power. Moreover, this would save utilities from having to invest at least $38 billion (in 1985 dollars); instead they would have to invest only about $8 billion in end-use efficiency (Geller et al. 1988).

During 1988–1989 the World Bank was considering a $500 million loan to Brazil for planning and constructing 145 major hydroelectric dams, more than 20 of which would have been in the Amazon Basin. These dams would have flooded more than 60 million acres of tropical rainforest. At the urging of conservation groups, the US Treasury Department opposed this loan. In March 1989 the Bank announced that it had withdrawn the power sector loan and was instead considering an environmental protection loan to Brazil for some $350–$400 million. About $100 million would be invested in energy conservation and efficiency; the remainder would support a new Brazilian environmental protection agency. The withdrawal of the power sector loan came after a two-year delay in loan approval and strong pressure from international environmental and human rights groups and from the Brazilian Indians whose culture would have been jeopardized by some of the proposed dams.

The World Bank is managing an Energy Sector Management Assistance Program (ESMAP) in collaboration with the UNDP and several bilateral aid agencies. The ESMAP, created in 1983, provides technical assistance for energy sector development in member countries and has been especially active in preparing preinvestment studies for energy-efficiency and renewable-energy projects. However, in 1987 less than 1 percent of the Bank's energy sector lending projects made use of ESMAP services. Conservationists have criticized the Bank for not making sufficient use of this facility (VanDomelen 1988, 27–28).

The Bank has been making a series of loans to India for hydroelectric power, including one for the Sardar Sarovar dam. Over the past decade the Indian government has spent nearly $50 billion on its energy sector, accounting for 30 percent of all federal spending. However, even with India's installed electrical capacity doubled during this period, it has not kept pace with demand, and the country has an estimated 10 percent shortage of supply over demand. The recent rate of expansion of India's energy capacity is unlikely to continue. According to one estimate, if it did, 99 percent of India's total federal budget would go to the energy sector alone by 2020, and all of India's hydropower potential would be tapped. Indian NGOs and US conservationists have pressured MDBs against making further power loans to India because of their environmental effects and because of the growing capital costs in both rupees and foreign exchange. India's investment must shift from projects designed to create new energy capacity to ones requiring less energy.

CONCLUSIONS

Energy conservation and reduced demand in both industry and households can make an important contribution to the environment and to efficient resource allocation in Third World countries. Subsidized power encourages urban households in poor countries to consume electricity that the country cannot afford if it is to allocate its limited capital resources for sustainable development. Subsidies also promote the use of energy- and capital-intensive technology in countries with surplus labor. MDBs should encourage energy conservation by shifting the majority of energy sector lending from power production to energy conservation; requiring recipients of all energy loans to adopt long-term social marginal cost pricing and eliminate all subsidies; investigating alternative energy projects less damaging to the environment; and requiring energy-producing companies (whether public or private) to internalize all costs associated with the generation and transmission of power.

Industrial Pollution

Industrialization in the Third World has brought with it rapidly increasing air, water, and land pollution and other adverse environmental conditions such as occupational health and safety hazards. Most of the larger metropolitan areas in Asia and Latin America are subject to high levels of air pollution; adjacent rivers are loaded with industrial and household sewage; and hazardous waste accumulates in dumps. Although automobiles and households are responsible for much of the air pollution, industrial plants in metropolitan areas have also contributed to it. In 1980 in Malaysia 39 percent of total pollution came from industries, with power plants contributing more than half the SO_2 (Carpenter & Sani 1983, 342–343). In Manila, where air quality is among the worst in Southeast Asia, only half of the one thousand industrial plants comply with minimal air-emission standards. In Egypt, the Alexandria harbor, contaminated by chemicals and oil, is one of the most polluted areas on the Mediterranean.

Loans to industry have averaged about 6 percent of World Bank and IDA lending since the beginning of operations and were about 9 percent of lending in FY 1989. Industry loans accounted for about 4 percent of ADB lending and 13 percent of IADB lending (including mining) since the beginning of operations. All three institutions have formulated environmental guidelines (including emissions standards) for industrial plants, disaggregated by major industrial sectors (ADB 1987; Environment Department 1988). But only recently have EIAs been required for most industrial projects supported by MDB financing.

The industries that benefit most from MDB project loans are pulp and paper, fertilizer, steel, petrochemical, pesticide, and textile. Each of these industries presents special problems for air, water, or ground pollution. Pulp mills, for example, often emit offensive odors, but they do their greatest damage to the rivers and lakes that supply the water for their operation (and to which their waste water returns). Many pulp-and-paper-mill effluents are toxic to organisms such as fish, and when the toxins accumulate in the fish, they may injure humans. Chlorine used to bleach paper gives rise to dioxins, which are believed to be harmful even at very low levels.

It is important that industrial projects include equipment for pollution control and treatment and proper operating instructions for meeting specific standards for each type of pollutant, and that arrangements be made to assure proper equipment operation by trained workers when a plant goes on stream. The MDBs usually set such requirements in their loan agreements, but unless provision is made for a local environmental authority to monitor the plants, there is no guarantee that the standards will be met. This involves legislative and institutional arrangements to ensure compliance with environmental standards set forth in the EIA and the loan agreement.

Even the best possible project design will not assure proper environmental operation. The private industry must also be willing to observe environmental standards, and government policies must induce private cooperation. For example, a 1980 agreement between the World Bank, Brazilian federal and state governments, and the US government provided for a $58 million loan to be used for pollution-control projects in greater São Paulo. The loan proceeds were to be re-lent to private industry for pollution control at subsidized interest rates. But few applied for the loans, largely because government control standards and enforcement were lax and private firms lacked the incentive to control pollution (Pearson 1987, 215). It should also be noted that much of the industrial pollution in developing countries is created by government-owned and -managed plants.

Where industry projects are identifiable an MDB can insist that a plant be equipped with pollution-control and monitoring equipment or with the "best available control technology" (BACT), using standards developed by the industrial countries. Standards should be applied to discharges into air and water bodies as well as to the treatment of solid waste, including hazardous materials. However, pollution control applied only to a few individual plants receiving assistance from MDBs is unlikely to do much for the environment. Pollution control involves maintaining ambient standards and requiring that abatement regulations be applied to all industrial plants within a given area, not just to those receiving MDB assistance.

MDBs can apply guidelines and environmental loan conditions to relatively few identifiable industrial projects that they finance. Virtually all the $1.9 billion in World Bank and IDA loans to industry in FY 1989 were "industrial sector loans." They were not loans to construct individual plants but rather were for financing a broad range of improvements in a number of industrial plants by providing for such things as credits for the purchase of inputs, technical assistance, rehabilitation and modernization, and environmental-control and monitoring equipment. Some World Bank and IDA credits for the industrial sector are provided from the proceeds of loans to "development finance companies"; these are different from industry loans. Structural adjustment loans (SALs) or other forms of nonproject loans provide other support for industry. To a considerable degree, the ADB and the IADB follow this same lending pattern.

These conditions suggest that MDB efforts to promote environmental protection and resource conservation should include agreements with borrowing governments to establish environmental controls on all industries operating in entire metropolitan areas or regions. These agreements might be part of the negotiations and disbursements of sector loans, or they might be included in the conditionality for SALs.

Mining Projects

Mining and associated mineral processing are among the most environmentally harmful activities. Developing countries produce more than half the minerals consumed by the market-economy countries, but until recently the environmental impacts of mines received little attention. These impacts include soil destruction; sedimentation in rivers and lakes; toxic chemicals discharged in rivers, lakes, and groundwater; deforestation; large scars on the land; and air pollution. Multinational mining enterprises, some nationalized and now operated by government corporations, have built most of the large metal mines in developing countries, but state-owned mining companies have built others, such as the Brazilian iron mines, and still others have been joint ventures involving both multinational enterprises and governments.

Prior to 1977 MDBs made few loans for mineral development. Financing petroleum and nonfuel minerals production was mainly regarded as the province of multinational firms and private banks. Several events led to a change in this policy. One was the widespread nationalization of foreign-owned mining enterprises that took place in Third World countries in the late 1960s and early 1970s. Not only was it considered the right of sovereign countries to expropriate foreign-owned properties in the resource industries, Third World governments argued that international agencies should facilitate such actions. This position found expression in a UN resolution (UN 1974) that called on "agencies of the UN system to meet requests for assistance from developing countries in connection with the operation of nationalized means of production." A second development was a reduced flow of private equity capital to Third World mineral industries brought on by the wave of expropriations. MDBs became concerned that sufficient capital and technology would not be forthcoming for exploration and for development of mineral-producing capacity. Finally, during the early 1970s there was widespread fear of a world shortage of nonfuel minerals, induced in part by a sharp rise in metal prices. As a consequence, a World Bank staff report (unpublished) assessed the growing capital requirements of the nonfuel mineral industries and recommended a large World Bank Group assistance program for mineral projects (Mikesell 1987, 130).

The US government and the governments of several other industrial countries believed that MDB financial assistance for mining projects should mainly serve as a catalyst for attracting private international equity and loans, rather than provide financing to state mining enterprises (SMEs). The US government also argued that the IFC could bolster the confidence of private investors in Third World countries by taking a minority equity position in, or making loans to, private domestic and foreign mining firms. Beginning in July 1977, the World Bank's executive directors announced a policy of increasing loans for nonfuel mineral development, with emphasis on loans serving as catalysts for the flow of private equity and loan capital (World Bank 1978, 21). The World Bank Group planned to lend about a billion dollars over the 1978–1982 period in support of Third World investment in nonfuel minerals. Actually, the amount loaned was short of the announced goal. During the period July 1978 to June 1983, World Bank and IDA loans to the mining sector totaled $550 million, mainly to SMEs. During the years 1978–1983, the IFC made loans and equity investments for private metal mining and processing projects totaling about $287 million. Most IADB loans to the mining sector have also been made to SMEs. For example, they include several loans to the Peruvian SME Centromin (owned by a US company, Cerro de Pasco, before it was expropriated in 1974). The IADB's largest mining loan ($268 million) went to the Chilean SME CODELCO in 1983 for expanding copper production.

CODELCO has also received substantial loans from the World Bank (Mikesell & Whitney 1987, 161–163). MDB loans to the mining sector have mainly financed the production of copper, iron ore, bauxite, nickel, tin, lead, and zinc. The US government has opposed some of these loans to the copper industries of Peru and Chile, with its representatives on MDB boards voting against them (Mikesell 1987), but the US cannot veto them. The US government has not opposed IFC assistance to the mining sector even though some IFC loans or equity investments have been made to joint ventures involving both private and state mining enterprises (Mikesell & Whitney 1987, 162).

During the 1970s the World Bank made several loans to mining enterprises developed by multinational mining companies but with minority ownership by a government. For example, in 1972 the Bank made a $32 million loan to finance water facilities and other infrastructure for the Selebi-Phikwe mine in Botswana, which is majority owned by AMAX and Anglo-American with a minority interest held by the Botswana government. In 1979 the World Bank made an $80 million loan to the Cerro Matoso nickel mine in Colombia, which is majority owned by US and foreign mining companies. The loan is guaranteed by the Colombian government. Again, there is no evidence of an EIA.

Since 1983 MDBs have made few loans to the mining sector, largely because of low world metal prices during the 1980s. World Bank loans in the 1980s have financed iron production in Brazil and Liberia, and two loans helped finance copper mining in Zambia. The IADB has made few loans for mining since its loan to Chile in 1983. Many MDB loans to the mining sector have been for processing equipment and for the expansion of existing mine complexes rather than for new mines. In such cases, EIAs are rarely required, although environmental problems are nearly always present. For IFC loans and equity participations in mines developed by multinational mining companies, EIAs were not required before 1990. It is impossible to believe that environmental problems were not present in these projects.

In 1985 the IADB made a $108 million loan to finance bauxite mining in Venezuela, but the mine was still only 40 percent completed by 1989. Evidently reflecting its interest in the environment, the IADB sent a special mission to review the environmental impacts of the mine on the soil, the forests, and the Indian tribes in the area (IADB 1989, 109–110). This is one of the few cases where environmental action has been taken with respect to MDB loans for mining investments.

ENVIRONMENTAL PROBLEMS

Mines are distinguished as surface (or open-pit) mines or underground mines. Surface mining is widely used for bauxite, coal, copper, gold, iron ore, nickel, tin, uranium, and industrial diamonds, among other minerals. Underground mines are also sometimes used for copper, gold, nickel, and coal, as well as for silver, lead, and zinc. Surface mining is more environmentally destructive than underground mining and requires a larger commitment of funds for reclamation. It disrupts a large land area and adversely affects forests, wildlife migration, natural hydrology, and soil. At most mines in developing countries ore is processed through the concentration stage, but a few mines include smelters that may produce serious air pollution. Since most mines are in mountainous areas far from cities, they require special construction of large communities, complete with power, transportation, water, and living facilities. Usually the mining area is sparsely inhabited so that a local population is not forced to resettle. When a modern mining complex is located in an area inhabited by a tribal society, it creates serious cultural and economic disruption, often leading to conflicts. This is perhaps best illustrated by Conzinc Riotinto of Australia's mine on the island of Bougainville in Papua New Guinea, where tribal protests stopped mining operations during 1989 and 1990.

Surface mining requires removing millions of tons of overburden to expose the mineable ore. Disrupting the topsoil this way can send a large volume of sediment into adjacent waterways. Sediment clogs stream channels, destroys aquatic habitat, and carries with it other pollutants. Roadways function as conduits for sediment to wash down from other areas into natural drainage systems. Mining on steep terrain can create substantial sediment damage. In recent years a number of mining operations have involved the removal of entire mountains, with consequent soil loss from rainfall and runoff, accompanied by chemical and acid pollution. The Ok Tedi gold-copper mine in Papua New Guinea and the original Ertsberg mine in Irian Jaya, Indonesia are examples of mountaintop mining in tropical areas with heavy rainfall. Technology exists to limit soil erosion by controlling water runoff and by stabilizing the soil during mine preparation and operation. Following surface mining of a particular area, the land should be reclaimed, returned to a condition capable of supporting prior land use. All surface areas should be stabilized and protected to control slides, erosion, and accompanying water pollution. To prevent water pollution, mine wastes must be properly disposed of.

In underground mining, solid waste from digging required to reach the mineral seams is transported to the surface and dumped in piles. Ore is taken to the surface by belts or carts and transported to treatment plants. In some cases, it is leached or otherwise treated by liquids. Steps should be taken to insure that the leached material and surface runoff from the piles do not pollute surface or groundwater.

In most mineral operations the ore is finely ground and placed in concentrators to separate the metal from the waste material. The concentrate, usually containing about one-third metal, then goes to a smelter. This process leaves behind a great deal of waste material. The material seriously pollutes waterways, either when it is dumped into streams and lakes or when it is left in piles and runoff pollutes watercourses or groundwater. Tailings are generally acidic and contain various toxic materials, including metals. The case study of the Ok Tedi mine in Papua New Guinea illustrates some of these problems (see Appendix 7-A).

Smelters also produce waste materials of a toxic nature and, more importantly, produce sulfur dioxide and other gases harmful to humans, livestock, and vegetation. The amount of pollutants depends on the type of smelter and on the use of antipollution devices such as scrubbers. Smelters in developing countries should be required to meet the same air-quality standards now required in industrial countries.

IMPLEMENTING ENVIRONMENTAL REGULATIONS

Most developing countries have laws and regulations relating to mining and a department of the government charged with administration. However, environmental authorities are often weak in dealing with the mining industry. Large mines are under the control of either SMEs or multinational corporations whose activities and initial agreements to operate in the country are controlled by the ministries of mines and finance. SMEs often have considerable independence and political influence, in part because they are foreign exchange earners.

Several factors make it difficult to implement sound environmental policies in mining. First, comprehensive environmental impact assessments made during a feasibility study are costly, are subject to substantial uncertainty, and frequently lead to differences between the mine developer and the government agency responsible for environmental practices. Second, capital expenditures for building waste rock and tailing dams can be very large, constituting a substantial percentage of the capital required for the mine. Not only is the cost of these facilities uncertain, but they are subject to frequent breakdowns and destruction because of landslides. Appendix 7-A illustrates this well. Regardless of whether the state or a multinational company owns the mine, the return on investment is highly sensitive to capital expenditures, and whether a project goes forward depends upon the expected total capital outlay. Because the tax structure makes government returns from the project highly dependent on net profits, both the government and the private company are anxious to limit capital outlays for environmental protection. Private firms will not agree to go ahead with a project without some limit on their liability for environmental protection expenditures. Since both the government and the private mining company have a common interest in limiting these expenditures, the government is willing to make compromises on environmental safeguards to prevent either a breakdown in negotiations on the project or a substantial reduction in the expected net profits of the enterprise.

A further problem with implementing environmental standards in developing countries is that NGOs cannot sue a government when it violates environmental legislation, either in its own operations or in its agreements with private enterprise. In most developing countries the judiciary is not independent from the administrative branch. Therefore, it is unlikely that the judiciary will decide in favor of NGOs in important cases brought against the government.

Some of these issues complicate MDB efforts to impose rigid environmental standards in loans that support mining enterprises. Environmental hazards are frequently discovered only after a costly period of exploration and, in some cases, only after construction is well advanced and hundreds of millions of dollars have already been spent. As illustrated by the Ok Tedi case study (Appendix 7-A), serious complications may arise when a mine is to be developed by a multinational corporation (MNC). The MNC may be willing to undertake only a minimal amount of environmental investigation before entering into a mining agreement, and may also insist on a limit to its environmental expenditures before and during the construction period. Perhaps the answer is that a mine should not be constructed if it poses severe environmental risks and if neither the government nor the private investor is willing to underwrite these risks.

Petroleum

Prior to the petroleum crisis brought about by the Organization of Petroleum Exporting Countries (OPEC) oil embargo and the sharp increase in world oil prices in 1973–1974, MDBs provided little assistance for petroleum development. As in mining, financing petroleum production and exploration was considered the province of multinational petroleum companies and private banks. The sharp rise in oil prices was especially harmful to the balance of payments of oil importing developing countries (OIDCs), some of which had oil-producing potential. In 1974 a UN agency was proposed to finance exploration and development of energy resources in the OIDCs. The US and other industrial countries rejected the idea. However, they were interested in having the World Bank finance certain petroleum activities, provided such financing complemented rather than substituted for private petroleum exploration and development.

In July 1977 the executive directors of the World Bank approved a program calling for expanded lending for the development of fuel and non-fuel mineral resources in member countries (World Bank 1978, 20–22). In a report dated August 1980, the Bank outlined an assistance program for energy development for 1981–1985 that included (1) assisting in energy sector review; (2) promoting oil and gas exploration; and (3) investing in oil and gas production. The report stated that "we shall seek to maximize participation by private companies which have traditionally provided risk capital and necessary knowhow. However, in some cases . . . international oil companies may seek the presence of the Bank at the exploration stage, or the Bank may be requested to participate in financing exploration programs undertaken jointly by private and national oil companies, or by national oil companies alone" (World Bank 1980, 74–75).

The Bank envisaged a lending program of about $4.0 billion for the period 1981–1985 for oil and gas development. In late 1980 World Bank President Robert S. McNamara proposed a new energy facility with capital of about $10 billion to be subscribed by the governments of industrialized and OPEC countries. Early in 1981 the Reagan administration declined to participate in this proposed Bank affiliate, and it was dropped. However, the Bank did go ahead with a program for financing petroleum in both non-OPEC oil-exporting developing countries and OIDCs. About $1 billion was made available to national governments or state-owned enterprises (SOEs) for exploration and development projects in which no domestic private or foreign equity was invested. SOEs could borrow smaller amounts so that they could participate in joint petroleum ventures with foreign companies; and about $100 million went to promote exploration. The World Bank made loans to SOEs in India (more than $550 million), Turkey, Peru, Morocco, Argentina, Egypt, and Tanzania. Most of these funds were loaned before 1983, when the price of oil dropped sharply from the levels reached in the early 1980s. During the early 1980s, the IADB also made loans to SOEs in several Latin American countries — Jamaica, Brazil, Colombia, and Peru — for petroleum exploration and development.

ENVIRONMENTAL IMPACTS

Despite the pictures in petroleum company advertisements of oil wells and pipelines operating alongside nesting birds and grazing deer, oil exploration and production can be very destructive. Development frequently takes place in tropical forests, wetlands, delicate Arctic environments, or offshore areas. On land, oil development usually requires roads for transporting drilling equipment, pipe, and other materials. The roads and pipelines themselves create ecological damage when trees are felled and wildlife habitat disturbed. Spontaneous settlers may do even more damage when provided access to primitive areas. Settlers may also have an adverse impact on indigenous forest people, whose lands may be taken from them or whose lives may be so disrupted that they cannot continue their traditional way of life as hunters and gatherers.

Developing countries are often desperate either for foreign exchange or to save exchange by producing oil domestically to replace oil imports (which sometimes account for 25 percent or more of their import bill). Governments of these countries are often willing to sacrifice forest reserves and nature parks for exploration. MDBs should discourage petroleum development in environmentally vulnerable areas — certainly in areas that have been set aside as national parks or wildlife reserves. The World Bank Group has formulated guidelines for protecting such areas from destructive development, but even very recently these guidelines have been violated. A good example is the Ecuadorian government's decision to negotiate contracts with international petroleum companies for production in the Yasuni National Park, a decision facilitated by funds from a World Bank loan to construct a 175-kilometer road into the park. This appears to directly violate the Bank's policies on investment in wildland areas and on investment having an adverse impact on the rights and welfare of indigenous people.

Yasuni National Park is a tropical rainforest with some of the greatest biological diversity in South America. It is the habitat of harpy eagles, macaws, jaguars, anacondas, manatees, freshwater dolphins, monkeys, and hundreds of endangered species. It is also inhabited by the few remaining tribes of the Huaorani, most of whom have had little or no contact with the outside world. Experience with similar situations has shown that the construction of a new road will very likely increase colonization, resulting in destruction of vast tracts of tropical forest. As in the case of the Brazilian Amazon, such colonization leads to destruction of valuable species of flora and fauna while contributing little to agricultural production because of poor-quality soil. In a letter[1] to the president of the World Bank, a number of Ecuadorian NGOs vigorously protested petroleum exploration and development in the traditional territories of Ecuador's Amazonian indigenous peoples. As a minimum, the government of Ecuador should be required to legalize the traditional territories of these people and guarantee that petroleum development will not pollute their environment or have adverse economic or sociocultural impacts. Officials of the Sierra Club and other conservation groups have also strongly protested to the US-based Conoco Corporation, which negotiated the oil contracts. An alternative to constructing the road would be building an oil pipeline with helicopters and cargo planes. A US petroleum company in the Marona Santiago province of Ecuador is using this method.

In 1990 an environmental law group in Ecuador, CORDAVI, brought suit to stop the Conoco project, arguing that issuing oil leases in a national park is illegal. The government then moved the park boundaries so that areas in which oil leases had been issued could be classified as "native lands." As of late 1990, plans were going ahead for oil drilling in the area. However, both the government and Conoco have promised to limit the environmental damage by expelling settlers and minimizing access roads and forest clearing ("New Effort" 1991, B8). Local NGOs remain unconvinced that the proposed measures will protect the environment or the way of life of the Huaorani Indians.

Transportation

Cumulative World Bank and IDA loans for transportation before FY 1989 represented nearly 15 percent of total lending. This percentage declined in recent years, so that transportation represented about 9 percent of total lending during FY 1989. Loans to this sector include support for highways, ports-waterways, railways, airlines-airports, and pipelines. Lending for highways is by far the most important, followed by railways and ports-waterways. All of these project categories present environmental problems, but the most serious are those generated by highways. Most highway projects consist of paving or modernizing roadways that have existed for many years; hence, construction does not generate many new problems associated with surface hydrology, erosion, silt runoff, or encroachment into fragile ecological areas. Highways do create major environmental problems in that they facilitate population movement to frontier areas, as when Highway BR-364 was paved in Rondônia, Brazil. Highways need to be part of well-considered plans for resettlement and the protection of forested areas, coastal areas, wetlands, and so on, especially when they provide access to less populated regions.

Location of railways may present some of the same problems. Railways into frontier areas are usually established to serve new mines or other resource industries, but they may also provide access for populations greater than those required to operate the mines. A good example of this is the railway built to serve the Carajás iron ore mining complex in Brazil.

In 1982 the World Bank loaned the SME Companhia Valle do Rio Doce (CVRD) $304 million to construct an iron ore mine at Carajás, an 890-kilometer railroad, and a deepwater port. The Bank's loan agreement stipulated that cofinancing covering total project costs would be arranged, and with Bank help, CVRD obtained loans for the project totaling $3.6 billion from both public and private sources. Although the Bank accepted responsibility for requiring measures to protect the environment within its project area—a 100-kilometer radius around the mine and railway—the railway and other CVRD investments resulted in a large migration into the area, substantial deforestation, and the creation of environmentally destructive industries such as charcoal-fired metallurgy projects that used charcoal converted from the native forest for fuel (Bank Information Center 1989, 17).

Constructing ports and waterways for ship traffic invites pollution from oil spills, from ships at port facilities, and from destruction of shoreline ecosystems and aquatic habitat through dredging and clearing operations. Ports and waterways also affect natural bird migration patterns and cause saltwater intrusion into groundwater systems. In addition to requiring actions that reduce environmental damage, it is important to select sites that will avoid damaging beaches and delicate ecosystems such as coral reefs and mangrove swamps.

APPENDIX 7-A

Case Study: The Ok Tedi Mine in Papua New Guinea

The Ok Tedi Project makes an interesting case study, partly because the Papua New Guinea (PNG) government at the time of its independence in 1975 was especially conscious of the adverse environmental impacts of mining. In 1978, the PNG parliament passed several laws that formed an environmental regulatory framework for the nation. PNG's awareness of environmental problems created by mines was enhanced by its experience with the Bougainville copper mine initiated during the early 1970s while PNG was still under Australian sovereignty. Despite the environmental legislation and strong support within parliament and the administration, PNG's Office of Environment has virtually no control over either the Bougainville or the Ok Tedi mines, since both were exempt from environmental legislation. This is because the foreign investors who developed the mines dealt with environmental requirements in their agreements, and the Minerals and Energy Department controls implementation of these agreements.

Although no MDB credits helped finance the Ok Tedi mine, official government institutions provided nearly $650 million; this includes export credits from Australia, Austria, the United Kingdom, and Canada. In addition, the German government financial institution Kreditanstalt für Weideraufbau made a loan, and the US Overseas Private Investment Corporation extended a credit guarantee.[2] There is no record that any of these institutions was involved in the environmental issues or took into account the environmental problems when it decided to make credit available. If any of the government agencies were to do so, the logical choice would have been the Australian government's Export Finance and Insurance Corporation, which provided the largest credit, $250 million. In addition, the Australian government was quite familiar with the Ok Tedi property, since negotiations for its development date from the 1960s when PNG

was still an Australian territory. Had the World Bank or the ADB participated in financing the project in 1980, the outcome of the negotiations
on the environmental issues would probably have been no different.

The Ok Tedi mine is 80 percent owned by a consortium, consisting
of BHP Minerals (Australian), AMOCO Minerals (US), and a group of
German firms, and 20 percent owned by the PNG government. Before
the final negotiations on the mining agreement, the Ok Tedi consortium
agreed to undertake an EIA as part of the feasibility study, but it insisted
on a budgetary ceiling of $180,000. Actually, the government spent several
times the consortium commitment on its own environmental investigation; the consortium refused to make larger expenditures until the feasibility study was completed and it had an agreement to build the mine (Pintz
1984, 138–141).

The Ok Tedi mine is on Mt. Fubilan in the Star Mountains of north-
eastern PNG near the Indonesian border. Mt. Fubilan, which is to be mined
to its base, consists mainly of copper oxide ore with a gold-bearing cap
characterized by soft face rock. Initially, only the gold cap was mined,
at the rate of 15,000 metric tons per day; in stage II, gold and copper
were mined; and in stage III only copper is being extracted, with a through-
put of 45,000 metric tons per day. Gold is leached with cyanide and copper is processed to concentrate.

The area has extremely heavy rainfall—between 450 and 550 inches
per year—severe seismic activity, unstable geology, and volatile hydrology. Massive landslides are common, and the river fluctuates up to 25
feet overnight. The people of the region where the mine is located have
a primitive culture and depend heavily on fish and certain reptiles found
in the Fly and Ok Tedi rivers. They practice subsistence agriculture using
riverbank gardens that are vulnerable to flooding, which can be exacerbated by sediment deposited in the rivers. Metals, chemicals, and other
substances discharged into the rivers impair the quality of the water for
consumption and adversely affect the native population.

The feasibility study of the ore body suggested a profitable but high-
risk investment costing $1.5 billion, including infrastructure. During the
negotiations between the consortium and the government, the government
expressed concern about the effects of the leached materials from the gold
cap on the river system, river sedimentation and turbidity, and the biological effects of cyanide and heavy metals in the rivers. Both the consortium and the government analyzed the effects of waste rock on the rivers
from samples of riverbed materials. The consortium concluded that the

Ok Tedi waste rock would simply wash through the river system to the Papuan Gulf. By contrast, the government studies concluded that the deposition could raise river levels by up to 10 meters in areas adjacent to important native settlements. One source of uncertainty regarded the quantity of waste rock and the size and composition of the materials that would be discharged.

Another source of uncertainty was the toxic effects of the cyanide released, both chemical-free and in combination with minerals in mine tailings. Free cyanide is known to undergo a rapid natural decomposition, but cyanide in the tailings, which is considerably less toxic, is environmentally more persistent. The consortium concluded that the cyanide effluent posed no threat to public health or aquatic life, but in a report to the government, the Australian National University suggested that river disposal of leached capping rock was environmentally risky. Given the uncertain impacts of river dumping, the government decided that a maximum limit of 60 million metric tons of waste rock should be set for dumping into the river. Continued river dumping beyond this level would require a specific variance from the government, which would be granted only with evidence that the river system was not being adversely affected. Although there was no scientific basis for the dumping limitation, the consortium accepted it because it feared that a delay in determining a less arbitrary limit would increase costs. There was also contention over the neutralization of the cyanide, which would substantially increase operating costs. The consortium agreed to construct facilities to chemically destroy the cyanide with the understanding that the facility would not be operated if it could be demonstrated that cyanide toxicity was not an environmental threat. Also at issue were environmental monitoring and compensation for injuries or damages arising from the environmental consequences of the project. The government proposed establishing an independent agency administered by jointly appointed scientists to handle the problems of both monitoring and liability compensation. This was not acceptable to the consortium and the issue was dropped.

Another environmental problem concerned the construction of a tailings dam to retain several hundred million tons of fine-grained material in an area of seismic disturbance and heavy rainfall. The consortium had agreed to build the dam, but due to many delays, the tailings disposal system fell behind the overall construction schedule for stage I of the project. In November 1983 the consortium proposed to the government that an alternative retention system be adopted to permit production to start nine months earlier than under the original plan. The PNG Cabinet considered the proposal but rejected it as environmentally less certain than the approved plan. However, in January 1984 the tailings dam became a moot issue when a massive landslide dumped some 50 million tons of debris into the center of the dam site. To get the gold mine operating without a waste disposal dam, the PNG government agreed to let the Ok Tedi Mining Company try a temporary method of chemically neutralizing the waste before releasing it into the river.

In the first months, there were two accidental releases of untreated cyanide into the rivers. Villagers found dead fish and even dead crocodile floating in the water. The company argued that until metal prices recovered it could not afford additional construction. In February 1985 the government ordered the mine shut down, not only because of the failure to construct the tailings dam, but also because the company had delayed construction of a hydroelectric power plant, which was part of the mining agreement. The government feared that the company would mine the gold cap and then withdraw without proceeding to stages II and III, during which the copper was to be mined and processed. The government allowed the mine to be reopened the following month under an agreement that the company would build a permanent tailings waste dam and a single copper processing line capable of handling 3,000 metric tons of ore per day. A second copper unit with the same capacity, and an additional hydropower facility, would be subject to an economic test (the price of copper) to be applied at the beginning of 1987. Completion of the tailings dam was delayed because of construction difficulties and financial problems resulting from cost overruns. Meanwhile, the company was allowed to release treated tailings into the rivers.

Since the mining of gold cap first began in 1984, between 30 and 50 million tons of untreated waste rock and soil have been dumped annually into the river system. At planned peak production (1990–1992), this is expected to increase to 50 to 70 million metric tons per year. In December 1988 the Department of Environment and Conservation submitted to the Cabinet a paper setting forth environmental protection and preservation goals. Among other things, the study called for protection of human health, social welfare, and preservation of aquatic life and fisheries. In June 1989 the Department proposed to the Cabinet the setting of maximum particulate levels with penalties for violation. The native population lodged serious complaints regarding the decreased fish catch in the Fly River and tried to bar company shipping on the river.

By September 1989 the PNG Cabinet again faced the option of shutting down the mine or allowing continued disposal of tailings and waste rock into the river system. Shutting down the mine would have meant a loss to the federal government of $35 million in 1990, and $860 million for the remainder of the life of the mine. The provincial government, Ok Tedi landowners, and PNG businesses that relied on purchases by the mining company and its employees would have lost additional amounts. Affecting the decision of the Cabinet was the fact that the Bougainville copper mine was forced to close in 1989 because of civil disturbances by the native population, who demanded independence from PNG and were critical of the environmental damage being done by the mine. Balancing the potential loss of revenue and jobs against the environmental damage, the PNG Cabinet decided in favor of the mine. The company did agree to commit between $6 and $11 million to compensate the people inhabiting the areas of the Ok Tedi and Fly Rivers and set up a $29 million village development fund. The government considered the option of requiring that tailings be retained by a dam while allowing the disposal of waste rock into the river system. This would have moderated the fish loss and reduced other biological damage. Because of the financial position of the Ok Tedi mining company, however, requiring a tailings dam costing an estimated $440 million would probably have led to closure of the mine.

Could a mine have been constructed to provide the government with revenue without damaging the environment? It is by no means clear that, given the unstable geological conditions and the enormous rainfall, a profitable mine that provided adequate protection for the adjacent river system could have been constructed. Clearly, this would not have been possible at the price of copper prevailing when the mine began operating in 1984, but it might have been possible at the price of copper in 1988–1990. It certainly would have been more efficient — from the standpoint of making the investment decision — if there had been an adequate independent EIA at the time of the feasibility study instead of two inadequate studies. If it had been decided that little or no waste should be discharged into the river system, the feasibility study probably would not have favored construction of the mine. In addition, an EIA would have needed to take into account the probability of a large landslide that would have destroyed any tailings dam or rock retention arrangement.

But an adequate EIA might have cost $25 to $30 million, and who was going to pay for it? The consortium would not have been willing to advance that amount of money without knowing whether the mine would be profitable, without permission from the government to develop it, and without a limit on its obligation to make additional environmental expenditures. On the other hand, the government probably could not have afforded to commit itself to pay for the EIA. Fortunately, most mining projects do not present comparable problems of high risk and uncertainty — but many have similar problems on a smaller scale.

NOTES

1. The "Open Letter to the Ecuadorian State and to the World Bank," dated 27 January 1990, was signed by officials of leading Ecuadorian NGOs. It has not been published, but copies are available from the Washington, D.C. office of the Sierra Club.
2. The US Overseas Private Investment Corporation insures private equity and loan investments in the mining industry and currently accepts some responsibility for screening the environmental effects of projects.

REFERENCES

Asian Development Bank. 1987. *Environmental Guidelines for Selected Industrial and Power Development Projects.* Manila, Philippines: ADB.

Bank Information Center. 1989. *Funding Ecological and Social Destruction: The World Bank and International Monetary Fund.* Washington, D.C.: Bank Information Center.

Carpenter, Richard A., and Sham Sani. 1983. "Urban Air Pollution." In *Natural Systems for Development: What Planners Need to Know,* edited by Richard A. Carpenter. New York: Macmillan.

"Company/Government Disputes May Close Ok Tedi." 1985. *Engineering and Mining Journal* (March).

Environment Department. 1988. *Environmental Guidelines.* Washington, D.C.: World Bank.

Geller, H.S., J. Goldenberg, J. R. Moreira, R. Hukai, C. Scarpinella, and M. Ysohizawa. 1988. "Electricity Conservation in Brazil: Potential and Progress." *Energy* 13, no. 6: 469–483.

"Giant Mining Project in Papua New Guinea is Beset by Calamities." 1985. *Wall Street Journal* (24 April).

Goodland, R.J.A., E.O.A. Asibey, J. C. Post, and M. D. Dyson. 1990. *Tropical Moist Forest Management: The Urgent Transition to Sustainability.* Washington, D.C.: World Bank.

Inter-American Development Bank. 1989. *Annual Report 1989.* Washington, D.C.: IADB.

Mikesell, Raymond F. 1987. *Nonfuel Minerals: Foreign Dependence and National Security.* Ann Arbor: Univ. of Michigan Press for the Twentieth Century Fund.

Mikesell, Raymond F., and John W. Whitney. 1987. *The World Mining Industry: Investment, Strategy, and Public Policy.* Boston: Allen and Unwin.

Natural Resources Defense Council and Indonesian Environmental Forum. 1990. "Bogged Down: The Tragic Legacy of the World Bank and Wetlands Transmigration in Indonesia." Mimeo. June.

"New Effort Would Test Possible Coexistence of Oil and Rainforest." 1991. *New York Times* (26 February).

"Ok Tedi Mining will Help with a Fly River Trust." 1989. *Coast Courier* (5 October).

"Ok Tedi Resumes under Tenuous Pact." 1985. *World Mining Equipment,* June.

Pearson, Charles S., ed. 1987. *Multinational Corporations, Environment and Third-World Business Matters.* Durham, N.C.: Duke Univ. Press for World Resources Institute.

Pintz, William S. 1984. *Ok Tedi: Evolution of a Third World Mining Project.* London: Mining Journal Books.

_____. 1987. "Environmental Negotiations in the Ok Tedi Mine in Papua New Guinea." In *Multinational Corporations,* edited by Charles S. Pearson. Durham, N.C.: Duke Univ. Press for World Resources Institute.

Reed, David, and Jennifer Smith. 1990. *A Review of World Bank Forestry Sector Projects to the Republic of Côte d'Ivoire.* Washington, D.C.: World Wildlife Fund, March 20.

Rich, Bruce M. 1990. "Statement on Behalf of the Environmental Defense Fund and National Wildlife Federation before the Subcommittee on Foreign Operations, Committee on Appropriations, US Senate, July 25." Mimeo. Washington, D.C.

United Nations. 1974. General Assembly Resolution 3202 (S-VI). New York: UN, 1 May.

VanDomelen, Julie. 1988. *Power to Spare: The World Bank and Electricity Conservation.* Washington, D.C.: Osborn Center (a joint program of the World Wildlife Fund and the Conservation Foundation.

World Bank. 1978. *Annual Report 1978.* Washington, D.C.: World Bank.

_____. 1980. *Energy in Developing Countries.* Washington, D.C.: World Bank.

CHAPTER 8

Structural Adjustment Loans and the Environment

Using structural adjustment loans (SALs) to promote specific environmental and resource management objectives is important for two reasons. First, SALs and other nonproject loans have constituted an increasing percentage of MDB lending. Limiting environmental conditionality to project loans, therefore, reduces the relative influence of MDBs on the environmental policies of their members. Second, achieving sustainable development requires changing a range of economic and social policies within a country, not simply adopting environmentally sound practices for individual projects financed by MDBs. Before exploring ways to give SALs an important environmental content, we must understand how they have been used in the past and how effective they have been in accomplishing their objectives.

The Origin of SALs

The World Bank initiated SALs in response to a series of economic shocks experienced by non-OPEC developing countries during the late 1970s and 1980s. Average real per capita growth in GNP for all developing countries in 1960–1970 was 3.5 percent and even the low-income countries had average annual growth rates of 2.7 percent. These rates declined by nearly 25 percent for all developing countries in the 1970s; the decline was even sharper during the 1980–1988 period, with sub-Saharan African and Latin American countries experiencing negative growth.

The first shock was the fourfold increase in petroleum prices in 1973–1974, followed by another increase from about $13 per barrel to $35 per barrel in 1979–1981. Since oil constituted 25 percent of total imports for some developing countries, these increases had a devastating impact. Many developing countries borrowed heavily in the world capital markets to maintain their oil imports, usually at interest rates that varied with world market rates. A second shock was the decline in the real prices for primary commodities beginning in the mid-1970s and lasting into the late 1980s. Third, a worldwide recession in 1980–1982 reduced developing countries' demand for imports. Recessions are usually accompanied by declining prices and lower interest rates in the industrial countries, but the US and certain other industrial countries experienced both inflation and high interest rates during 1979–1982. Higher prices for manufacturers in the industrial countries reduced the terms of trade of the developing countries, while higher interest rates increased the cost of carrying their large external debts. Developing countries' private capital imports, which had financed much of their growth in the 1960s and 1970s, declined sharply in the 1980s, so that by 1987 *net* transfers of private capital (gross disbursements minus the sum of interest and principal repayments) were negative, contrasted with positive net transfers of $53 billion in 1981. The result has been widespread default on external debt by Latin American and African countries and a drying up of foreign private investment in these countries.

Before the 1980s, when a developing country experienced a large balance-of-payments deficit, the IMF would make a loan of three- to five-years' maturity, accompanied by an agreement that the country reduce its demand for imports by tightening domestic credit and reducing fiscal expenditures and encourage exports by depreciating its currency. Unfortunately, the standard medicine could not heal the balance-of-payments problems resulting from the economic shocks of the 1970s and 1980s without reducing investment so far that GNP and levels of living would decline. Conservation measures and the development of domestic energy sources can reduce the need for oil imports, but they cannot offset a multiple rise in the oil import bill, except possibly over a decade or two. The external debt constituted another inflexible element in the balance of payments, especially in the context of sharply rising interest rates on both old and new debt. (By the mid-1980s much of the new borrowing simply went to finance interest and capital repayments on old debt.) Had the large capital imports of the 1970s been invested productively, instead of used for petroleum, military hardware, nonproductive urban structures, and large subsidies to inefficient state enterprises, developing countries might have been able to service their debt. Even so, it would have been necessary to make substantial changes in their patterns of production, especially in their systems of taxation and fiscal expenditures.

The Bank's executive directors approved structural adjustment lending in 1980, largely in response to the balance-of-payments problems brought about by the sharp rise in petroleum prices. Initially, SALs were designed to provide longer-term financing "in order that the current account deficits of many developing countries do not become so large as to jeopardize seriously the implementation of current investment programs and foreign exchange-producing activities" (World Bank 1980, 67). Balance-of-payments problems continued for many developing countries throughout the 1980s, even after petroleum prices fell to quite low levels in real terms. During this period conditions of the SALs were broadened from monetary and fiscal policies to include energy and agricultural pricing, industrial policies, and the elimination of deficits of public enterprises. The banks attempted to reduce the impact of adjustment programs on the poor by avoiding across-the-board reductions in fiscal expenditures and giving priority to investment in human resource development activities. Thus agreements with countries receiving SALs have been steadily broadened to encompass a number of aspects of public policy affecting the direction of production and the distribution of income (World Bank 1989b, 78–82).

In FY 1989 the World Bank and IDA made structural and sectoral adjustment loans totaling $6.4 billion, or about 30 percent of total loans during that year (World Bank 1989a, 39). Sectoral adjustment loans are similar to SALs, except that funds are directed to particular areas, such as agriculture and industry, and the conditions attached to loans are designed to achieve changes in the structure of a particular sector. More than fifty countries have received SALs from the Bank and IDA, and many received *sectoral* adjustment loans.

In 1986 the IMF initiated its own structural adjustment facility providing longer-term repayment schedules and accompanied by agreements obligating borrowers to undertake policies and measures in many ways similar to those in Bank SAL agreements. The Bank and the Fund often collaborate in dealing with the problems of countries that receive SALs from both institutions (IMF 1989, 30–38). Both the ADB and the IADB have been making SALs, but not on the scale of the World Bank and the IMF.

The Effectiveness of SALs

How well SALs are able to achieve their objective of reducing or eliminating structural balance-of-payments deficits (deficits not amenable to short-term financial measures) depends on four factors: (1) the ability of the policy instruments (such as fiscal, foreign exchange measures, trade, and industrial policies) to achieve structural adjustment; (2) the willingness and political ability of the government of the borrowing country to implement the conditionality set forth in the SAL; (3) the adequacy of the loans for carrying out the conditionality; and (4) the emergence of unforeseen developments that might impair the adjustment process. All four of these factors may have contributed to the SALs' failure to achieve significant balance-of-payments adjustments during the 1980s. Factors (1) and (2) have probably been the most significant, however.

Evaluations of the effectiveness of SALs based on recipient countries' performance are inconclusive. A World Bank report (1989b) compared the experience of thirty countries receiving Bank adjustment loans before 1985 with a control group of sixty-three countries that did not. Among the group of thirty, the relative growth of about half improved; the real exchange rate depreciated more than average in about two-thirds; inflation fell in about half; and external debt indicators improved for about half. On the other hand, the investment to gross domestic product ratio for nearly two-thirds of the group of thirty worsened relatively, suggesting that the burden of adjustment fell heavily on investment, which determines future growth. A 1990 Bank working paper, using a different sample of countries receiving SALs and control countries not receiving SALs, reached the following conclusion: "We found no evidence of a statistically better (or worse) performance for loan recipient countries." Performance is measured in terms of growth for the countries that received loans. This report also pointed out that "the positive effects on growth and resource mobilization expected from adjustment with growth packages has not yet occurred" (World Bank 1990, 21).

When we look at individual countries that received large SALs from both the IMF and the Bank during the mid-1980s, such as Argentina and Brazil, we find that some have been plagued with double- and triple-digit inflation, have price distortions of all kinds, and have been miserable performers in terms of growth. This does not mean, of course, that SALs could not be more effective if governments were more willing (and perhaps more politically able) to live up to the conditions, and if MDBs were more zealous in enforcing the conditions necessary for both adjustment and growth.[1]

To induce compliance with the loan conditions, the proceeds from SALs are released in stages, with additional amounts withheld, depending on the country's performance. Since SALs are frequently made in periods when the country is experiencing a severe balance-of-payments crisis, however, much of the fund is often made immediately available for the purchase of imports or for making other payments. In the case of project loans, approval can be delayed until the environmental requirements for the project design are met and loan payments for use on the project or program are released as implementation proceeds under the supervision of the lender. This principle is difficult to apply in the case of SALs since the borrower needs to count on a certain level of foreign exchange receipts at the time important changes in economic policy are instituted, such as currency devaluation or import liberalization. This problem would not necessarily constrain withholding the loan proceeds conditioned on the adoption of policies and measures to improve the environment, however.

Criticisms of SALs

Critics of SALs say that political opposition has impeded economic reforms and that the loans simply enable countries to perpetuate their uneconomic policies. Judging from the poor performance of the recipient countries, this criticism has some merit. Unless a government demonstrates a will and an ability to carry out the measures that the SAL is designed to facilitate, the loan may be counterproductive and simply add to the recipient's external debt. Some also say that the fiscal and monetary policies that SALs impose on recipients may cause unemployment and a reduction in social services available to the poorest segment of the population. Elimination of price controls and subsidies on essential imports may also reduce the real income of the poor.

These two criticisms together seem to say that SALs are unlikely to achieve their purpose since governments will not adopt the reforms, and that even if they do, the policies will have an adverse impact on low-income families. The banks can overcome the first criticism by insisting that recipient countries undertake specific measures with respect to their budgets, money supply, subsidies, exchange rates, and internal and external trading practices before, or at least at the time SAL funds are released. This is not the same as requiring performance in the sense of achieving the ultimate objective of the policy reforms; it may take several years before inflation is greatly reduced, exports expanded, and production and investment increased. The loan funds are intended to enable countries to undertake the desired reforms without having to experience high rates of unemployment and loss of output as a result of reduced imports or to cut back on social programs and technical assistance that benefit the poor. Reducing fiscal deficits does not require that all categories of expenditures be reduced. Most large budget deficits in developing countries are caused by inefficient state enterprises, failure to tax large corporations and wealthy individuals, heavy military expenditures, outlays on buildings in urban areas, and high payrolls supporting bloated military and civilian bureaucracies. Eliminating overvalued exchange rates favors poor farmers by giving them world prices for their products, as does eliminating government marketing boards that hold farm prices artificially low to subsidize urban consumers. Economic reform associated with SALs should involve not just an aggregate reduction in expenditures, but a reallocation of resources. It is in this latter function that SALs have tended to fail. Indeed, effective resource reallocation is necessary to eliminate external and internal maladjustments and to facilitate growth.

Incorporating Environmental Conditionality in SALs

As far as we are aware, neither the MDBs nor the IMF has made policies and actions for improving the environment or for sustainable resource management a major component of SAL conditionality. SAL agreements sometimes mention environmental issues—most frequently erosion control, deforestation, pesticide use, and desertification. In some cases the measures set forth have important implications for sustainability, even though the primary purpose of the measure is balance-of-payments adjustment.

For example, the forestry component of the third Ivory Coast SAL explicitly addresses guidelines for conservation, incentives for replanting, promotion of agroforestry, soil conservation, and land tenure reform (World Bank 1986, 15–16). A recent IMF structural adjustment loan agreement with Haiti notes that "the combination of import restrictions on grains and export taxes on coffee generated high producer prices for grains and low ones for coffee, compared to world levels. This encouraged grain production on the hillsides in place of coffee; these practices, together with deforestation, aggravated soil erosion" (IMF 1987, 2). In these and other cases the guidelines in the loan agreement for the elimination of import restrictions, export taxes, and overvalued exchange rates had as their stated purpose the adjustment of the country's trade balance. These same measures would also contribute to a more sustainable agriculture.[2] What we are saying is that environmental improvement and sustainability can readily become a primary objective of SALs, not simply an incidental consequence of pursuing a balance-of-payments objective. Moreover, in the majority of cases, pursuit of environmental objectives will not be inconsistent with balance-of-payments and growth objectives.

This analysis suggests that the traditional argument of many World Bank and IMF officials—that the introduction of environmental objectives in SAL conditionality is not feasible because it complicates and weakens the basic objectives of the SALs—is untenable. We have yet to see a case in which growth, *properly defined,* and balance-of-payments adjustment are inconsistent with sustainability. Of course, if growth measurement includes resource depletion as part of the national product, there could be a conflict. However, World Bank officials have come to recognize that resource depletion, whether in the form of soil mining or deforestation or a steady deterioration in air and water quality, can only be temporary and is not true growth.

SAL DEVELOPMENT POLICIES
AND RESOURCE MANAGEMENT

SALs should seek to influence the recipient's development policies in a way that will contribute to external adjustment without impairing growth on a sustainable basis. Since MDBs have now adopted the goal of *sustainable development* in their official statements, MDB loan policies should be consistent with this goal. A country's balance of payments is affected by a whole complex of development policies, not just those affecting exchange rates and fiscal deficits—the traditional instruments for influencing the balance of payments. Development policies influence what and how much is produced; how a nation's human, natural, and human-made resources are allocated; and how the nation's output is distributed. The management of natural resources, broadly conceived to include all natural inputs (land, air, and water), plays a crucial role in development policies directed to the goals of sustainable growth and balance-of-payments adjustment. This should be admitted as a general proposition, but it is often forgotten. A country cannot achieve sustainable growth if its farming practices degrade the soil or if its water resources become so polluted that they are not fit for irrigation, industrial, and human use. Can there be sustainable growth if overcutting for timber or clearing land for crops in areas where the soil soon loses its fertility depletes the forests that protect the watersheds? The following two examples illustrate the relationship between development policy, structural adjustment, and the environment.

A recent unpublished study of the Tunisian economy found that dryland farming on marginal lands is destroying the productivity of areas formerly used for grazing, and that a rapid rate of growth in population has fostered these activities because the people cannot find employment in agriculture in areas with better soil. Such a development path is unsustainable because eroding the marginal land will eventually impair the fertility of the good land as well. Tunisia has rapidly growing industries in the large cities, but the cities are overcrowded and highly polluted as a result of industrial activities and inadequate facilities for waste disposal. The authors conclude that Tunisia should not try to expand agricultural production with labor working on marginal lands, but that development policy should favor industrial expansion in a number of smaller cities with production oriented to foreign markets. Tunisia's relatively well-educated and skilled workforce could produce a higher-value output in this way than in nonsustainable agriculture in marginal areas. This recommendation illustrates the integration of development strategy with sustainability of the resource base.

Egypt's principal resource problem is a shortage of water, which is heavily used for agriculture, industry, and households. The major source of water is the Nile, but given the country's present water consumption pattern, the available water will not meet Egypt's demand by the year 2000. Water pollution from agriculture, industry, and municipal use limits the degree to which water can be recycled and exacerbates the problem. To compensate for nutrients formerly supplied by silt but now retained in the Aswân reservoir, the Egyptians have rapidly expanded their use of fertilizer, which has caused a rapid growth of aquatic weeds (particularly water hyacinth) in canals and drains. The weeds slow water flow in canals, clog and deteriorate water pumps, and increase water evaporation.

The Egyptian government places a high priority on increasing land reclamation to expand irrigated cotton agriculture. An unpublished World Bank report recommends that Egypt drop this objective in favor of increasing agricultural productivity through better land use and expanding export-oriented industry. Egypt could employ its reasonably well-educated and skilled labor force to produce industrial goods for the world markets, which, given the water situation, would have a comparative advantage over producing cotton. (The productivity of Egyptian labor is indicated by the fact that several million Egyptians work in other Middle East countries and are in demand.) Egypt may also have a potential comparative advantage in producing cheap, nonpolluting energy from wind and almost-constant sun. To deal rationally with its resource problems, the country needs a different set of development priorities.

If sustainable development is to be a meaningful objective and not simply a slogan used by MDB officials, SALs and project loans must support sustainability objectives. Thus, if expanding water-intensive agriculture or creating energy-intensive industries is not consistent with a country's sustainable development, loans for these purposes should not be made. Instead, banks should make loans that would shift the country's resources to other industrial categories. For MDBs to follow this policy, MDBs, government officials, NGOs, and the general public must fully understand the directions necessary for a country to achieve sustainable development. The World Bank and the regional banks have sponsored many country development studies in the past, and other agencies such as USAID and OECD are also preparing such studies. Yet the typical country development study rarely takes sustainability into account, or considers severe pollution conditions in making development recommendations. Moreover, planners generally neglect to consider *social* benefits and costs and the depletion of resources when formulating recommendations for maximizing growth. Therefore, these studies do not provide MDBs with guidelines for promoting sustainable development, nor do they help officials of the countries to adopt appropriate policies for realizing this objective.

Recognizing the need for adequate studies to integrate environmental and resource management with the formulation and implementation of development strategies, the World Bank recently initiated a program for preparing environmental action plans (EAPs) for member countries. It developed this program in part as a response to the IDA 9 replenishment, which stipulates that an EAP must be prepared for each IDA borrower (see Chapter 9). In addition, EAPs are to be prepared for as many non-IDA borrowers as possible. A number of draft EAPs have been prepared, but they have not been made public. We hope that these plans will induce the World Bank Group to focus on sustainability in the allocation of loans and on influencing the development strategies of members.

Environmental Conditionality in World Bank SALs

The Environment Department of the World Bank is quite aware of the limitations of the project approach to environmental reform. In a recent article, Jeremy Warford and Z. Partow state that the "Bank is now convinced that the pervasive nature of environmental problems dictates a new approach: integrating environmental management into economic policy-making at all levels of government, supplementing the traditional project-by-project approach" (1989, 5–8). The authors go on to say that the Bank is implementing its new policy through a series of activities, one of which is compiling a set of environmental studies for each country and then preparing EAPs. The next logical step, although not spelled out in the article, would be to apply environmental policy conditionality to SALs and sector adjustment loans. The article does say that "structural adjustment lending has not, until recently, paid specific attention to environmental issues . . . Nevertheless, more explicit consideration of the effects of adjustment lending on the environment is necessary, not only to avoid possibly damaging environmental consequences, but also to fully use the potential of adjustment lending in improving environmental conditions" (7).

Since environmental and resource management issues are an integral part of development policy for achieving adjustment and growth, why has it taken so long for the Bank and the other MDBs to adopt this approach?

The IMF and Structural Adjustment

In the mid-1980s the IMF began making longer-maturity loans under its structural adjustment facility for much the same purposes as the World Bank's SALs. For several years environmental groups have been arguing that the Fund should include in its loan conditionality a requirement that borrowers adopt proper environmental policies. Generally, IMF officials have rejected these arguments. They say that the IMF charter constrains the Fund to pursue a rather narrow set of financial policy objectives, and that getting into the complexities of environmental policies would constitute a departure from its basic objectives. However, the IMF's concern for structural adjustment has broadened the focus of its conditionality to include policy issues that go well beyond the traditional financial content of its loan operations. As we have shown, environmental and resource management issues are very much a part of structural adjustment. Thus, there seems no reason for the Fund not to incorporate the environment into its operational and policy objectives.

Section 594 of the FY 1990 US Congress's Foreign Operations Appropriations Bill (HR 2491) requested that the secretary of the treasury recommend (1) the addition of environmental and natural resource specialists to the Fund's staff; (2) the establishment of a systematic process to take into account the impact of IMF lending activities on the environment, public health, and poverty; and (3) the creation of lending terms that would promote sustainable management of natural resources, as well as measures that would reduce external debt in exchange for domestic investment in conservation and environmental management. The US IMF executive director believes that a small environmental and social assessment unit could be created within the Fund, and he has proposed that the best way to begin incorporating environmental concerns into the Fund's operations would be through Policy Framework Papers (PFPs), which are prepared for many of its borrowers. (PFPs are prepared for low-income countries that borrow from the Fund's structural adjustment or enhanced structural adjustment facilities.) The IMF staff prepared memoranda on ways to bring environmental considerations into the Fund's activities; the IMF executive board discussed the issue in early April 1991. According to an IMF press release, "the Board concluded that the IMF staff should develop a greater understanding of the interplay between economic policies, economic activity, and environmental change. This would help to avoid the possibility that the Fund might recommend policies that could have un-desirable environmental consequences, while insuring that the thrust of its actions—promoting sustainable growth and reducing poverty—also helps mitigate environmental concerns" (IMF 1991, 124). This decision does not commit the IMF to using conditionality in its loans for achieving environmental objectives. Nevertheless, we believe the decision will lead the Fund to consider environmental and resource management issues in dealing with its members, including negotiating conditionality agreements.

NOTES

1. The questions may be asked, "Why is it so important for developing countries to achieve balance-of-payments adjustment? Why not continue to let them run deficits?" If deficits are not financed, they will automatically disappear because countries cannot go on indefinitely buying goods from abroad without paying for them. But when deficits are adjusted in this way, the goods actually imported may not be those determined as the country's priorities for development and for maximizing social welfare. In addition, the country may make little effort to expand exports by promoting production of goods for which it has a competitive advantage in international markets.
2. For additional examples of SAL agreements concerned with resource issues, see Stein Hansen (1988).

REFERENCES

Bouis, R. D., and Lawrence J. Haddad. 1990. *Effects of Agricultural Commercialization on Land Tenure, Household Resource Allocation, and Nutrition in the Philippines.* Washington, D.C.: International Food Policy Research Institute, January.

Hansen, Stein. 1988. *Structural Adjustment Programs and Sustainable Development.* Unpublished paper prepared for annual session of Committee of International Development Institutions, 13–17 June 1987. Washington, D.C., May.

International Monetary Fund. 1987. *IMF Haiti—Policy Framework Paper.* EDB/87/286. Washington, D.C.: IMF, 5 November.

_____. 1989. *1989 Annual Report.* Washington, D.C.: IMF.

_____. 1991. *IMF Survey.* Vol. 20, no. 8. Washington, D.C.: IMF, 15 April.

Warford, Jeremy, and Z. Partow. 1989. "Evolution of the World Bank's Environmental Policy." *Finance and Development* (December): 5–8.

World Bank. 1980. *Annual Report 1980.* Washington, D.C.: World Bank.

_____. 1986. *World Bank Report and Recommendations of the President of the IBRD to the Executive Director on the Proposed Third Structural Adjustment Loan in the Amount Equivalent to $250 Million to the Republic of Côte d'Ivoire [Ivory Coast].* Washington, D.C.: World Bank, 12 May.

_____. 1989a. *Annual Report 1989*. Washington, D.C.: World Bank.

_____. 1989b. *World Bank Adjustment Lending: An Evaluation of Ten Years of Experience*. Policy and Research Report I. Washington, D.C.: World Bank, March.

_____. 1990. *Growth Oriented Adjustment Programs: A Statistical Analysis*. Policy Research and External Affairs Working Paper. Washington, D.C.: World Bank, June.

CHAPTER 9

External Influences on MDBs

The principal influence on the environmental policies and practices of MDBs is from member governments who elect the MDB president and appoint or elect the executive directors who vote on each loan proposed by management. Although nominally the board of governors elects the president, the US government has traditionally nominated the president of the World Bank Group, while individual regions select the presidents of the banks that serve them. Since the governors normally meet only once a year, the president and his staff and the executive directors who approve the loans largely control lending operations. Voting is weighted in accordance with the capital subscriptions of the member countries represented by the executive directors. The World Bank has twenty-two executive directors, five appointed by the member governments with the largest subscriptions and seventeen elected by the remaining 132 governments. The IADB and the ADB have twelve executive directors each, with forty-four and forty-seven member countries respectively. The AfDB has twelve executive directors and twenty-seven member countries. Except for the large industrial countries that appoint their executive directors (the US and Japan in the ADB, the US in the AfDB, and the US and Canada in the IADB), the directors are elected and may represent several member countries. The industrial countries together have a majority of the votes in the World Bank, but the developing countries together have a majority vote in the ADB, AfDB and IADB.

The influence of individual member country governments on the MDBs is not measured by their votes alone. For example, the US government has only 16.5 percent of the votes in the World Bank (34.6 percent in the IADB, 12.4 percent in the ADB, and 7.36 percent in the AfDB), but its influence on the president and senior staff of the Bank is substantial and, on some issues, dominant. Except for the AfDB, the US must approve the president of all of these institutions and, although presidents of the regional banks are not US citizens, US citizens hold the senior vice presidential positions in all but the AfDB. Moreover, as the largest stockholder in the World Bank and the IADB (the US and Japan have equal shares in the ADB), the US has significant influence over the approval of proposals for increased capital subscriptions. Although developing-country members participate in decisions to increase capital subscriptions, only the subscriptions of the wealthy industrial countries represent effective loan resources for these institutions. This is true because most of the capital subscriptions are not actually paid to the banks but serve as a guarantee for the indebtedness of the MDBs when they borrow in world capital markets. The US is occasionally outvoted on a loan approval, but if an MDB makes a series of loans over US objections, the US could very well refuse to approve proposals for increased capital subscriptions for that MDB. Such increases have taken place every few years for all the MDBs, and concessional loan affiliates must also be replenished from time to time. If the US government refuses to increase its capital subscriptions, other industrial countries generally reject the proposed increase as well.

A more recent source of influence on the MDBs is the public of member countries (and to a much more limited but growing extent in the borrowing countries), whose views are often mobilized and expressed by national environmental organizations. The NGO exercises its influence either through various branches of the member governments or directly with the officials of the MDBs. However, direct lobbying of bank officials is most effective if member governments also take up the issue at hand. In the US and other developed countries, NGOs exert the greatest influence by pressuring their governments to express certain positions through the executive director representing the country. NGOs in the US also monitor the activities of MDBs and express their views directly to the officials of these institutions.

NGOs in developing countries are usually concerned with the environmental consequences of projects financed by MDBs in their own countries. In some cases, the people directly affected by proposed projects have organized the NGOs. Their first recourse should be with their own government, which must approve all projects financed by the MDBs. However, petitions to their governments to avoid certain projects or to modify them in ways that will not cause environmental damage or harm certain groups within the country often go unheeded. In such cases, NGOs may express their views directly to the presidents and staffs of the MDBs, often with support of NGOs from developed countries. Alternatively, NGOs may express their views to MDB representatives in their own countries. (To date this option has not proved to be a very effective avenue of redress.) The World Bank has about forty-five permanent representatives in developing member countries; both the ADB and the IADB also maintain offices and representatives in a number of their member countries. MDBs have begun to respond to borrower-country NGOs by arranging to consult with them on proposed loan projects in which NGOs have a special interest. Since implementation of the EIA process, the borrower-country governments must formally consider the concerns of NGOs on individual projects. Still another approach is for NGOs in developing countries to make their views known to MDBs through NGOs in other member countries or through international NGOs.

A third type of influence on the MDBs is from the international organizations—both intergovernmental agencies, such as the UNDP or the Committee of International Development Institutions on Environment (CIDIE), and nongovernmental organizations, such as the International Union on Conservation of Nature and Natural Resources (IUCN), the World Commission on Environment and Development (Brundtland Commission), and the International Institute for Environment and Development (IIED). Governments (and/or government agencies) and NGOs are members of IUCN, and government officials are frequently members of nongovernmental international organizations in a personal capacity. International organizations hold conferences attended by representatives of various private environmental organizations and groups of MDBs, as well as by government officials. They prepare studies on environmental practices and policies that MDBs should follow. These organizations have undoubtedly increased the awareness of MDBs, governments, and the public concerning environmental problems in developing countries, but they rarely address specific procedures or particular projects that may be environmentally flawed. For example, in 1977 the UNEP and the Canadian International Development Agency financed a study by the IIED on the environmental procedures and practices of MDBs (UNEP 1980). Another study, *Banking on the Biosphere* (Stein & Johnson 1979), criticized the environmental policies and practices of MDBs. The IIED also prepared a number of recommendations that were incorporated in the "Declaration of Environmental Policies and Procedures Relating to Economic Development." In 1980 the nine development assistance agencies, including the MDBs, signed this declaration. The recommendations had little impact on the environmental quality of the MDB projects, however. None of the banks undertook a rigorous examination of the environmental consequences of the individual projects that they financed as standard operating procedure until late in the 1980s.

The Brundtland Commission was created in response to UN General Assembly Resolution 38/161 (adopted at the 38th Session of the United Nations in the fall of 1983). That resolution called on the secretary general of the United Nations to appoint a chair and vice chair of the commission who, in turn, were to appoint remaining members, at least half from the developing world. The commission functions as an independent body, and all members serve as individuals, although many are government officials. Its report, *Our Common Future* (1987), was very critical of the MDBs, especially of their approach to the management of natural resources. The direct impact of this report on procedures has been limited, but it did help to legitimize NGO criticisms and galvanize public opinion regarding the magnitude of the problem.

Individual scholars, either in association with NGOs or on their own, have been a fourth influence on MDB environmental policies. At least as far back as the 1960s, books and articles have exposed the destruction of the Amazon forests and the adverse environmental impacts of large multipurpose dams and other MDB-supported projects. In 1968 the US Conservation Foundation and Washington University, St. Louis, sponsored a conference; the proceedings contained a collection of fifty case studies of ecologically destructive development projects, many of them funded by MDBs during the 1960s and earlier (Runnals 1972). This conference influenced Robert S. McNamara, then president of the World Bank, to establish the Office of Environmental Advisor (Runnals 1972). Another book, *Only One Earth* (Ward & Dubos 1972), emphasized the need to minimize the adverse environmental effects of development and also greatly influenced the highest levels of government and external aid agencies. Over the past two decades, hundreds of books and scholarly articles have detailed cases of environmentally flawed MDB-assisted projects, bringing these cases to the attention of the MDBs and the governments supporting them.

All these external criticisms have influenced the MDBs, and they are recognizing past mistakes. In a report on its environmental activities for FY 1990, the World Bank (1990b, 64–71) discussed the criticisms of some of its controversial loan projects, including the Sardar Sarovar dam and the Singrauli power generation projects in India, the Kedung Ombo multipurpose dam in India, and the Carajás iron ore and Polonoroeste projects in the Brazilian Amazon Basin. While the Bank admitted to errors and lax oversight, the review was not to self-criticize, but rather to say that the Bank has learned from past experience, is in the process of adjusting problems created by the projects, and plans to greatly reduce problems in the future by implementing new procedures for environmental assessment and project monitoring. The Bank's report might well have added that it might have avoided some of these problems if it had provided adequate information to and consulted with NGOs.

US Government Influence on Environmental Policies of MDBs

Of the member governments of MDBs, the US government has had the strongest influence on environmental policies and practices. Certain other governments, notably those of Canada and the Scandinavian countries, have been at least as outspoken in condemning environmentally flawed projects, but they carry less clout. It should be said that the prime movers behind US government initiatives are the US NGOs, whose leaders have brought to the attention of government administrators and legislators the MDBs' failure to pursue sound environmental practices in their loan operations.

On the administrative side of the US government, the Department of the Treasury has the predominant role in influencing MDB policies and operations. The secretary of the treasury serves as the US governor on the MDB boards of governors, and US executive directors are usually former Treasury officials. This is also true for US participation in the IMF. The Assistant Secretary of the Treasury for International Affairs chairs the Working Group on Multilateral Assistance (referred to as WGMA, pronounced wigma), which was formed in 1978 to coordinate US policy on MDBs. The WGMA includes representatives from the US Departments of State, Agriculture, and Commerce; the US Agency for International Development; the Export-Import Bank; the Federal Reserve Board; the White

House Office of Management and Budget; the National Security Council; and, recently, the Environmental Protection Agency (EPA). The WGMA meets weekly to discuss US positions on upcoming loan proposals and policy issues, and the Treasury Department transmits its decisions to the US executive directors in the MDBs. Representatives of Treasury and State, USAID, and EPA meet monthly on an informal basis with representatives of the environmental organizations to review upcoming environmentally controversial loans. These informal meetings are the result of legislation passed by Congress in 1986 to establish the so-called early warning system (EWS) (Public Law 99–951, Section 539). This system attempts to provide advance notification about projects thought to pose environmental problems. USAID's extensive network of missions located in the developing countries transmits information from the WGMA. (The system was developed because member governments cannot go directly to an MDB to request specific information on a pending project without violating MDB policy on project secrecy.)

During the early 1970s there was a debate between environmentalists and the US government regarding the applicability of US environmental laws to US government activities abroad. The Environmental Policy Act of 1969 (PL 91–90, 42, USC 4312–4347) required the US government to prepare EISs on all proposed federal projects that would have a major impact on the human environment. In 1975 the NRDC, on behalf of several other environmental organizations, brought suit in a federal district court, asserting that the National Environmental Policy Act required USAID to prepare an EIS for the financing of sales of pesticides to developing countries. According to the settlement reached in December 1975, USAID was required to prepare an EIS for sales and to institute pesticide regulations. In 1976 USAID adopted general environmental regulations to be applied to its project loans.

In 1979 President Jimmy Carter issued Executive Order No. 12114, which set forth general requirements for federal agencies concerning the environmental effects of their activities abroad. In spite of this order, USAID is still the only US government agency to regularly prepare EISs on federal activities abroad. In 1990 the US Justice Department responded to pending legislation in the 101st Congress that would have required the government to prepare EISs on extraterritorial projects. The department claimed that such a requirement would "apply burdensome procedural requirements in areas where the President, to meet his own constitutional responsibilities, must be able to act with flexibility and dispatch" (Navarro

1990). In addition, international organizations to which the US government belongs were exempt from this executive order because the US government does not have jurisdiction over independent international bodies. The US Justice Department also argued that it would be administratively unworkable to require US officials to participate directly in environmental investigations relating to loan decisions by MDBs. However, this did not preclude the US government from directing its MDB executive directors to take positions reflecting US policies on loans and other MDB activities. Nevertheless, before January 1985, no US executive director voted against any loan on environmental grounds.[1]

THE ROLE OF CONGRESSIONAL COMMITTEES

At the urging of three national environmental organizations, six different congressional subcommittees held extensive hearings on MDB activities during 1983–1984. In the course of hearings by the House Banking Subcommittee on International Development Institutions and Finance, representatives of the National Wildlife Federation, the Environmental Policy Institute, and the NRDC reviewed a number of World Bank– and IADB–financed projects with serious environmental problems. As a result of these hearings, the Treasury Department undertook an investigation of the environmental policies and procedures of the MDBs. This investigation included extensive questionnaires regarding World Bank, IADB, and ADB policies and practices. After receiving responses to the questionnaires, in September 1983 the subcommittee held hearings to review a series of draft recommendations regarding MDB environmental policies and procedures, which the subcommittee staff had prepared in consultation with the national environmental groups. In December 1984 the subcommittee issued a set of recommendations calling upon the US Treasury Department "to monitor environmental aspects of bank activities, to facilitate constructive US involvement in assuring that sound environmental policies are implemented by multilateral lending agencies supported by the US, and to expedite the flow of information between the banks and the US Congress, other relevant federal agencies, and the public regarding environmental considerations." The Committee called upon the US executive director of each MDB to press the banks to work with NGOs and to give "heightened consideration of environmental factors" in their operations. The subcommittee also urged the US directors to vote against any projects that would result in unacceptable environmental damage, such as those involving sustainable resource exploitation, species extinction, pesticide misuse, degradation of protected areas, and disturbance of the habitat of indigenous people (Rich 1985, 729). In December 1985 Congress restated, strengthened, and placed into law (PL 99–190) these recommendations.

In January 1985 the IADB was considering a loan of $73 million to pave a road in the Brazilian Amazon. This road was to be an extension of a highway that was a component of the World Bank Polonoroeste Project. The US executive director expressed serious concern about the project's impacts on the environment and on the region's indigenous inhabitants. When the loan went before the board, the US director vetoed the use of that portion of the loan that was to come from the Bank's Fund for Special Operations (Rich 1985, 734–735). In June 1986 the US executive director in the World Bank, on instructions from the secretary of the treasury, voted against a $500 million loan for power projects in Brazil.

While the congressional directive and subsequent legislation had a decided effect on the US Treasury Department, they appeared to have little impact on the MDBs. In the spring of 1985 environmental groups consulted with Rep. David Obey (Chair of the Appropriations Subcommittee on Foreign Operations, which controls the House of Representative bills for funding MDBs) and Sen. Robert Kasten (who held the same position in the Senate) regarding future strategies to keep pressure on the MDBs. Obey and Kasten agreed with the environmentalists that a case-study approach would be an effective means of pressing the banks to reform their lending practices. The Polonoroeste road in Brazil, supported by the World Bank and the IADB, was the first project to be studied. A turning point came early that summer when a letter to World Bank President A. W. Clausen from the three environmental organizations regarding the Brazilian project failed to elicit an adequate response. Sen. Kasten sent a letter to Clausen threatening congressional economic reprisals if the Bank did not take the environmental concerns seriously. As a result of this letter and of a subsequent meeting between Clausen and Kasten, the World Bank started responding.

Recent legislation passed by the US Congress directed the secretary of the treasury to promote environmental reforms in the MDBs by requiring the US executive director on the board to take recommended positions and report back to Congress on MDB compliance. PL-202, Section 537(h) (September 1988), required USAID to monitor MDB projects likely to have adverse environmental impacts. PL 101–240, Section 521 (December

1989), directs the secretary of the treasury to instruct the US executive directors for each MDB "not to vote in favor of any action proposed to be taken by the respective bank which would have a significant effect on human environment, unless for at least 120 days before the date of vote (a) an assessment analyzing the environmental impacts of the proposed action and of alternatives to the proposed action has been completed by the borrowing country or the institution, and been made available to the board of directors of the institution; and (b) . . . such assessment or a comprehensive summary of such assessment has been made available by the MDB, to affected groups, and local nongovernmental organizations." The act further states that the US executive directors are to initiate discussions and propose procedures "for the systematic environmental assessment of development projects for which the respective bank provides financial assistance, taking into consideration the guidelines and principles for Environmental Impact Assessment promulgated by the United Nations Environmental Programme and other bilateral or multilateral assessment procedures." The act also requires MDBs to make environmental assessments or comprehensive summaries of the assessments available to "affected groups, and local nongovernment organizations."

PL 101–240 (December 1989) also authorized an increase of $9.2 billion in the US subscription to the capital stock of the IADB, and an increase of $82.3 million in the US contribution to the Bank's Fund for Special Operations. These authorizations were conditioned on the Bank's establishing "an environmental unit with responsibility for the development, evaluation, and integration of Bank policies, projects and programs designed to promote environmentally sustainable development in borrowing countries." That law also required the Bank to provide increased staff with environmentally oriented responsibilities and training; increase the number of environmentally beneficial projects and programs it financed; and insure the access of indigenous nongovernmental organizations to the process of designing projects and programs (Title II, Section 33). PL 101–240 also directed the secretary of the treasury to instruct US executive directors in the MDBs "to support development that maintains and restores the renewable natural resource base so that present and future needs of debtor country populations can be met, while not impairing critical ecosystems and not exacerbating global environmental problems" and to "promote the maintenance and restoration of soils, vegetation, hydrological cycles, wildlife, critical ecosystems (tropical forests, wetlands and coastal marine resources), biological diversity and other natural resources essential to economic growth and human well-being and . . . when using natural resources . . . to minimize the depletion of such natural resources" (Section 1614). In addition, "US executive directors should encourage borrowers to develop national plans and strategies to eliminate poverty and enhance human resources."

While the US Treasury Department has been supportive of NGO environmental concerns in general, it strongly opposed legislation sponsored by Representative Nancy Pelosi that the US executive directors of the MDBs not support funding of any proposed MDB project having a major impact on the environment unless an EIA was available at least 120 days in advance of the vote. The Treasury Department feared that the banks would not respond to the law and that the US would then be excluded from supporting a majority of future requests, thereby losing its power to influence the MDBs. The Sierra Club, which lobbied the legislation through Congress, contended that none of the MDBs could afford to have the US excluded from participating in loan decisions and that they would move quickly to implement EIA requirements rather than risk the loss of US funding. While many problems with MDB implementation of the EIA process remain, the Sierra Club's prediction has proved to be correct. Most MDBs have instituted EIA procedures, and the World bank is establishing training programs for borrower-country governments on assessments preparation.

REASONS FOR STRONG CONGRESSIONAL SUPPORT

In light of the difficulties in securing congressional approval for environmental reform legislation for the domestic economy, how can we explain Congress' strong support for sound environmental principles by our foreign economic assistance organizations? US conservation organizations have in testimony and publications made legislators aware of the adverse environmental consequences of projects supported by MDBs. In addition, thousands of members of these organizations have written their congressional representatives in support of these revelations. But this is also true of domestic environmental problems, which have been the subject of far greater lobbying activities by private environmental organizations and their members.

Congress has been more receptive to efforts to preserve foreign environments in part because efforts to protect tropical forests or victims of large dam projects are not controversial in the United States. Its members have no constituents abroad whose votes they seek to attract. They support foreign economic assistance as a means of promoting the well-being of developing countries. They are not interested in promoting the special interests of foreign bureaucracies dominated by dictators, or of industrialists or large landowners. Nor are they interested in short-term increases in output at the expense of the resource base. The US administration often supports US bilateral foreign aid that will keep a political group in power because it is friendly to US interests or because its downfall might mean a takeover by an unfriendly government. This motivation has never influenced the MDBs a great deal in setting policies. Some legislators have never trusted multilateral aid and therefore welcome efforts to control MDB operations. Others favor multilateral assistance but sincerely believe that MDBs have made many mistakes in the past, particularly by supporting unsound government projects and inefficient state enterprises or by providing nonproject loans to governments that persist in controlling prices and trade.

The 1990 Agreement for the Ninth Replenishment of IDA between the governments of the contributing countries and IDA places a direct obligation on IDA to follow the policies and procedures set forth in US legislation. Specifically, the agreement obligates IDA to improve and implement EIAs; to insure public access to information on specific projects and programs; to invite public participation in reviewing projects that IDA is considering for financial support; and to increase lending for end-use energy efficiency, renewable energy programs, and least-cost energy planning in borrowing countries. Congress will likely tie all future increases in US contributions to MDBs to conditions similar to those set forth in the 1990 IDA agreement.

The former communist countries of Eastern Europe have long suffered from extreme environmental degradation as a result of government failure to enforce even minimum standards of air and water pollution. Therefore, it is important that the new European Bank for Reconstruction and Development (EBRD), which will make loans to these countries, adopt a strong environmental component in its lending activities. The US Treasury Department, with strong backing from US NGOs, worked to incorporate language in the EBRD charter that would make the Bank responsible for assuring environmental soundness of projects it supports, and for assigning a high priority to projects designed to restore the environment.

MDB Environmental Procedures

Pressure by the US government in cooperation with the governments of other developed countries has caused MDB officials to reexamine their environmental performance. However, most environmental organizations still contend that the quality of the projects funded by MDBs has shown little if any improvement. Major problems arise in procedures, especially those involving the relationship between the lending agency and the government of the borrowing country. These procedures include not only the assessment of the environmental impacts of projects, but the changes in projects and in modes of operations that must be made to eliminate or mitigate identified adverse impacts. They involve monitoring the preparation of projects and their subsequent operation to make sure that the environmental components are implemented. This, of course, involves the MDBs' relations with government agencies engaged in completing and operating the project. In many cases MDB support of a large project, such as a multipurpose dam, is confined to a small segment, such as a road, that may represent less than one-tenth of the value of the entire complex. In some cases the MDB may not take responsibility for the environmental consequences of the other elements. It can well be argued that a road financed by an MDB contributes to the adverse impacts of a multipurpose dam, and, therefore, the bank has a responsibility for making sure that all elements of the project complex are free from environmental flaws. But the bank may argue that its responsibility should be limited to the element it has financed. Even more removed are the environmental impacts of hundreds of projects financed by sectoral loans or SALs, both specifically excluded in the World Bank's operational directive on environmental assessment (World Bank 1989).

These issues raise the question of the Bank's responsibility for the general environmental policies of the borrower. What leverage does an MDB have in carrying out this responsibility? As we discussed in Chapter 2, we believe that MDBs must move toward applying broad environmental and resource management conditionality in all loan programs. MDBs should consider environmental conditionality for a loan just as important as any other kind of conditionality.

MDB Relations with NGOs in Developing Countries

Few of the NGOs in developing countries that are concerned with the environment are primarily environmental organizations. They include charitable and religious associations that mobilize private funds for development, distribute food and family planning services, and promote community health and sanitation. They also include independent cooperatives, community associations, water-user societies, and citizens groups that raise public awareness of a variety of social issues.

On an NGO–World Bank committee composed of senior Bank managers and twenty-six NGO leaders from around the world, about three-fifths of the members are from developing countries and none are from an environmental NGO. NGO members of the committee serve five-year terms and are elected by other NGO members. The secretariat for the NGOs on the committee is the International Council of Voluntary Agencies (ICVA) based in Geneva, Switzerland. Environmental organizations have often criticized the committee for not pressing the Bank hard enough on needed reforms, such as more public participation in the Bank's development planning. During the World Bank's 1990 annual meeting in Washington, DC, representatives of the NGO–World Bank committee met with a world-wide gathering of NGOs to discuss the formation of a new advisory committee to focus solely on the environment. While generally receptive to the idea, the environmental organizations pointed out that the current NGO committee has had little impact on Bank operations, and they were not convinced that yet another committee was the answer. Rather, the NGOs urged the Bank to initiate an aggressive effort to establish more direct consultation between bank officials, the borrowing-country governments, and the NGOs of the member countries.

NGOs have enormous potential for promoting the environment in developing countries, but they operate under severe handicaps in most countries. In the United States, groups of private citizens operating at the local, regional, and national levels often initiate and heavily influence the enactment of environmental laws and the formulation and issuance of environmental regulations by the EPA or other governmental regulatory agencies. National and local legislatures, regulating bodies, and courts provide remedies against government or private activities believed to violate environmental standards; this is an important element of constitutional democracy, permeating government at all levels. Such conditions do not exist in most developing countries, in part because of governmental constraints and the absence of legal facilities, and in part because of economic and social impediments to the mobilization of citizens for group action.

In recognition of the role of developing-country NGOs in identifying environmental problems, US and international NGOs have, both directly and through US government agencies, brought pressure on MDBs to consult with and provide information to NGOs. The MDBs have responded in several ways. They sometimes directly involve NGOs in the projects they finance, especially those involving rural or urban development, family planning and health, education, low-cost housing, and vocational training. The World Bank sometimes makes direct grants to NGOs, or it enables the NGOs to undertake specific projects. For example, a Bolivian NGO participated in an IDA-supported slum-upgrading project providing improved urban services for about 100,000 people. Some fifteen NGOs in Kenya joined with the government in efforts to provide information and family-planning services under the auspices of the National Council for Population and Development. The NGOs received IDA funds to carry out information and education activities for family planning, to operate family-planning clinics, and to distribute contraceptives (World Bank 1990a, 9–11). The ADB has also enlisted NGOs as administrators of social welfare programs, small credit programs, and small agricultural and rural development programs.[2] However, direct financing of NGO activities tends to be small, and an NGO's involvement in projects depends upon the willingness of a government to allow its participation.

We are especially concerned in this book with the NGOs that have opposed certain MDB-supported projects they regard as having adverse consequences for the physical environment or for the health and economic welfare of certain populations. These organizations are often small and confined to the specific region where a project is located. In some countries national agencies represent and provide information and other services to such organizations: Examples include the Ecumenical Center for Documentation and Information, the Institute for Social and Economic Analysis, and the Institute for Socio-Economic Studies in Brazil; the Center for Tribal Conscientiousness, Kalpavrksh—The Environmental Action Group (Hindu College Nature Club), and the Center for Science and Environment in India; the Indonesian Environmental Forum and SKPHI in Indonesia; and Sahabat Alam—Friends of the Earth in Malaysia. MDB literature on dealings with NGOs rarely mentions this type of NGO, although these groups do see MDB representatives and obtain information from them. This type of NGO seeks to get its reports published in the press and lobbies for support from legislators. It is frequently at odds with the government, and its actions are sometimes illegal, especially in opposition to projects favored by the government. This often poses a problem for officials of MDBs whose policies call for consultation with and provision of information to NGOs on projects on which the MDB and the government are negotiating. Such information is necessary for an NGO to determine the environmental or human impact of a proposed project. NGOs cannot wait until they receive a summary of an environmental study, which may not be available until just before the loan is up for approval by an MDB board. Generally, MDBs do not release internal reports on a project unless the government agrees to their doing so, but the government may not agree if the reports can be used to undermine the government's position. Local officers of an MDB may, of course, provide information orally to NGOs, or NGOs may be able to obtain it surreptitiously from government officials with whom they have friendly relations. Sometimes they can obtain information more readily from the headquarters of the MDB through US or international NGOs. Frequently NGOs in developing countries depend on US NGOs for information on projects that may be environmentally flawed; this dependence is reciprocal.

An NGO in a developing country seeking information on proposed projects that its own government refuses to reveal may take the following steps:

1. NGO officials may obtain documents released by MDBs on projects in which they have an interest. The World Bank's *Monthly Operations Summary* gives brief descriptions of all projects being prepared for Bank financing; quarterly summaries give more detailed background on projects calling for environmental assessment. The Bank mails these summaries free of charge to any NGO that requests it. The IADB publishes a similar monthly entitled *Summary of Operations*.

2. The World Bank, IADB, and ADB maintain resident representatives in many of their member countries; their names and addresses are listed in annual reports. These representatives take requests for information and listen to expressions of concern about proposed projects on a confidential basis and without the knowledge of government officials. In addition, MDB staff frequently make missions to member countries. To obtain information on these missions, write to the bank's headquarters or, in some cases, the embassy of an industrial country.

3. A US NGO or an international NGO that maintains close contacts with the MDB headquarters can often provide information on proposed projects. Alternatively, a US NGO can frequently obtain information from the US executive director of the MDB.

4. Some countries have consultative committees consisting of MDB and NGO representatives. In India, for example, a World Bank–NGO committee meets regularly. These committees can facilitate dialogues.

Although all MDBs have policies and procedures for promoting dialogues with NGOs regarding proposed projects, MDBs cannot make full use of NGOs in preparing their own evaluations and recommendations for appropriate changes in project designs unless NGOs have adequate information. A World Bank document makes the following statement: "To preserve its close working relationship with member governments, the Bank does not release many of its internal reports to the public. However, partly in response to NGO queries, the Bank recently modified its policy on access to information. When government officials and the Bank's country director agree, requesting groups may now receive country economic, sector and project appraisal reports" (World Bank 1990a, 14).

We believe that MDBs should be free to provide NGOs with whatever information they need regarding projects affecting their interests—together with the Bank's own appraisals of the environmental problems associated with them—without having to obtain the permission of the borrowing government. This should be a condition of MDB financial support of a project or program.

US NGOs generally have better access to information from the World Bank and IADB than NGOs in developing countries. Frequently, information is available on an oral basis that is not provided in official documents. In addition, US NGOs can use congressional or US administrative channels both to raise questions and to express positions. Nevertheless, even US NGOs often have not been able to obtain EIAs and other internal evaluations of projects, partly because EIAs have not been systematically prepared for projects; the World Bank only recently established a systematic method of determining which projects should be subject to full environmental investigation. While US legislation passed in December 1989 should help remedy this problem, it is difficult to judge the adequacy of the new procedures before a full case history can be prepared.

NOTES

1. For a discussion of the history of US administration and congressional activities in promoting environmental and resources management principles in the MDBs, see Bruce M. Rich (1985).
2. An ADB study (1989) describes more than one hundred NGOs in Asian countries that collaborate with and receive donations from various external agencies, including MDBs and USAID.

REFERENCES

Asian Development Bank. 1989. *Cooperation with NGOs in Agriculture and Rural Development.* Vols. I and II. Manila, Philippines: ADB, August.

Brundtland Commission. 1987. *Our Common Future.* Oxford, England: Oxford Univ. Press.

Navarro, Bruce C. 1990. Letter from the Deputy Assistant Attorney General to George Mitchell, Majority Leader of the United States Senate. 9 October.

Rich, Bruce M. 1985. "The Multilateral Development Banks, Environmental Policy, and the United States." *Ecology Law Quarterly* 12, no. 2.

Runnalls, David. 1972. "Factors Influencing Environmental Policies in International Development Agencies." In *Environmental Planning and Development,* the proceedings of the Regional Symposium on Environmental and Natural Resources Planning, 19–21 February 1986. Manila, Philippines: ADB.

Stein, R. E., and B. Johnson. 1979. *Banking on the Biosphere.* New York: Lexington Books.

United Nations Environment Programme. 1980. "Declaration of Environmental Policies and Procedures Relating to Economic Development." New York: UN.

Ward, Barbara, and Rene Dubos. 1972. *Only One Earth.* New York: Norton.

World Bank. 1989. *World Bank Operational Manual.* Operational Directive 4.00, Annex A: Environmental Assessment. Washington, D.C.: World Bank, October.

_____. 1990a. *How the World Bank Works with Nongovernmental Organizations.* Washington, D.C.: World Bank, June.

_____. 1990b. *The World Bank and the Environment: First Annual Report Fiscal 1990.* Washington, D.C.: World Bank, September.

CHAPTER **10**

Conclusions

The single most important conclusion of this study is that MDBs should adopt the principle of sustainable development in determining and evaluating their loan programs and in their efforts to influence the policies and development strategies of their members. In its fullest connotation, sustainable development means integrating environmental and resource-use principles with economic-growth strategies directed to achieving enduring economic and social progress. Noneconomic factors often constrain pursuit of this objective. Everlasting growth is not possible under all conditions. Continued high rates of population growth, corrupt and self-serving political leaders, military armaments and conflicts, and physical disasters may defeat the realization of the objective no matter how a nation allocates its resources. Performance toward the objective is sometimes difficult to quantify because we have no fully satisfactory measures of economic and social progress. We need a measure of real per capita national product that includes nonmarket amenities and is adjusted for social disservices and natural resource depletion. Such measures will be available in time. Meanwhile, we do have sufficient monetary and nonmonetary indicators (such as levels of education, health, and mortality) to distinguish between sustainable progress and the absence of it.

MDBs have come a long way from the time when the first MDB, the World Bank, viewed its primary mission as a source of bankable loans for well-formulated projects in countries that "had put their financial house in order." This approach might be satisfactory for a modern Korea well on its way to sustainable growth through export-oriented industrialization. But it is largely irrelevant for the countries of Sub-Saharan Africa or the Indian subcontinent, where population expansion presses against the productivity of a limited resource base. By the 1970s the MDBs had come to regard themselves as development institutions responsible for promoting broadly based economic and social development in countries that were desperately poor and whose governmental policies were generating even further economic and social degradation. This responsibility included not only supporting projects and programs appropriate for an ameliorative development strategy, but also inducing governments to adopt monetary, fiscal, price, trade, and investment policies that would create a framework within which private economic forces could be productive.

This positive role for the MDBs has been only partially successful because of several things: (1) economic shocks generated by the world economy; (2) governments guided more by political motives than by a desire to promote national welfare; and (3) an emphasis on short-term gains in output rather than on sustainable development. Occupation with adverse environmental impacts at the project level has been slow to emerge in the MDBs, and even slower in the governments of client countries, which often see environmental protection and sustainable growth as constraints on the achievement of particular objectives rather than as objectives in themselves. Herein lies the difference between identifying and modifying possible adverse environmental impacts of proposed projects, on the one hand, and pursuing sustainable development, on the other. Much of our critical review of the policies and practices of the MDBs in the foregoing chapters defines this difference.

A Summary of the Major Shortcomings of MDBs in Past Environmental Administration

The following paragraphs summarize our findings of the major shortcomings of the MDBs in their past administration of environmental problems. Recently the MDBs have established policies and administrative procedures designed to correct some of these deficiencies. We will evaluate these new procedures in a later section.

FAILURE TO REQUIRE EIAS

Until recently MDBs did not regularly require EIAs as a part of project preparation by prospective borrowers, nor did their staffs follow standard procedures for environmental assessments and evaluations. Descriptions of environmental administration in World Bank and other MDB publications rarely mentioned EIAs before 1989 (see, for example, Baum 1982; World Bank 1984). However, by the mid-1970s the US required comprehensive EIAs for its government-funded or licensed projects, and the preparation of these EIAs was well known; by the late 1970s a number of other industrial countries were requiring them. By 1990 some forty-three countries required EIAs. In the mid-1980s, UN agencies, the OECD, and MDBs themselves published several sets of guidelines for preparing EIAs, both general and for projects in major sectors. Nevertheless, there is little evidence that comprehensive EIAs were required for most MDB-supported projects. Prior to 1989, at least, MDB staff members handled environmental administration mainly through reviews of project proposals.

Although the existence of an EIA does not guarantee that a project will be free of environmental flaws, preparation of an EIA under carefully formulated guidelines and terms of reference is an important first step. Making an EIA a part of the process of project formulation enables the project design to take into account the preliminary findings of the assessment. This has a distinct advantage over delaying environmental assessment until the project is fully formulated. A properly prepared EIA requires detailed economic and social studies by environmental specialists who simulate the resource and environmental conditions that would be changed by the project from the baseline conditions. EIAs should also receive inputs from the nongovernmental groups that would be most affected by the project. MDB staffs should become familiar with the preparation of EIAs and, where appropriate, offer assistance to the government of the borrowing country. MDB staff should review EIAs with respect to their completeness under the terms of reference and the MDB guidelines. The public in the borrowing countries should also have the opportunity to review EIAs before MDB loans are approved.

A well-prepared EIA should include recommendations for mitigating adverse environmental impacts or for implementing the project in a manner that would minimize adverse environmental consequences. It should also include alternative development scenarios as well as a "no action" option. This would provide the bank's staff, the donor government, and the public with analyses of several alternatives. Such recommendations and alternative actions provide a basis for environmental safeguards in a loan agreement. An EIA, released well in advance of the vote on the loan, also provides information needed for the final evaluation of the project by the MDB board, which must determine whether the environmental impacts from the project are sufficiently serious to warrant disapproval of the loan.

INSUFFICIENT MDB TECHNICAL STAFF
FOR CARRYING OUT ADMINISTRATION

Prior to the 1980s, MDBs either had no professional environmental staffs or had staffs of only a few people who lacked the range of professional training needed to judge the soundness of proposed projects. Regardless of the environmental procedures and guidelines adopted, two or three environmental officers could not possibly have done an effective job of administering hundreds of project loans each year.

FAILURE TO INCLUDE THE FULL SOCIAL COSTS
OF ENVIRONMENTAL DAMAGE

Financial feasibility has always played a predominant role in MDB decisions on loans for projects. However, MDBs have traditionally failed to include in project costs the social costs of resource degradation and depletion and the adverse impacts on human health, living standards, and social conditions. In addition, studies have regularly overstated the social benefits of projects by failing to apply probability coefficients to account for risk, especially in projects such as multipurpose dams. In many cases projects that appeared to meet the World Bank's standard of a return in excess of 12 percent on invested capital would have yielded no return, or a negative return, under proper SBCA. But MDBs apparently have not used such analysis to evaluate projects with substantial environmental risks. This is not because bank staffs lacked the knowledge to apply SBCA. The World Bank has published several first-rate studies on the subject (Squire & van der Tak 1975; Ray 1984).

Even where banks have included some expenditures in the cost of the project, such as compensation for people displaced by a large reservoir, the actual expenditures have proved inadequate to compensate for property loss and rehabilitation. Usually, this has meant that the government has not paid the compensation budgeted for the project.

FAILURE TO APPLY THE PRINCIPLES OF SUSTAINABLE DEVELOPMENT IN SUPPORTING PROJECTS

Quite apart from the direct environmental damage of projects, MDBs have tended to allocate too many of their loans to a particular sector. For example, a high proportion of the loans has supported power development. The heavy demand for power in poor countries is often due to a price for power well below its social cost, in some cases even below its current world market value. Such policies discourage conservation and result in a transfer of income from poor rural people to the urban middle- and upper-class. Most power projects are environmentally damaging, and the income transfers work against alleviating poverty, which in turn creates further damage to natural resources. Undervaluation or failure to charge for irrigation water encourages the inefficient use of water through over-irrigation and damages the soil. MDBs that allow the projects they support to misallocate resources violate the principle of sustainable development (OECD 1990, 36–37).

Critics also accuse the MDBs of failing to allocate their loans to sectors that could make the greatest contribution to sustainable development in poor countries. The International Food Policy Research Institute (IFPRI) recently published a study showing that the World Bank reduced the real value of its project lending for agriculture and rural development (ARD) by 19 percent between 1977–1979 and 1986–1988 (Lipton & Paarlberg 1990, 10). This means that ARD disbursements declined from 30 percent to 17 percent of the Bank's total disbursements between the two periods. The IFPRI report attributes this decline to a shift in emphasis from sustainable development to quick-disbursing SALs that favor debt service and overall maintenance of imports. Certainly for the poorest countries, sustainable agriculture is the most critical need.

FAILURE TO USE SANCTIONS TO INDUCE GOVERNMENTS OF BORROWING COUNTRIES TO MEET CONDITIONS IN LOAN AGREEMENTS

Perhaps the most serious violations of environmental principles have resulted from governments' failure to live up to their commitments in loan agreements designed to avoid environmental damage during the project construction or operation phase. This has frequently occurred in loans for multipurpose dam, resettlement, and forestry projects. The World Bank has, on occasion, temporarily withheld disbursements of loans, such as for the Narmada dam, after substantial NGO protests. MDBs might further declare a moratorium on new loans to a country that violates a conditionality agreement.

FAILURE OF MDBs TO CONSULT WITH RESIDENTS MOST SERIOUSLY AFFECTED BY PROPOSED PROJECTS BEFORE LOAN APPROVAL

Many project proposals by Third World governments are motivated by special economic or political interests and benefit one group largely at the expense of another—particularly the rural poor. While the disadvantaged group may not be able to get a hearing from its government, an MDB considering a loan has an obligation to consult with all those affected by the project to make sure that any disadvantaged groups are compensated and the harm minimized. The MDBs have not always provided such recourse in the past. Even if it can be shown that a particular project will increase total national output, it violates an important social welfare principle if it benefits some groups in a manner that makes others worse off. This concept is called the *Pareto optimality rule*.

FAILURE OF MDBs TO TAKE ACCOUNT OF ALL THE DIRECT AND INDIRECT ENVIRONMENTAL CONSEQUENCES OF A PROJECT THEY SUPPORT

Sometimes MDBs arbitrarily limit their responsibility for the environmental consequences of projects they support to, say, a certain area or certain categories of consequences. For example, financing a highway or railroad into a frontier area may facilitate the movement of land speculators, cattle ranchers, or miners into a primary forest but may also cause the wasteful destruction of tropical forests and disturb the economy of the indigenous tribal people. MDBs need to see these potential consequences and take actions to avoid them before making a loan commitment. Loans for large irrigation projects have been made without adequate attention to the management of the system. Consequently, soil has been salinized and waterlogged, downstream water contaminated, reservoirs silted, and wildlife destroyed. These consequences often result in nonsustainable agriculture, even when output increases in the near term.

FAILURE OF MDBs TO PROVIDE INFORMATION TO NGOs

NGOs, both in countries where projects are located and in the US and other industrial countries, have experienced considerable difficulty in obtaining information on the potential adverse consequences of projects supported by MDBs, both from their governments and from the MDBs themselves. This has greatly handicapped NGOs lobbying against certain projects in their own countries, as well as NGOs in industrial countries expressing opposition to environmentally flawed projects in Third World countries. In many cases the governments of countries in which projects are located seek to suppress opposition by refusing to provide information. Although some problems still remain, the procedures newly adopted by the MDBs at the insistence of board members representing the US and other industrial countries are expected to expand public access to information on proposed projects.

Environmentally Flawed MDB-Supported Projects by Major Sector

Most of the environmentally flawed projects supported by MDBs have involved irrigated agriculture, power, forestry, or land resettlement. Loans for these activities have tended to be large, the projects controlled by governments—with little if any private business or other nongovernmental participation. They have also tended to affect significant numbers of people, often adversely. A high portion of these loans have been criticized, not only by NGOs but by research institutions and scholars, including those associated with MDBs themselves. Although World Bank officials are not known for self-criticism, we have taken a significant number of our findings on environmental shortcomings of projects in these sectors directly from studies published by the Bank. Thus we have referenced several World Bank studies criticizing large multipurpose dam projects in general, or particular Bank-supported projects. In some cases, the Bank studies attribute responsibility for the environmental problems to governmental failure to meet conditions set forth in the loan agreement rather than to the Bank's failure to fully anticipate the problems. Yet the Bank has continued to make loans for the same kinds of projects with the same environmental failings to the same governments. The hydroelectric power component of multipurpose dams has generated criticism from both Bank and non-Bank sources, not only on environmental grounds, but also on grounds of misallocation of resources when cheap power benefits the urban sector at the expense of the rural sector. As we discussed in Chapter 4, professionals in the MDBs themselves are expressing doubts as to whether constructing more large dams is consistent with sustainable development.

Professionals, again including those associated with MDBs, have particularly criticized the forest harvesting programs supported by MDBs. Forestry specialists, such as Robert Goodland of the World Bank's Environment Department, have questioned whether sustainable yields are possible in tropical moist forests. The Bank should limit its forestry loans to those that support conservation and afforestation. Likewise, the large land resettlement projects supported by the World Bank not only have proved disappointing in terms of productivity and ability to raise the incomes of settlers, but have had disastrous impacts on indigenous people in the newly settled areas as well as on the forests and other resources.

Is there something inherent in large, state-operated projects that renders them environmentally unsound and perhaps economically unjustifiable? We cannot prove that a large multipurpose dam or land resettlement program involving thousands of settlers cannot be consistent with sustainable development and poverty alleviation. But the record of past projects does suggest that the probability of failure is too high to justify the social risks. One explanation may be that Third World governments simply cannot manage such projects and carry out all the conditions that MDBs should impose to assure their success. A corollary may be that large measures of private or nongovernment organization initiative and control are necessary for such projects to be both sustainable and productive. We frankly do not know whether nongovernmental control would be feasible for very large undertakings involving many thousands of participants. But we would like to see it tried.

What Succeeds?

What kinds of projects succeed in promoting sustainable development? Let us look first at agriculture, since output in this sector must expand on a sustainable basis if the countries containing more than half the world's population can hope to realize higher levels of living, or even to avoid a Malthusian paradigm. For these countries the challenge is to combine agricultural expansion and resource protection. Our reading of the literature on Third World agriculture, including that published by the MDBs, does not reveal a demand for large irrigation or resettlement projects. Nor do agricultural specialists suggest a reduction in external financing of ARD, such as would justify the decline in its financing by the World Bank over the past decade.

In Chapters 4 and 6 we find agricultural specialists advocating donor support for improving smallholder productivity and soil management by generating new production technology through research and pilot programs tailored to the conditions in the local areas, and by bringing this technology to the farmer. Adaptation and modification of existing techniques can also help achieve agricultural growth. Agricultural extension needs to be improved by a greater use of national and local NGOs. In countries with irrigation systems, improving existing systems—rehabilitating canals and ditches, for example—yielded far more for each dollar invested than creating new irrigation systems. Labor-intensive investments, such as for terracing and agroforestry, increase employment and prevent soil erosion. Assisting small farmers to develop their output for the export market is another way to increase agricultural value-added. Limiting the use of chemical inputs by introducing IPM programs and by teaching farmers to make more effective use of fertilizer will reduce agricultural pollution without impairing yields (Lipton & Paarlberg 1990, 26–30). An important challenge to the MDBs in supporting programs of this nature is to find NGOs and private farm associations that could manage them. In making ARD loans to governments, the MDBs might insist that funds be sub-lent to NGOs or private enterprises capable of carrying out the programs.

Other programs that have paid out well in terms of production or resource protection (or both) include watershed restoration projects; creation of wildlife reserves (including protection of biodiversity); afforestation projects; energy conservation projects (such as developing and disseminating improved woodstove technology); restoration of badly eroded lands; construction of ponds to introduce fish culture; and creation of small industries that use local raw materials and meet local demand for products such as food, cement, charcoal stoves, and fishing boats (Reid, Barnes, & Blackwelder 1988; Conroy & Litvinoff 1988; USAID 1987).

Most MDB-funded projects that have been generally successful in terms of promoting sustainable development are relatively small; a much larger portion of the total funding goes for large projects requiring total capital outlays of hundreds of millions of dollars and MDB assistance of more than $100 million. MDB staffs have been predisposed to finance large projects—pressured from management and client- and donor-member governments to meet total funding goals, and from the fact that large loans require lower staff commitments per dollar loaned. Traditionally, World Bank officials have argued that the Bank cannot afford the staff time to make small loans. During FY 1990 the World Bank approved only four loans of less than $10 million out of its total loan portfolio of 121 loans, and fifty of the approved loans were for $100 million or more.

For decades, small private foundations have been making effective use of their capital by promoting small projects with financing of under $1 million. Responding to the experience of private foundations in Latin America, in 1978 the IADB established a "small projects program." This program is designed "to carry out self-improvement projects designed to raise living standards through a more effective participation in the economy" (Economic & Social Development Department 1983). As of October 1987 the Bank had approved 166 small project loans totaling $72 million. By and large, these credits have succeeded in raising incomes of beneficiaries, and repayment rates compare favorably with typical commercial portfolios. These loans, which may not exceed $500,000 each, are channeled through intermediate organizations—private foundations, cooperatives, other NGOs, and some specialized government agencies. To cite examples, in November 1984 the IADB disbursed $300,000 to a foundation in Guatemala to help an estimated four hundred low-income women establish community orchards, poultry farms, hog-raising facilities, fish farms, fruit- and vegetable-processing facilities, bakeries, textile and clothing shops, and facilities for producing ceramics and silverware. In March 1984 the Bank loaned $500,000 to small-scale goat farmers in the state of Paraná, Brazil, to enable them to expand and upgrade their enterprise. In April 1986 a $500,000 loan helped an NGO in Honduras to provide credit and training to small businessmen lacking access to conventional credit sources. While these cannot be labeled as "environmental projects," they do represent small-scale enterprises that can be sustainable and have minimal environmental impacts.

For the past 15 years the World Bank has been making loans to commercial banks and development finance institutions for making subloans to small and medium enterprises (S/MEs). According to a recent World

Bank report (Webster 1991), average annual lending to S/MEs has been about $200 million during the 1980s, with subloans to S/MEs averaging $35,000. The average subloan repayment rate for completed projects was 80 percent, with the highest average rate in Latin America (92 percent) and the lowest in Africa (61 percent). Although the report judges the S/ME lending program to be a success in terms of job creation and strengthening the financial institutions making the subloans, "the majority of projects . . . have been unable to establish programs that can be sustained without some level of external funding" (Webster 1991, xxii). Success depends heavily on the lending capabilities of the financial institutions and the general environment in the country for small and medium private enterprise.

We are not suggesting that MDBs discontinue financing most of the traditional projects with which they have been associated, such as those in industry, transportation, population, health, urban development, energy, education, and ARD. We are recommending that they give greater emphasis to loans for projects that small private enterprise and NGOs can administer.

Current MDB Policies and Procedures

The new EIA procedures announced by the World Bank and the IADB in 1989–1990 (see Chapter 3) are an important advance over the unstructured environmental administration of the past. It will require several years before operations under these procedures can be evaluated, but at least environmental disasters sponsored by MDBs are less likely to occur. In reviewing the EIA procedures published by the World Bank, we have found that some elements are missing and some issues unclear, however. First is the absence of procedures for assessing nonmarket costs and benefits in the preparation of EIAs. The World Bank's Operational Directive (4.00 Annex A-1, October 1989) states that "Feasible and cost effective measures which may reduce potentially significant adverse environmental impacts to acceptable levels should be proposed" in the preparation of EIAs. Simply identifying adverse health effects or the loss of a primary forest ecosystem does not provide an adequate basis for evaluating the social costs of a project or for determining whether the proposed mitigation of an adverse environmental impact is worth performing. Only SBCA can satisfactorily address questions of feasibility and cost-effectiveness, and the Operational Directive makes no reference to this procedure. Nor does it mention the need to take account of natural resource depletion or degradation in the evaluation of adverse environmental impacts. The procedures lack objective standards and methods of measurements and leave a great deal to arbitrary judgment regarding acceptable environmental costs and the balance of full social costs against social benefits.

Nonmarket costs of potential health impairment or destruction of the way of life of an indigenous people are difficult to estimate, but environmental literature suggests methodologies for making such estimates. Using a very rough estimate of social cost is far better than ignoring that cost entirely. In some cases, guidelines can be employed in place of, or in combination with, SBCA. One suggested guideline might be that any project that significantly reduces the productive capacity of future generations is unacceptable, regardless of its contribution to current output. Another is that any project that reduces per capita income of a substantial number of people is unacceptable. Where wildlife is at risk, a guideline might be that no project resulting in the destruction of a significant number of an endangered species is acceptable.

Even under the new World Bank guidelines, environmental assessment of a project is not fully integrated with project design or with the determination of financial feasibility. Although the guidelines refer to the possibility that preliminary environmental assessment may influence project design, the environmental assessment is not likely to be available until the project has been fully formulated and tested for engineering and financial feasibility. Environmental feasibility should be on a par with technical and financial feasibility, and this cannot occur unless the feasibility studies take place simultaneously and interact in a multiple-objective process. This process should avoid a situation in which a fully formulated project that is both technically and financially feasible is subjected to an environmental test, with adverse impacts constituting a constraint on the project. Under these conditions, the benefits of the project are likely to be judged as overcoming each of a series of environmental costs arising from the constraints.

There is a danger that MDB officials who have been engaged in formulating a project for loan approval and are committed to it will minimize adverse environmental impacts or overstate social benefits in relation to social costs. Early US experience showed that agencies responsible for both the project and the environmental impact statement tended to minimize the adverse environmental impacts of proposed projects and play down the potential benefits of alternatives. In the US, a draft EIS must be made available for interagency and public review. Private individuals and organizations have recourse to the courts if their objections do not result in a satisfactory revision of the proposal. Except for public review, this mechanism is not available for those who object to projects proposed for MDB funding. Ideally, a body like the UN Environment Programme or a panel of consultants should do this. As a minimum, the environment departments of the MDBs should undertake an appraisal and prepare an independent report on the project, which would be available to the MDB board at the time of the loan review. This procedure does not exist for the Environment Department of the World Bank, but we understand it is a part of the new procedures adopted by the IADB.

Thus far the environmental activities of MDBs have been confined to projects they support. Just as the MDBs have broadened their economic involvement in client countries from project to sectoral to national development strategies, so also should they consider the environment and resource allocation in the context of a general development strategy. In promoting sustainable development it is not enough to assess the potential environmental damage of a hydroelectric power plant and to consider how the adverse environmental consequences might be modified in a cost-effective manner. It is necessary to consider whether the country's natural and capital resources might contribute more to the net social product through energy conservation or through the development of another source of power. These alternatives should be explored before a large multipurpose dam is proposed. In most cases economic justification depends on whether a project is likely to yield an acceptable rate of return on capital outlays. This traditional approach neither takes into account nonmarket values that may be destroyed or impaired by the dam, nor allows for the opportunity cost of alternative uses of the natural, capital, and human resources employed to produce the dam—that is, the net social output these resources might have produced in other uses. A project using natural resources should be evaluated in terms of optimum development strategy for the country.

The integration of sustainability with development strategy requires consideration of the long-term consequences of current patterns of resource use. An agricultural expansion strategy based on extensive cultivation and the use of marginal lands or the destruction of forests is not sustainable. A development strategy requiring an annual percentage increase in power supplied from environmentally destructive hydroelectric projects is likewise nonsustainable. MDBs should formulate an EAP for each client country, taking into account the interactions between development strategies and sustainability. As noted in Chapter 9, the Ninth IDA Replenishment Agreement requires the preparation of EAPs for each IDA country.

The success of this approach depends upon the governments' dedication to environmental and sustainability principles. The influence MDBs have in applying conditionality to isolated projects they support is too weak to accomplish the adoption of national sustainable development principles. Their most potent instrument is the SAL, currently used to influence broad development policies not directly associated with projects. SAL agreements should be expanded to include policies that support sustainable development. Past experience with SAL conditionality suggests that success in revolutionizing the environmental policies of governments will occur slowly, at best. This approach should be regarded as an educational endeavor, but banks should suspend disbursements to countries that do not make reasonable progress.

All MDBs include in their policy objectives the amelioration of abject poverty. This requires a rise in per capita income for one-fourth to one-third of the total populations of poor countries. Definitions of sustainability usually include this objective, and poverty correlates closely to the depletion of the natural resources base. MDBs need to take poverty into account in development strategy and in the formulation of projects. As a minimum, loans should not be made to facilitate an increase in per capita income of a country at the expense of the per capita income of its poorest members. Directives for preparing EIAs need to include this objective.

REFERENCES

Baum, Warren C. 1982. *The Project Cycle.* Washington, D.C.: World Bank.

Conroy, Czech, and Miles Litvinoff, eds. 1988. *The Greening of Aid: Sustainable Livelihood in Practice.* London: Earthscan Publications.

Economic and Social Development Department. 1983. *Program for the Financing of Small Projects.* Washington, D.C.: IADB.

Lipton, Michael, and Robert Paarlberg. 1990. *The Role of the World Bank in Agricultural Development in the 1990s.* Washington, D.C.: IFPRI, October.

Organization for Economic Cooperation and Development. 1990. *Development Co-Operation, 1990 Report.* Paris: OECD, December.

Ray, A. 1984. *Cost-Benefit Analysis: Issues and Methodologies.* Baltimore: Johns Hopkins Univ. Press for the World Bank.

Reid, Walter V., James N. Barnes, and Brent Blackwelder. 1988. *Bankrolling Successes: A Portfolio of Sustainable Development Projects.* Washington, D.C.: Environmental Policy Institute.

Squire, Lyn, and Herman G. van der Tak. 1975. *Economic Analysis of Projects.* Baltimore: Johns Hopkins Univ. Press for the World Bank.

United States Agency for International Development. 1987. *The Environment: Managing Natural Resources for Sustainable Development.* Washington, D.C.: USAID, Fall.

Webster, Leila. 1991. *World Bank Lending for Small and Medium Enterprises: Fifteen Years of Experience.* Washington, D.C.: World Bank.

World Bank. 1984. *Environment and Development.* Washington, D.C.: World Bank.

INDEX

Accra Plain, 96
ADB. *See* Asian Development Bank
ADF. *See* African Development Fund
AfDB. *See* African Development Bank
Africa: East, 200; river basins of, 82–85; Sub-Saharan, 37, 184, 188–89, 198, 199–202, 248, 279; West, 178–81. *See also* Botswana; Cameroon; Egypt; Gabon; Ghana; Guinea; Ivory Coast; Liberia; Malawi; Morocco; Niger; Nigeria; Sahelia; Senegal; Sudan; Tanzania; Togo; Uganda; Zaire; Zambia; Zimbabwe
African Development Bank (AfDB), 24–26. *See also* Multilateral development banks; Regional development banks
African Development Fund (ADF), 25
Agricultural credit loans, 186–88
Agriculture: effects of, on wildlife, 194; export, 191–92, 197–98; multipurpose dams and, 73–75, 86; successful projects in, 285–86; sustainable, 198–202; technology and, 188–89, 286; World Bank loans for, 11–12, 80–82. *See also* Fertilizers; Irrigation; Livestock projects; Pesticides
Akosombo Dam, 83, 193
Akrotiri Salt Lake, 212
Alaska Wildlife Refuge, 195
Alexandria harbor, 226
Algeria, 17
Alto Turi, 216
Amazon, The, 38, 43; in Brazil, 55, 123, 125–28, 165–67, 176–77, 188, 268; destruction of, 123, 264; in Ecuador, 236; energy in, 224–25; forestry in,

125–28. *See also* Amerindians; Grand Carajás Program; Jarí Project; Polonoroeste Project
Amazonia. *See* Amazon, The
Amerindians, 135, 165, 166, 213
AMOCO Minerals, 240
Amuesha Indians, 156
Animal health projects, 203–5
Archeological sites, 79, 100
Argentina, 2, 235, 250–51
Asher, Robert E., 13
Asian Development Bank (ADB), 21–24. *See also* Multilateral development banks; Regional development banks
Aswân High Dam, 79, 100, 193; reservoir, 255
Australia, 239–40
Australian National University, 241
Austria, 239

Balance of payments, 26–27, 34n.4, 46, 259n.1. *See also under* Structural adjustment loans
Bali, 135, 157
Banker, James A., III, 183
Bastar Wood Pulp and Paper Project, 153–54
Benefit-cost accounting, 47
Benefit-cost analysis, 48, 49–51, 143, 147
Benin, 95
BHP Minerals, 240
Bigot, Yves, 189
Bilateral Assistance Agencies, 27–28. *See also* US Agency for International Development

IFC. *See* International Finance Corporation
IMF. *See* International Monetary Fund
India, 75, 89, 107, 112n.3, 279; energy in, 224, 225; Five-Year Plans of, 12, 153; irrigation in, 81; petroleum development in, 235; waterlogging in, 76. *See also* Bombay; Dudhichua coal project; Gujarat; Madhya Pradesh; Narmada River Project; New Delhi; Orissa; Singrauli
Indigenous peoples, 135, 159–60, 205, 235, 236, 289. *See also* Amerindians; Amuesha Indians; Huaorani
Indonesia, 23, 107, 116; forestry policies in, 123–25; and involuntary resettlement, 138; and resource accounting, 41. *See also* Bali; Cirata hydroenergy dam; Indonesian Transmigration Plan; Irian Jaya; Java; Lombok; Kalimantan; Sulawesi; Sumatra; Timber Estates Development Project
Indonesian Environmental Forum, 164, 274
Indonesian Transmigration Program (ITMP), 135–36, 137, 157–64
Indus Basin, 85
Industry, 95–97, 194, 226–28
Infrastructure, 11–12, 222–28
Initial executive project summary, 15
Institute for Developmental Anthropology, 171
Institute for Social and Economic Analysis, 274
Institute for Socio-Economic Studies, 274
Instituto Brazileiro de Desenvolvimento Forestal, 128
Integrated pest management (IPM), 190, 286
Inter-American Development Bank (IADB), 18–21; Seventh Replenishment Agreement, 20. *See also* Multilateral development banks; Regional development banks

Inter-American Economic and Social Council, 19
International Council of Voluntary Agencies, 273
International Development Association (IDA), 4, 10, 15–17; Agreement for the Ninth Replenishment, 256, 271, 291. *See also* World Bank Group
International Finance Corporation (IFC), 4, 10, 17. *See also* World Bank Group
International Food Policy Research Institute, 191–92, 282
International Institute for Environment and Development, 263–64
International Monetary Fund (IMF), 4, 26–27, 32–33, 257–58
International Paper, 129
International Union on Conservation of Nature and Natural Resources, 263
International waters, 29
IPM. *See* Integrated pest management
Irian Jaya (Western New Guinea), 136, 157, 159–60, 162, 163, 231
Irrigation, 68–71, 193; criticisms of, 71–73, 80–82; effects on archeological sites, 79; environmental effects of, 75–79, 101–5; in Pakistan, 85–86; Rahad, 92–94
Islamic Development Bank, 170
Itapecuru River, 213
ITMP. *See* Indonesian Transmigration Program
Ivory Coast: Abidjan, 24; and agriculture, 188, 189; forestry in, 120, 129–30, 131–32; structural adjustment loans to, 253

Jamaica, 235
Japan, 21, 87, 91
Jarí Project, 120, 154
Java, 135, 157, 162, 163
Johnson, B., 21
Johnson, Lyndon B., 21

Kafue Hydroelectric II project, 214